The Jews in Business

The Jews in Business

STEPHEN ARIS

Jonathan Cape Thirty Bedford Square London

FIRST PUBLISHED 1970
© 1970 BY STEPHEN ARIS

JONATHAN CAPE LTD, 30 BEDFORD SQUARE, LONDON WCI

ISBN 0 224 61953 5

PRINTED AND BOUND IN GREAT BRITAIN
BY BUTLER & TANNER LTD, LONDON AND FROME

Contents

Illustrations

Acknowledgments

In writing this book I have accumulated more debts of gratitude than I can hope to repay. As a Gentile and a journalist setting out to explore a particularly sensitive area of the Jewish world, a certain amount of suspicion and wariness might have been expected. But in fact in almost every case I was treated with courtesy and attention. It would be invidious to single out individuals from amongst the many people I interviewed, but without their generous help this book would never have been started, let alone finished.

Gathering material has been a brain-picking operation on a large scale. And I am especially grateful to those who guided me through the by-ways of the early economic history of the Jews in England: to Mr Edgar Samuel who pointed me in the right direction, and to Mr Donald Samuel who lent me some of the personal papers of the Montagu family. Thanks also to the staff of the Mocatta Library at University College, London, of the London School of Economics, of the *Jewish Chronicle* and of the *Sunday Times*, who dealt with my inquiries with patience and expertise.

Much of this book was written in my spare time but I am more than grateful to Mr Harold Evans, editor of the *Sunday Times*, for allowing me leave of absence to do some of the work and to complete the task. I have shamelessly exploited the goodwill of my friends and colleagues. Mr Anthony Lester read the final chapter

ACKNOWLEDGMENTS

in its various drafts and I have incorporated a number of his invaluable and stimulating suggestions. Mr Oliver Marriott guided me through the intricacies of the property business, and Mr Anthony Vice's special knowledge of Sir Isaac Wolfson's career saved me from falling into a number of pits of my own making. Mr Leon Brittan and Mr Peter Wilsher read the entire manuscript in draft, but if there are any errors of commission or omission the fault is mine alone. My final debt is to my wife, Pepita, whose support and encouragement has kept me going.

Greenwich   STEPHEN ARIS
May 1970

TO MY FATHER

Chapter One

Introduction

1882 saw the beginning of one of the biggest mass migrations of modern times. Between then and the outbreak of the First World War something like a million Jews left their homes in Eastern Europe and fled westwards. The vast majority crossed the Atlantic to America but some 200,000, either from necessity or choice, came to settle in England. 'It seemed to me', one immigrant said, recalling how Tower Bridge opened as his boat approached St Katharine docks, 'that England herself was opening her arms to welcome me.' And so she was—up to a point.

The Jews were by no means the first immigrants to seek shelter from oppression in England: nor were they to be the last. In the previous three hundred years thousands of Flemings, Huguenots and Irishmen had been taken in, each wave in its turn affecting the pattern of England's social and economic life. In the last fifteen years Pakistanis and West Indians have arrived in such numbers that the politicians were finally persuaded to shut a door that had stood open for centuries. The problems of absorbing these successive waves into a small, densely populated island have been considerable, giving rise to ugly tensions and conflicts. But by and large the gains have outweighed the disadvantages. Britain's industrial history is shot through with examples of the fertilizing influence of the immigrants. It was Flemish weavers who laid the foundations of the textile industry; it was the shovels and the sweat of the Irish navvies which built the railways and today it can be argued that without Commonwealth immigrants, Britain's hospital service and the transport system of her cities would collapse.

The Jewish contribution is more complicated, more diverse and, in a way, more considerable. In fifty-odd years the Jews have come to exercise an influence on Britain's commercial, and to a much lesser extent on her industrial, life out of all proportion to their numbers. To many people, especially the Jews themselves, such a statement must sound both familiar and distasteful. For centuries it has been the economic activities of the Jews that have been seized upon by the anti-semites and used as a stick with which to beat them. The idea of the Jew as usurer and money-lender is so entrenched in popular mythology that even as respectable an authority as the Oxford Dictionary defines a Jew first as a 'person of the Hebrew race' and secondly as an 'extortionate usurer, a driver of hard bargains'. 'To jew', the dictionary says, 'is to cheat, to overreach.'

One of the purposes of this book is to try to shovel this prejudice to one side and take a cool look at Jewish economic activity, assessing its importance and demonstrating where and why and how its influence has been felt. To say that 'their influence has been out of all proportion to their numbers' is not, in my view, the same as saying, as the Fascists did, that the Jews 'dominate and control' all or even a large part of British industry. The first is, I think, demonstrably true, the second demonstrably false.

It has often been suggested both by friends and enemies of the Jews that there is something unique and entirely singular about Jewish success in business; that the Jew, unlike the Christian, the Moslem or the Negro, possesses an inherent, instinctive gift for business which is denied to other religious, national or racial groups. Doubtless I myself, hard though I have tried to put the Jews' economic achievements into perspective, to describe not only their successes but their limitations and failures, will be accused of fostering this impression. The subject is such an emotive one for Jews and Gentiles alike, that merely to single out Jewish businessmen, to describe, as I do in the next ten chapters, their careers and to speculate on the reasons for their success is to run the risk of being accused of anti-semitism. The Jews' own neuroses about their achievements is so strong, their understandable dislike at being singled out for special mention is so marked, that it is difficult to remain unaffected. As Paul Ferris remarked in his book on the City, in writing about the Jews it is very hard to remain neutral: one is forced either on the offensive or the defensive.

On balance my own posture throughout this book is a defensive one in as far as I try to indicate the complexity and variety of Jewish economic activity and to avoid the crude 'all Jews are money-grubbing millionaires' stereotype which occurs again and again whenever Jews and their money are discussed. But at the same time I have not attempted, as nearly all Jewish spokesmen and some of the businessmen to whom I talked would have liked, to play down their genuine achievements in the pretence that the Jews have had little or no impact on Britain's business history over the last three hundred or so years. Their achievements have been remarkable and, in my view, are well worth examination.

This is neither a book about Jewish success in general nor an anatomy of the Jews in Britain today. If I have ignored the contribution of the Jews in the arts, in the sciences, in literature and in politics, it is not because I think it inconsiderable but because it is outside the scope of my inquiry, which is concerned with only one dimension of the Jewish character and personality. I have written as a business journalist who happens to be fascinated by the phenomenon of the Jewish businessman. In attempting to put their achievements into perspective and to explain their behaviour, I have been forced to stray outside my area of professional competence and to look to the historians and the sociologists for guidance. But though this departure may have been rash I think it was worth making. It would, of course, have been possible simply to retell a series of already well-documented success stories and leave the readers to draw their own conclusions. But that does not seem to me to be a very fruitful or illuminating approach.

In my view it is impossible to understand the achievements of the Jews as businessmen unless one knows a little more about the circumstances in which they came to this country, the mores and culture of the society which they left and the nature of the external and internal pressures which still bear upon them. It is considerations of this kind that have determined the structure of this book.

Part One is mainly historical. In the early chapters I have devoted a good deal of space to a description of the main wave of immigrants from the 1880s onwards, to an examination of the reasons why they left and to a portrait, based largely on eye-witness accounts, of life and labour in the East End and elsewhere. Not all Jews are, of course, the product of this particular tradition. The City financiers and bankers, the backbone of the Jewish aristocracy, arrived much earlier, not in one great apocalyptic rush, but in dribs and drabs. The City owes a great deal to its Jewish bankers. And because no account of the Jewish contribution would be complete without this side of the picture I have included a short sketch of their history.

Part Two is contemporary. I have chosen to concentrate in some detail on a handful of individuals and institutions whose activities seem to bring into sharp focus some of the differing aspects of the Jewish economic character. In looking at the careers of such men as Lord Marks, Sir Isaac Wolfson and Sir John Cohen, the question of their Jewishness and its relationship to their business is one that I have consistently tried to answer. But it is not the only theme that runs through these chapters. Can the family firm survive? Can entrepreneurial flair be handed down from generation to generation? Is Jewish success in business largely a matter of historical accident or is there something in the Jewish make-up that can explain it? These questions—to which by the nature of things there can be no definitive answers—continually recur.

Much of the final section deals with a quite separate subject which though apparently unconnected has a bearing on the main theme. The chapter on charity gives me an opportunity to discuss the Jewish businessman's attitude to wealth while in the concluding chapter the various strands which run through the book are drawn together. It is here that I attempt to explain Jewish economic behaviour and answer the question that underlies the whole discussion: are the Jews different?

In Britain, just as in America, there are large areas of commerce and industry which remain the preserve of the White Anglo-Saxon Protestant and in which the Jews hardly figure at all — either as entrepreneurs or managers. For example they play little or no part in banking proper.* There are Quakers like the Barclays and the Lloyds; there are Catholics like Lord Longford; and there are aristocrats of all shapes and sizes on the boards of the clearing banks — but hardly any Jews. Nor is Jewish involvement in merchant banking (which is after all a polite word for money-lending) anything like as great as it used to be.

The accents of the shipbuilders at John Brown, of the engineers at Guest, Keen and Nettlefold and of the motor-men at the British Leyland Motor Corporation or at Ford are often Scottish, Yorkshire or American but they are very rarely Jewish. It is true that the chairman of the British Steel Corporation, Lord Melchett, is half Jewish with merchant banking connections, but the steel masters of the old companies that make up the corporation are exclusively Gentile — as are the majority of their colleagues in the heavier end of British industry. Of the five hundred companies listed in *The Times*'s index only twenty-three could fairly be described as Jewish.

It is a situation that is beginning to change. Just as some of the largest firms in the country such as Shell and I.C.I. owe their initial inspiration to Jewish scientists like Mond or Jewish traders

* The only clearing bank where a Jew has played a significant part is the Westminster, one of whose founders was Sir David Salomons (1797–1873), a stockbroker and the first Jew to become Lord Mayor of London.

and financiers like Marcus Samuel, the first Lord Bearsted; so the Jews are now playing a part in the rebuilding and refashioning of the great entrepreneurial constructs of the late nineteenth and early twentieth centuries—a process which has been enormously accelerated by the wave of mergers and takeovers that have occurred in the last ten years. The growth of Viyella International, now part of I.C.I., is indicative of this trend. It was very much the personal creation of Joe Hyman, the volatile son of a prosperous Manchester textile dealer—'We were rich enough to have servants and that sort of thing.' Within some ten years Hyman has transformed the rather sleepy textile company, which he took over in 1961; in the process he has shaken up a large part of Lancashire's traditionally fragmented, product-orientated industry. 'My vision', he says, 'was to conceive of a multi-fibre, multi-process industry. When everybody else was thinking of single units producing different bits of the process—spinning, weaving, or finishing—I saw it as an integrated whole.' And the fact that the vision has yet to be fully realized does nothing to detract from the boldness of the conception. Nor has Hyman's vision necessarily been vitiated by the fact that in December 1969 he lost his job as Viyella's chairman and chief executive after a dramatic and sudden boardroom coup. The reasons for his expulsion were apparently largely personal and though he may have been a demanding man to work for, his commercial judgments were on the whole soundly based.

The most spectacular example, however, is provided by Sir Arnold Weinstock, the son of a North London tailor who, after joining his father-in-law's electrical and radio business has gone on after a series of dazzling takeovers to become the head of a mammoth company with annual sales approaching the thousand million pound mark and embracing three of the proudest names in British engineering—General Electric, English Electric and, biggest of them all, Associated Engineering Industries. On paper Weinstock's career looks like the classic Jewish rags-to-riches success story. In one sense it is: he started with very little and he is now a millionaire several times over. But in other respects it is not. Weinstock's skills and ambitions are, as far as one can tell, managerial rather than entrepreneurial. He has not got where he is by building his own business—that job was done for him by his father-in-law—but by reorganizing other people's. English Electric and A.E.I. succumbed to G.E.C. not because Weinstock was offering a fancy price for the businesses but because, in the last resort, their shareholders came to believe that Weinstock would make a better job of managing their companies than anybody else. And in this respect Weinstock is an entirely modern figure, seemingly quite unmarked by the memories of the East End ghetto on whose fringes he was brought up.

Despite the emergence of men like Weinstock, Hyman and Sir Jules Thorn, a Viennese refugee who has built up an electrical appliance business second only in size to G.E.C.'s, Jewish involvement in the mainstream manufacturing industries remains comparatively small. They are, however, heavily involved in business.

Statistics about Jewish economic life are a very scarce commodity in Britain; Anglo-Jewish sociologists (unlike their American counterparts), reflecting the nervousness of the community at large, have preferred to concentrate on such comparatively barren and inward-looking subjects as Jewish identity and the extent (or lack) of Jewish cohesiveness. Nor are the census figures much help, as respondents are deliberately not classified according to religion. But such figures as there are do seem to indicate that as a community the Jews are more business-minded than most. When the Trades Advisory Council, a Jewish body set up in 1938 to combat anti-semitism, set out in 1948 to survey 71,675 firms in London, Manchester, Leeds, Cardiff and Newcastle, it discovered that about 11,000—some 14 per cent of the total—were owned by Jews who then as now represent about one per cent of the country's population. These trades were not spread across the spectrum but concentrated in a relatively narrow band. In Manchester the Jews were involved in 24 per cent of the trades covered by the trade dictionaries; in Liverpool in only 13 per cent, and in Glasgow in only 8 per cent. By far the commonest activity was textiles and drapery, followed by furniture, jewellery, boots and shoes and fur, and only in the last did Jewish-owned firms have anything approaching a monopoly.

Over the years this economic base has become a good deal broader. Wherever opportunities have opened up the Jews have taken them, so that today they are almost as likely to be found running machine-tool companies or commercial television combines as they are building supermarket chains or dress businesses. Time has blurred the lines but the original profile is still discernible. Though the membership of the Trades Advisory Council has dwindled almost to vanishing point (from 9,100 in 1946 to 559 in 1968), reflecting the decline of anti-semitism and a corresponding increase in the Jews' feeling of security, the main trades represented are still textiles and clothing, fur, jewellery, food, furniture and footwear. An analysis of the changes in the occupational background of the parents of children at Carmel College, the only exclusively Jewish public school in England, from 1964–9 gives, perhaps, a more rounded picture.

	1964	1969
Textiles	22%	18%
Various businesses	39%	30%
Furniture	8%	4·5%
Property/Finance	5%	5%
Medicine	3%	5·5%
Law	3%	5%
Engineering and Pure Science	3%	5%
Teaching (University and School)	3%	5%
Miscellaneous Professions (Architects, Dentists, Opticians, Diplomats, Pharmicists)	6%	10%

	1964	1969
Widowed, divorced, maintained by the London Education Authority	4%	5%
Miscellaneous	4%	7%

What emerges is the extent to which these middle-class families still have a textile or other business background—despite the continuing drift away from business and into the professions. The explanation is quite simple: textiles and shopkeeping, drapery and shoemaking were the trades of the immigrants, the ones by which they had earned their livings in Russia and Poland. According to a survey made between 1895 and 1908 by the Poor Jews' Temporary Shelter, a body started by a Jewish baker to look after the newly arrived immigrants and later taken over by the middle classes, 29 per cent of the 9,000 immigrants questioned had worked in the garment trade in their own country; 23 per cent were in what could loosely be described as trade and commerce; 9 per cent had made boots and shoes; 7 per cent were carpenters and 2 per cent had come off the land. There was an acrobat too but he was in a minority of one.

There is another reason why the Jews have played such a small part in the life of the great, bureaucratic institutions that now dominate British industry: they are, as innumerable surveys have shown, individualists who prefer to work for themselves rather than for other people. It is an attitude of mind that seems to run right through the social scale, from the taxi driver (approximately 25 per cent of London's taxi drivers are Jewish) to the multi-millionaire. When the Jewish Chronicle surveyed the community in 1952 it discovered that of the 1,244 men employed in trades of one kind or another, no less than 921—69 per cent or just over three out of every four—were working on their own account: a figure which compares strikingly with the 6 per cent self-employed in the country as a whole.

The image of the Jewish businessman is not of a smooth, grammar-school boy whose vision of success is an expense account, a Rover 2000, a nice house in the suburbs and a steady job, pensionable of course; but of a restless, individualistic character, anxious to make his own way and determined to be master of his own fate. It would be stretching truth far too far to suggest that all but a handful have made it. While the majority of the 200,000-odd immigrants who flooded into the country were, as I show in Chapter Five, undoubtedly ambitious and business-minded, no more, I would reckon, than 250 of them or their children have become millionaires. Not all Jews are businessmen and only a minority of those that are (as the number of tailoring businesses which go bust every year would seem to indicate) are any good at it.

Often they were not even the first in the field. It was John Sainsbury and Thomas Lipton who began the mass marketing of groceries; Express Dairy was a supermarketeer several years before Sir John Cohen's Tesco and it was the Gentile firm of Hepworth's, not Sir Montague Burton, who initially led the way into multiple tailoring. But, as many pioneers have discovered to their cost, to be first in the field is no guarantee of success.

The early Jewish entrepreneurs were not always wholly attractive figures; they were often, just as Henry Ford and Alfred Krupp were, autocratic and domineering people. Like most self-made men they were often keen on material possessions which, once acquired, they were not slow to display. But they were also men of exceptional ability and energy. They had, as Cecil King put it, 'no pull, only push'. And in the pushing process men like Lord Marks of Marks and Spencer, Sir Isaac Wolfson of Great Universal Stores, Sir Siegmund Warburg of the merchant bankers, S. G. Warburg, Sir John Cohen of Tesco Stores and Sir Harold Samuel of Land Securities have not only built up size-able fortunes of their own, rivalling those of the industrial magnates of the nineteenth century, but they have had a revitalizing effect on the sectors in which they have operated. Marks and

Spencer is widely admired not because it sells three out of every five pairs of panties bought in Britain but because it is patently such a good business—an exemplar for all its rivals. When the shareholders of Woolworths, disappointed in the company's progress over the last twenty years, wished to complain to the company's management, it was to Tesco and to Marks and Spencer that they pointed to make the painful comparison.

Business is often thought of as a rather dull, boring affair, devoid of intellectual content and excitement and infinitely less preferable as an occupation for gentlemen than the professions and the Civil Service. The third generation of Jews, the grandchildren of the immigrants are, as far as I can judge, beginning to think that way too. But their grandfathers and in many cases their fathers did not have the benefit of a public-school education and they were not gentlemen. For them business was absorbing because it had to be and for the most part they enjoyed their work. The results of their, often extraordinary, talents is the subject of the next nine chapters.

Chapter Two

The Coming of the Immigrants

The upheaval which was to transform the lives of millions of Jews began with an explosion. On March 1st, 1881, the reforming and liberal-minded Tsar, Alexander II, was assassinated in a St Petersburg street by a dynamite bomb, thrown by a group of terrorists. There was only one Jew among them, a young woman called Hesia Helfman whose job it was to provide a hide-away for the men afterwards, but that did not prevent the Russian authorities from using the assassination as a heavy stick with which to beat the 5 million Jews then living within the boundaries of the Russo-Polish empire. That the blows were so heavy and the injuries so great was largely the responsibility of the new Tsar, Alexander III, and his former tutor and chief lieutenant, Constantine Petrovitch Pobyedonostzev, whose official title was Procurator-General of the Holy Synod, whose name meant 'Victory Bearer', but who was often called simply: 'The Grand Inquisitor'.

The autocratic nature of the new regime quickly became apparent. On April 29th, 1881, just eight weeks after the death of his father, Alexander proclaimed: 'The voice of God hath commanded us to take up vigorously the reins of Government, inspiring us with the belief in the strength and truth of autocratic power which we are called upon to establish and safeguard.'

'Hideous sedition', Alexander said, was to be 'eradicated'. By this he meant anything or anybody who challenged the political, religious and economic orthodoxies of the regime. And though the Imperial Proclamation did not specifically mention the Jews, it was perfectly plain to those responsible for law and order in the provinces that it was the Jews that St Petersburg primarily had in mind. To the autocratic politicians and clerics of St Petersburg the Jews were offensive for two reasons: in pursuing a separate religion they were flouting the all-powerful Greek Orthodox Church, and in carrying on their daily lives as small shopkeepers, tradesmen and the like, they dominated, so the Government said, the commercial life of the country, competed unfairly with Christians and generally exploited the peasantry.

Trouble broke out even before Alexander's proclamation. And though there is little evidence that the authorities deliberately planned or fostered it, once it had started they were certainly in no hurry to stop it. The wave of anti-semitic riots that swept through Southern Russia, reaching Warsaw by the summer of 1881, began in April at Elizabethgrad, a town with a population of 15,000 Jews. On April 15th a crowd collected outside a Jewish shop: a drunken Russian was sent inside and when the shopkeeper, as expected, threw him out into the street, the people cried: 'The Zhyds are beating our people.' The account of the Elizabethgrad pogrom given in Dubnow's *History of the Jews in Russia and Poland* tells what happened next:

During the night from the 15th to the 16th April, an attack was made upon Jewish houses, primarily upon liquor stores, on the outskirts of the town, on which occasion one Jew was killed. About seven o'clock in the morning, on April 16, the excesses were renewed, spreading with extraordinary violence all over the city. Clerks, saloon and hotel waiters, artisans, drivers, flunkeys, day labourers in the employ of the Government, and soldiers on furlough—all of these joined the movement. The city presented an extraordinary sight: streets covered with feathers and obstructed with broken furniture,

which had been thrown out of the residences; houses with
broken doors and windows; a raging mob running about
and yelling and whistling in all directions and continuing
its work without let or hindrance ...

Ten days later after similar outbreaks in towns and villages
around Elizabethgrad the violence spread to Kiev.

The pogroms alone were not responsible for the exodus. In
fact the central Government in St Petersburg attempted to put
them down, sternly warning the provincial governors in the
following spring that it was 'firmly resolved to prosecute invariably any attempt at violence on the person and property of
the Jews', who, as it reminded them in case they had forgotten,
were 'under the general protection of the general laws'. The
warning seems to have been effective. Apart from one or two
isolated incidents there was no major pogrom for another twenty
years. Serious trouble did not break out again until the Kishinev
massacres of 1903, nine years after Alexander III's death.

Why then the exodus? The answer is contained in two words:
May Laws—or as the Government preferred to call them:
Temporary Rules. Under the new laws they now had to prove to
the authorities' satisfaction that they had been living on the land
before May 3rd, 1882. For many peasants this was more difficult
than it sounds. No Jew was allowed to have his own land or
house, so all the peasants were leaseholders; and very often the
terms of the lease were verbal, not written. So when the local
officials from the nearest town came round asking the Jews for
proof, there was nothing they could show. If they failed to
provide that proof they were expelled from the villages where
they had lived all their lives and packed off to the towns. The
inevitable result was that the towns were overrun by thousands
of poor, homeless and hungry Jews all looking for work.

The May Laws were openly and deliberately anti-semitic and
Pobyedonostzev, the Grand Inquisitor, was for one quite clear as
to their effect: 'A third of the Jews will emigrate,' he said, 'a third

will be converted and a third will die.'* It was in this fashion that the Government proposed to do away with what it called 'the aggravated relations between the Jews and the original [*sic*] population'.

Even before the introduction of the May Laws, the 4,750,000 Jews who lived in the fifteen westernmost provinces that made up the Russian Pale (an area about ten times the size of Ireland) were surrounded on every side by restrictions and regulations. Though military service was compulsory no Jew could rise higher than a private, most of the professions were closed to him and the places in which he was allowed to live were strictly limited. St Petersburg and Moscow were barred, as were most of the big cities. The only Jews allowed to live outside the 350,000 square miles of the Pale were a few of the richer merchants, university students, long-serving soldiers, dentists, surgeons and skilled artisans who were allowed into the big towns—but only on sufferance. Sir Samuel Montagu, later Lord Swaythling, visiting Russia in 1886 to investigate conditions there on behalf of British Jewry, quickly discovered for himself just how precarious and unpredictable life was—even for the intelligentsia. The Russians, totally unimpressed by the fact that Sir Samuel was a distinguished member of the British Parliament, treated him exactly like his co-religionists and gave him twenty-four hours to leave Moscow.

But the misfortunes of the Jewish inhabitants of Moscow and St Petersburg were small compared to the disaster that overtook the hundreds of thousands of peasants and other small people in the villages and hamlets of the Russian countryside. According to Major William Evans-Gordon, the anti-alien M.P. who visited Russia as a member of the 1902 British Commission on alien immigration, in the eighteen months after the passing of the May Laws, the population of Tschernigo, a typical Russian town, rose from 5,000 to 20,000.

---

* His estimate of the number of conversions and deaths turned out to be a wild overstatement (there were few deaths and almost no conversions), but on emigration his forecast was too low.

Evans-Gordon was not the only person to be shocked by the conditions in the towns of the Pale. Arnold White, another anti-alien agitator, wrote in his report for the Royal Commission:*

A visit to the town of Berdicheff admits the traveller into a City of Dreadful Night. It is one dead level of gloom, decay and silence. The neglected streets are almost impassable from water holes. Ordure lies untouched, festering in the sun or washed by frequent rains. The very animals are afflicted by the blight that hangs over the town. The droskies and cars are falling to pieces, the ribs of the horses stand out. Emaciated dogs prowl about in search of food ... In Berdicheff 30 or 40 manufacturers might make a living. The number exceeds 500. Wages run as low as 4d. a day.

In 1902 the British Government, worried by the increasing flood of immigrants and the problems that this created in the East End, had set up a Royal Commission. Their inquiry lasted sixteen months, during which the Commissioners interviewed no less than 175 witnesses—local government officials from Whitechapel and Stepney, Board of Trade experts, leaders of the Jewish community, trade union spokesmen and other interested parties. They saw remarkably few immigrants. And those they did see were nearly all hand-picked by Arnold White to illustrate his point that the immigrants were dirty, improvident and generally undesirable. 'They are', he said, revealing the agitator's gift for the telling phrase, 'like a drop of prussic acid in a glass of water.' The Commissioners, though not notably sympathetic to the aliens, tried hard to be fair and rapped White over the knuckles for this singularly unpleasant remark. But they were, all the same, anxious to discover whether the immigrants had come to England of their own accord or whether, as the anti-alien camp was quick to suggest, they had been encouraged to come by the Anglo-Jewish community. On the whole the immigrants were not very satisfactory witnesses (partly because few of them spoke English)

* *Royal Commission on Alien Immigration: Report and Minutes of Evidence*, 1903.

but on this point they were unanimous and quite clear. As Libel Abramovitch told the Commissioners:

'I came here because the Government were cruel and have driven me away, because they do not allow Jews to be in the country and work on the land; therefore they have driven me out. I could not go into the towns and, therefore, I sold my horse and cow and came here.'

'How was the Government cruel?'

'Simply because they would not let me remain.'

'How long have you been on the land?'

'All my life; and suddenly a ukase came that I must no longer live there and I must go.'

'Were you driven off by the police, or how?'

'They have driven me out. Some people have hanged themselves and some have drowned themselves but I did not wish to do either.'

He was not the only one. Even before the accession of Alexander III and his May Laws, the Jews were leaving the Russian empire in considerable numbers. Between 1870 and 1880 it is reckoned that 350,000 emigrated—in the early years the majority going to America. By 1888 when Sir Robert Giffen, the distinguished economist and head of the Board of Trade's commercial department, testified to a House of Commons' Select Committee investigating immigration, he estimated that about 40,000 people were leaving every year.

Exactly how many of those 40,000 settled in England is impossible to say, for though the machinery for counting immigrant heads had existed since George IV's day, it had grown rusty with disuse. The best anybody could do was to make guesses and there were plenty of these. Everybody, from the Jewish Board of Guardians, the body set up by the Jewish community in 1859 to co-ordinate the work of poor relief, to the British Brothers' League, an embryonic East End Fascist organization, joined in the guessing game. But it was the Board of Trade who probably got closest to the mark. Basing its estimate on the rise in relief given by the Board of Guardians, it reckoned that between 1881 and 1886 the numbers of Russian and Polish immigrants (nearly all of whom must have been Jews) rose by 50 per cent. It sounds a lot until one remembers that in 1881 there were only 15,000 alien Jews in the whole of England and Wales; three-quarters of them in London, Manchester and Leeds. The dramatic leap came in the next ten years when the number of Russians and Poles soared by 212 per cent to just over 50,000; and by 1901, five years before the flood was stemmed by the Aliens Act, the number had almost doubled again to 95,000. And so with an average influx of 4,000 a year, over a period of twenty years the Jewish population had increased by some 600 per cent.

The people who profited most from the flood were not the taskmasters of the East End sweat shops but the shipping companies and the travel agents. When the traffic was at its height, a Mr Kendall of Adelaide Street handed over to the Elder Dempster Line £44,000 which he had collected in one year from immigrants travelling from England to America. It might seem odd that so many should stop off in England on their way to America but they did so for one very good reason: the travel agents made more money that way. Throughout this period the commercial policies of the shipping companies oscillated wildly: at one moment they were setting up cartels and the next they were at each others' throats, slashing prices to the bone. During the 'Atlantic Rate War' which raged between 1902 and 1904, the cost of travelling steerage from England to America fell from £6 10s. to £2. But in the 1890s the companies were passing through one of their cartel-making phases. In 1895 the companies working the Atlantic agreed that the English price should be fixed at £2 below the German rate. The Germans, for their part, agreed to pay the extra £2 that they received into a central fund on condition that the British did not carry immigrants who intended to stay in the country less than six weeks. The objective was to prevent immigrants from taking advantage of the cheaper British prices and thus travelling on to America on a cut rate.

This restriction did nothing to deter the agents who had spotted an easy way of making an extra £2. To the agent in Russia the immigrant paid the full fare to America; all he got in return was a ticket to England, the address of an agent there and instructions that he was, on no account, to tell the English customs he was travelling on to America. The idea was that while the immigrant was travelling to England the Russian agent, having collected £7 10s., would send £5 10s. to his English partner. And that by the time the immigrant arrived in London the tickets for America would be ready and waiting. Sometimes it worked like that but more often the immigrant was cheated: the money was never sent or the tickets never bought. Occasionally the defrauded immigrants were brave enough or desperate enough to hit back. In October 1895, a party of six Russian immigrants who had had the wit to obtain the support of a Jewish paper tried to sue the London agent, a Mr Meczyk with whose brother-in-law they had dealt in Russia. They told the court:

'On arriving in London a man came to us and asked us if we were going to America. We were, of course, afraid and answered that we intended to stay on in London ... Mr Meczyk told us that as it was Friday it was too late to send us away this week but he would send us by the first ship that sailed the next week. After the Sabbath we began to understand how great our misfortune was. Mr Meczyk would not send us away. One day he said that no money had arrived, and the next day that money had arrived for three only ... So he led us by the nose from day to day. We made a disturbance in the synagogue, and he had us turned out by the police. We are three weeks in London and we are starving.'

They lost their case.

The travel agents were not the only hazard the immigrants met on arriving in England. As the ships drew in all manner of sharks were waiting on the quayside. Tired and dirty after four days in the holds of ships which were often designed to carry cattle, not passengers, and speaking only three English words—'Board of Guardians'—they were easy meat for the hundred or so Yiddish-speaking con-men who gathered to meet them. There are lurid stories of young Jewish girls being whisked off the immigrant boats and away into the brothels of Cable Street and the Totten-ham Court Road. Undoubtedly some were. But the ticket touts were a far greater hazard. In the early years of the immigrant boom, before the Jewish community in England realized what was going on and rallied round to stop it, they were extraordin-arily brazen. 'You want to go to America?' they asked the immi-grants. 'Yes,' they replied. 'Well, follow me,' said the touts, leading them off to Liverpool Street Station. There, after ex-tracting fifty shillings or so, the touts packed them, in a state of high excitement, into a train—which twenty minutes later ended its journey at Tottenham.

While the shipping companies and the travel agents welcomed the immigrants with open arms—and outstretched hands—their reception from nearly everybody else in England varied from the cool to the openly hostile. As the numbers of the immigrants grew, so did the chorus of protest. It was one in which all sectors of society joined. On November 24th, 1902, the Bishop of Stepney addressed his flock. It was a speech that made quite a stir. He said:

East London was [*sic*] growing more and more poverty stricken. In some districts every vestige of comfort has been wiped out, the Jews coming in like an army, eating up Christian Gentiles or driving them out. I prophesy that before my hair is grey the old parish church of Stepney would be [*sic*] standing amid an alien population. I recognize the vigour and intelligence among the aliens but the fact remains that they are swamping whole areas once populated by English people and our churches are continually being left like islands in a sea of aliens.

If the Bishop voiced the fears of the East End's Christian community, then Mr James Johnson, a labourer by trade and chairman of the executive committee of the British Brothers' League, spoke for the tailors, the costermongers and the ordinary working people of the East End, who saw the Jews as a threat to their livelihood. Encouraged by Major Evans-Gordon, some sixty years before Mr Enoch Powell began his anti-alien campaign, Johnson expressed the view that this country was 'too small' to take in any more foreigners. 'The object of the League', Johnson said, 'is to prevent any further incursion into this country of destitute aliens, no matter who they are or where they come from ... We, the British Brothers' League, think, and believe, that this country is too small to take any more in, that its own natural increase will be, and is quite sufficient; therefore we say there is no room for foreigners.'*

The Jews were accused of every kind of crime and misdemeanour: from prostitution to not observing the Christian Sabbath. They were even accused of causing the death of Mr Chadbourne, of 39 Varden Street, whose rent was raised after his house had been bought by a Jew. Mr Chadbourne, so a friend of his told the Royal Commission, suffered from asthma and 'was not a robust man'. 'A wet night came; he had to travel outside, caught a chill and was dead within a few days. I say, emphatically, that man's death was mainly attributable to this influx of aliens.'

Even from their co-religionists the poor immigrant Jews received only a qualified welcome. Many of the stockbrokers, the bankers and the bullion brokers who provided the main support for such pillars of Anglo-Jewry as the United Synagogue and the

* The similarities between the reactions in certain quarters to the arrival of the Jews in the 1880s and to the coming of the West Indians and Pakistanis in the 1960s are striking. In the spring of 1968, shortly after Mr Enoch Powell made his famous 'Wolverhampton' speech, I happened to read out Mr Johnson's remarks which were made to the Royal Commission in 1902 to some friends in a railway carriage. Some strangers overheard the remarks and when I had finished they volunteered a loud 'Hear, hear'.

c

Board of Guardians had travelled the same route not two generations back. But now wealthy, respected and established, they were
torn by conflicting emotions: a natural sympathy for their fellow
Jews was combined with a fear that an uncontrolled horde of
poor, extremely *foreign* immigrants would undo in a moment all
their patient and successful efforts to assimilate into British society.
In the end they compromised: the doors of the Jewish charities
were partially but not fully opened (nobody could claim a penny
of relief from the Jewish Board of Guardians until he had been
in the country for a minimum of six months) while at the same
time the leaders of the community did everything possible to
persuade the immigrants not to come—or having come, to go
back again. In its annual report for 1901 the Board wrote:

> In the main, the only relief it could offer to applicants arriving
> in a hopeless condition would be to assist them to return to
> the country they had left with such absence of foresight ...
> It is an outrage against the dictates of common sense and
> humanity that such a senseless and hopeless movement
> should ever have been directed to these shores; and the
> responsibility is heavy on those who encouraged and
> assisted it.

What worried both Jewish and non-Jewish authorities alike
was not so much the number of the immigrants but their poverty
and their habit of concentration. A number of abortive attempts
were made to divert the newcomers from the already over-
crowded East End and to persuade them to settle elsewhere. In
May 1902 the Jewish community set up a special committee to
head the fathers of immigrant families away from London,
Manchester, Liverpool and Leeds which were already over-
crowded. They were given interest-free loans to encourage them
to go to towns like Chatham, Reading, Blackburn and Dover.
Likewise the Royal Commission, after finding that 'the greatest
evils produced by the presence of the alien immigrants here is the
overcrowding caused by them in certain districts and the con-

sequent displacement of the native population', toyed with the idea of declaring certain districts a prohibited area. This suggestion was never adopted as it was obvious from the beginning that it could never be enforced*. The Jews were determined to settle in the East End and little could be done to stop them.

There were Jews in and around the East End long before the arrival of the immigrants. The well-to-do merchants who arrived from Holland in the latter half of the seventeenth century settled in the City itself, round Finsbury Square and in Angel Court, just across the road from where the Bank of England now stands. They moved into the tall houses, now occupied by the ship-brokers, round St Mary Axe, and they bought comfortable mansions among the bankers along Leadenhall Street. The City welcomed these rich Jews but when it came to their poorer co-religionists the City Fathers were not nearly so hospitable. The poor Jews were not only forbidden to trade in the City—they were not allowed to live there either. But they were never far away. Never more than half a mile separated the rich City Jews from the poor rag-dealers and second-hand clothes men in the slums of Whitechapel. Though there was a small outpost in Tenter Ground, just south of Whitechapel High Street, the main community was packed in among the narrow alleys that led off Middlesex Street (better known as Petticoat Lane) and it was so compact that one could have walked from side to side of the quarter in under five minutes.

With the community so firmly established in the East End, only a few hundred yards from the docks, it was only natural that the newly arrived Russians and Poles should make for the one part of London where they knew they would find their own

* Mr James Callaghan, the then Home Secretary, came to much the same conclusion. When it was suggested by the Labour borough of Ealing in a letter to the Prime Minister that 'in view of the number of immigrant children already in the schools no more should be allowed in', he replied: 'Just stop and think a moment. How do you stop them? They only have to buy a ticket at Charing Cross and they are there.' B.B.C. Panorama, April 29th, 1968.

people—speaking the same language, and sharing the same religion and customs. Sometimes the immigrants arrived with just a name and an address. Sometimes, as happened in Leeds, the immigrants arrived at the railway station, waving placards on which was written simply 'Vilna' or 'Lodtz'—meaning that they wanted to be taken to that part of the town where the Jews from Vilna or Lodtz lived.

By 1889 the Jews had burst out of the old ghetto; crossing over Commercial Street which had marked the eastern boundary and moving farther eastwards into Fashion Street and Thrawl Street —a notorious red light district—and on into Chicksand Street and Old Montagu Street. As the thieves and prostitutes of Fashion Street moved out, the Jews moved in. To their great alarm, the public health inspectors, the local authorities, the costermongers, the shopkeepers and the stockbroking and banking leaders of Anglo-Jewry saw the character of the East End change almost overnight. By 1894, the Board of Trade calculated no less than 53 per cent of the 75,000 or so Russians and Poles in the United Kingdom were to be found in an area not two miles square, bisected by the Whitechapel Road. By the turn of the century Dr Shirley Foster Murphy, London's level-headed health officer, calculated that nearly one person in every three in Whitechapel, and more than one in four in the parish of St George's in the East, was Jewish. It was a phenomenon that did not escape the notice of that diligent investigator Charles Booth. He began his famous inquiry, the *Life and Labour of the people of London*, in 1883—just about the time the immigrant rush was beginning to swell. By 1898 he could write:

The whole district has been affected by the increase in the Jewish population. It has been like the slow rising of a flood. Street after street is occupied. Family follows family. No Gentile could live in the same house with these poor foreign Jews, and even as neighbours they are unpleasant; and since people of this race, though sometimes quarrelsome among themselves, are extremely gregarious and sociable, each small street or group of houses invaded tends to become entirely Jewish. Houses are bought or rented, however dilapidated they may be or with however short a lease to run. The previous tenants are ejected nominally for repairs and their place is taken by the new owners or their new tenants, the houses being sub-let and packed full of poor Jews. The crowding that results is very great ... House and land values rise, however. Rents are paid punctually by the tenants-in-chief and without doubt no less punctually collected from their sub-tenants.

Booth was not merely voicing his own feelings when he harped on the over-crowding in the East End: it was the central issue; the one that bothered more people, and caused more anti-semitic feeling than any other. Housing conditions in the East End in the 1890s were indeed grim. Nor did public bodies like the London County Council or private ones like Lady Rothschild's Four Per Cent Industrial Dwellings Company, hard at work clearing the slums, do much at first to improve them, as they knocked down many more buildings than they put up. According to the Registrar-General, any house of less than five rooms in which there were more than two people living in any one room, was classified as over-crowded. In 1901, so Dr Murphy calculated, 83·3 per cent of the houses in Whitechapel came into that category. In other words eight out of every ten Whitechapel tenements housed more than a dozen people. 'At one of our Xmas teas', said the rector of Spitalfields in 1901, 'about 200 children were assembled. After tea, as they sat together, I asked: "How many of you live in a one-roomed home?" Every hand but seven went up. "How many live in a two-roomed house?" Seven hands went up. "How many live in three rooms?" None. "How many of you live in a furnished room?" All but twelve.'

It may have been uncomfortable for the immigrants but it was highly profitable for the landlords, both Gentile and Jewish, for whom the twenty years straddling the turn of the century was boom time. So strong was the demand that between 1890 and 1908 it was difficult to obtain a house of any kind without paying around £25 in 'key money' and the few landlords who did not demand it hung notices outside their properties advertising the fact. But even if he had paid his 'key money' the immigrant had no guarantee that over the next few years the rent would not rocket beyond his reach. In the twenty years of the housing boom property changed hands with unusual speed: and each time it did so the new landlord, in the hope of recovering the inflated price he had paid for the freehold, raised the rent. In Cadiz Street, Stepney, to mention one of many examples, the rent nearly doubled in just four years. At the height of the boom, people, as they are prone to do, were asking totally ridiculous prices for freeholds. One man who owned a row of houses next to a vacant plot at Lomas Buildings in Stepney was asked if he would sell, as the plot could not be developed unless his houses were demolished. His asking price was £16,000 an acre. The deal did not go through.

Knowing that the immigrants had no option but to accept and pay for conditions that no native East Ender would tolerate, houses were packed from floor to ceiling in a fashion that offended local officials, concerned as much with the immigrants' morals as they were with the state of the drains. Describing an unannounced visit to an immigrant home, the manager of the Winterton Estate in Stepney told the Royal Commission: 'There were two young girls, about 23 to 25, sleeping on the left-hand side of the room, two young men lodgers were sleeping on the right-hand side in the same room, and the young men were talking to these girls in bed. A more disgusting thing I never saw in my life.' But though the public health people tried hard enough there was little they could do. As one of them said: 'Although we endeavour to prevent overcrowding as far as possible in dealing with these people it is very much like dealing with a large rabbit warren. We simply put the legal ferrets, if I may so call them, into the hole, the rabbits come out and go into another hole and the same operation is repeated.'

The arrival of the Jews certainly created very great problems for the local authorities, the health and factory inspectors and the other hard-pressed officials who had the almost impossible job of administering the East End. There were great abuses and injustices and for a short time conditions in a small corner of London and in equally small corners of the larger provincial cities were intolerable. But it could have been worse. The Jews were, most fair-minded officials agreed, cleaner, more God-fearing and more family-loving than those they had replaced. Nor, despite the fears of Mr James Johnson and his friends, was there much unemployment among the East End shopkeepers, costermongers and tailors. Even the worst fears of the middle-class Jews were not realized, for though the immigrants may have been foreign when they arrived, they lost no time in acquiring English characteristics. Considering their numbers, their poverty and their general disadvantages, the process of assimilation was astonishingly rapid. Their parents may still have worn funny clothes and spoken little English but the children were fast shedding their Eastern European background. So great was the thirst for education that they poured into the Board schools in such numbers that by the turn of the century nearly all the sixteen Church of England schools in Tower Hamlets were staffed by Jewish teachers and were observing Jewish holidays. The teachers were delighted with their progress. The headmaster of the Betts Street school told the Royal Commission:

The boys seem to be very proud to believe that they will become English. If you speak to the boys the general idea is that once they are here they mean to try and be English in everything. In the matter of English history they are most attentive and they seem highly delighted to listen to English history lessons. In fact, at my last examination of the class a fortnight ago the entry in my book, which will go to the

London School Board, was: 'The history of this class is in a highly creditable condition, and it is a very remarkable fact that the foreign children show an even better knowledge of English history than English children themselves.'

The long climb out of the ghetto had begun.

Chapter Three

The Englishmen of Jewish Extraction

> There is an upper class among Jews, the old English Jews,
> those families who have been in this country at least three
> to five generations. They have wealth, education and,
> most important, background — they are well brought up.
> We are all like diamonds, except that some of us are more
> polished than others. And they have polish. Carriage.
>
> A Hendon gown manufacturer
> on the Jewish aristocracy.

The Jewish community that the immigrants found waiting for
them with half-open arms was strikingly different from the one
that they had left behind in the small villages and towns of the
Russian Pale. The boys poring over their history books at the
Betts Street school in an attempt to become 'English in everything' were just beginning their climb out of the East End — an
ascent that was to take them first north to Stoke Newington and
Stamford Hill, then westwards to Cricklewood, north again up
the newly-built Northern Line to Hendon and Edgware, eventually finishing up among the elegant Nash Terraces that surround
Regents Park. For the dignitaries from the Board of Guardians,
waiting on the quayside of St Katharine docks to greet the new
arrivals, the ascent was already complete. They were still very
conscious of the fact that they were Jews, and as such had powerful
obligations to the newcomers, but as bankers, stockbrokers,

bullion merchants, lawyers and politicians they were equally conscious that they had become part of the fabric of late-Victorian society.

When Sir Robert Waley-Cohen, managing director of Shell, declared at the height of the bitter Zionist controversy which was to split Anglo-Jewry for more than a generation, that the English Jews were 'entirely British in thought, aspirations, interest and zeal', he was speaking for the greater part of the resident Jewish community whose oldest families had been living and working in England for close on 250 years—ever since 1656 when Cromwell reversed Edward I's 366-year-old decision to expel the Jews.

That Sir Robert should speak out on behalf of the English Jews was only natural. As president of the United Synagogue he was what his biographer, the late Robert Henriques calls: 'the last of the Grand Dukes of Anglo-Jewry'; a member of that tight, much intermarried group of families which at the turn of the century made up the Anglo-Jewish Establishment. It was a surprisingly small group of not more than half a dozen families, almost equally divided between those of Sephardic origin who came from Spain and Portugal (often via Holland) in the late seventeenth century and the Ashkenazim from Germany and Central Europe. The Ashkenazim, however, rapidly overhauled the Sephardic Jews and by 1730 were already outnumbering them by two to one. The Mocattas, the Sebags and the Montefiores had the dark brown complexions and thin, aquiline faces of the Sephardic Jew while the Franklins, the Keysers, the Rothschilds, the Samuels and the Montagus were smaller and stockier, often with black curly hair and heavy jowls. Initially the Sephardim regarded themselves socially as a cut above the solid, Yiddish-speaking Germans and Dutchmen, but though there are some differences in religious ritual, the two groups soon began to intermarry; and as they did so the physical characteristics became increasingly blurred and the Sephardim began to lose whatever claim they had to social superiority.

By the time Sir Robert had assumed the leadership of the community the leading families had become bound together in an incredibly complex network of marriage ties and alliances—so much so that they were practically one enormous family. Sir Robert himself, through his ancestor, Levi Barent Cohen who came to London in the 1780s as a linen trader and made his fortune as a stockbroker, was related to practically every family in Anglo-Jewry; to the Rothschilds, the Montefiores, the Goldsmids and the Samuels. Similar skeins connected nearly all the important families; the Franklins to the Montagus and the Sassoons to the Franklins. Only the Rothschilds remained aloof; the tribe was already extensive and they preferred to marry cousins—thus keeping the family in the family, as it were.

The older families monopolized the great offices of Anglo-Jewry which they administered in much the same autocratic, paternalistic spirit as their own family businesses, handing down responsibility from father to son. It was accepted quite as the established order of things that Sir Robert Waley-Cohen should succeed his father and his grandfather as president of the United Synagogue, and nobody thought it in any way remarkable that no less than six members of the Cohen family should have led the Board of Guardians (now the Franklin-led Jewish Welfare Board) since its foundation in 1859.

But it would be wrong to imagine that the Jewish aristocracy kept themselves entirely to themselves. Not only were the ramifications of what the Jewish author Chaim Bermant has described as The Cousinhood extensive but by the early 1900s its members were to be found in almost every segment of British society, involved in good works as much as in making money. Among the most powerful and influential of the families was the prolific Samuel–Franklin–Montagu clan, descended from an obscure foreign exchange dealer born in Breslau at the beginning of the eighteenth century.

When the family genealogist sat down in 1931 to compile the family tree—a task that took him over four years—he identified no less than 3,500 members; among them two cabinet ministers —Edwin Montagu and Lord Samuel, the Liberal peer; at least two more who were to become distinguished lawyers, Lord Cohen of Walmer and the Hon. Ewen Montagu (author of *The Man who Never Was*, one of the great cloak-and-dagger epics of the Second World War), and innumerable bankers (including Samuel Montagu, the first Lord Swaythling), philanthropists and academics. A page taken at random from the family genealogy gives some idea of the range and scope of this extraordinary family's interests and activities.

Franklin, Ernest Louis.
Educated at King's College School, London.
Partner in the banking and bullion firm of Samuel Montagu & Co. from 1885 until 1946, when he retired, remaining a limited partner. J.P., county of London. Fellow of the Statistical Society. Fellow of the Royal Economic Society. President for fifty years, subsequently Vice-President, Home for Aged Jews. Vice-President, Children's Country Holidays Fund, and president of Jewish branch for fifty years. Vice-President, Jewish Home of Rest. Publications: articles on Foreign Exchange in the 11th Edition and on arbitrage in the 14th edition, *Encyclopaedia Britannica*, and on finance in British and American periodicals over a long period. b. 16 Aug. 1859 at 39 Burton Crescent (now Cartright Gardens) London wc. d. 8 April 1950 at 50 Porchester Terrace, London, w2. b'd at Liberal Jewish Cemetery, Willesden.

Franklin, Frederick Samuel.
Partner in the banking and bullion firm of Samuel Montagu & Co. 1894. b. 9 June 1864 at 2 Leinster Terrace, London. d. 17 April 1918, b'd at United Synagogue Cemetery, Willesden.

Franklin, Geoffrey Montagu Ernest.
Educated at Bedales and at Lincoln College, Oxford. First

World War: Friends War Relief Organisation in France. A
founder of the Wayfarer's Travel Agency, 1920. b. 11 May
1890 at Pembridge Gardens, London w. d. 11 Sept. 1930 at
50 Porchester Terrace, London w2. b'd at Willesden.

Franklin, Hon. Henrietta.
C.B.E. (1950) Educated at Doreck College, Kensington
Gardens Square, London, w. President 1926 and 1927,
Hon. Vice-President, National Council of Women. Hon.
Secretary, Parent's National Educational Union since 1892.
Member of Council, Liberal Jewish Synagogues (formerly
Jewish Religious Union) since 1902, and other organizations.
Member of Advisory Committee, Liberal Jewish Synagogue,
since 1945. b. 9 April 1866 at 53 Cleveland Square, London
w. m. 7 Oct. 1885 at New West End Synagogue, London, w.

Franklin, Hugh Arthur.
Member, 1946-9, Chairman of Drainage Committee, Middle-
sex County Council. Member 1937-49, Chairman of Works
Committee, 1940-9, Metropolitan Water Board. Member of
Education Committee, London County Council 1934-46
and since 1952. Member Thames Conservancy 1946-9.
Member of Committee, Harefield and Northwood (Mount
Vernon) Hospital group since 1951. A governor of Regent
Street, Northern, Northampton, and Battersea Polytechnics,
of Wandsworth Technical College, and of secondary schools.
Candidate for Parliament, 1931 and 1935, for Labour Party.
b. 27 May 1889 at 28 Pembridge Villas, London, w.

The fact that most of the Franklins worked for Jewish causes,
were married in synagogues and were buried in Jewish cemeteries
is significant. Though some, like Geoffrey Franklin who became
a Quaker shortly before the First World War, abandoned the
faith altogether, the majority remained very conscious of their
Jewish traditions and inheritance. Abraham Goldsmid, the

banker, moved in the highest circles (he was an intimate friend of Nelson who stayed with him in Surrey the night before he left for Trafalgar) but he worshipped in a private synagogue in his grounds and set aside a piece of the estate to grow wheat for the Chief Rabbi's Passover cakes. The Keysers, yet another branch of the Franklin family, had it laid down in their articles of association that under no circumstances would the family bank do business on the Jewish Sabbath—a rule that was still in force in the late 1960s.

It was the same consciousness of Jewish tradition, plus a strong sense of duty towards the poor, that led the Jewish aristocracy to take up philanthropic works on a massive scale; an instinct which after an initial reluctance found full expression as the immigrants poured in from Eastern Europe throughout the 1890s. Occasionally business rivalry spilled over into philanthropy: one of Lord Swaythling's basic tenets was to do the exact opposite to anything the Rothschilds did, and when Lord Rothschild offered £20,000 to improve social conditions in the East End, it was Lord Swaythling who led the opposition. But such incidents were exceptional and in the face of the crisis created by the Russian pogroms most of the leaders were prepared to sink their differences. Nearly every family contributed to the appeal that the Lord Mayor of London launched at the Mansion House in 1882; many spent much of their spare time touring the East End setting up soup kitchens and youth settlements—several of which, though shadows of their former selves, still remain. The Rothschilds were particularly active. Charlotte, Lady Rothschild, formed a special company, the Four Per Cent Industrial Dwellings Company Ltd, to put up great tenement blocks which, grim as they look now, were a vast improvement on the slums they replaced.

The arrival of the immigrants created more than one crisis. Not only did it present the aristocracy with a very real challenge to their philanthropic zeal, it also threatened to undermine their hard-won social position by reviving the Englishman's latent belief that underneath that English veneer which Anglo-Jewry had acquired lurked an essentially 'different', altogether foreign being.

It was a danger that Anglo-Jewry was quick to recognize, and their consciousness of it does much to explain why their opposition to Chaim Weizmann and his Zionist ideals, which contained the implication that a Jew owed his allegiance as much to Israel as to England, was so bitter and so fierce. It was of the assimilated Jews of Anglo-Jewry that Weizmann said: 'They seem to live in an entirely different world.' What he really meant was that they had long lost the distinguishing traits of the ghetto Jew and had almost totally submerged themselves into British society, adopting the culture and mores of their new country.

Indeed they had. The older families thought of themselves, as Robert Waley-Cohen was at pains to point out, as Englishmen first and Jews second. Even the religion itself, as the new arrivals were horrified to discover, had been anglicized. Some fifty years before, in 1840, the Mocattas had led a movement to clothe the rabbis in English canonicals, to decorate the synagogues and to trim the services to a modest two and three-quarter hours. In the privacy of their own homes they may have observed the traditional Jewish customs, and in the streets of the East End they may have handed out soup to their afflicted co-religionists, but in every other respect the aim was to resemble the native-born Englishman as closely as possible. As Professor Maurice Freedman in an essay 'Jews in the Society of Britain'* has pointed out: 'To be an Englishman and a Jew, which is probably the aim of a very large proportion of Jews born in England, depresses Judaism to the level of one faith among many in a predominantly secular society … Flanking the Jewish Englishman is, as it were, the Englishman of Jewish extraction.' It is a description that fits the Rothschilds and the Montagus, the Samuels and the Franklins perfectly.

From the days of the great eighteenth-century speculator and loan contractor, Samson Gideon, onwards, bankers who had made their money in the City tended to invest it in the countryside

* In *A Minority in Britain.*

in the form of great houses, flocks of pedigree sheep and stables full of racehorses. It was not that the Jews were fonder of these luxuries than anybody else; merely that in reaching up towards the landed gentry and the aristocracy they were following the pattern set by the aspiring middle classes. The ranks of the English aristocracy have always been open to those successful, lucky or unscrupulous enough to be able to afford the entrance fee, as many nineteenth-century English gentlemen with a fortune in beer or railways discovered.

Nevertheless when the City bankers decided that the time had come to sink their roots in the land, the results were often magnificent and spectacular. Samson Gideon made an enormous fortune (he had by the time he was forty-one made £360,000 as a stock-jobber), much of which he used to buy Lord Baltimore's estate at Belvedere in Kent which he then proceeded to fill with a collection of Old Masters. He later acquired large estates in Buckinghamshire, Lincolnshire and Northamptonshire; the bulk of which he left, much to Horace Walpole's surprise, to the Duke of Devonshire. 'I forgot to tell you', wrote Horace in a letter to his cousin Henry Seymour Conway, 'that Gideon who is worth more than the whole land of Canaan, has left the reversion of his milk and honey, after his son and daughter and their children, to the Duke of Devonshire, without insisting on his taking the name, or even being circumcised.'

But splendid as Gideon's estates were, for sheer magnificence he was easily outshone by those nineteenth-century magnates the Rothschilds and the Sassoons—often called the Rothschilds of the East. They spent prodigious sums; both on their houses and the surrounding acres and on the pictures, the furniture and the racehorses to fill them. Lionel Rothschild, second son of Nathan Mayer, the founder of the British house, paid a quarter of a million pounds for Tring Manor, a beautiful seventeenth-century mansion designed by Sir Christopher Wren and given as a present by Charles II to Nell Gwyn as a recompense for her services. On fitting the house out Lionel spent many thousands of pounds more. The Sassoons too had territorial ambitions. Shortly after he arrived from Hong Kong in 1858, S. D. Sassoon bought Ashley Park in Surrey, a fifteenth-century estate of some 200 wooded acres, once occupied by Cromwell and containing a magnificent banqueting hall where Henry VIII had danced. Some fifty years later his nephew, Sir Edward, bought Trent Park, a 1,000 acre estate with its private golf course at the end of what is now the Piccadilly Line at Cockfosters, once supposed to be the hiding-place of Dick Turpin.

David Sassoon in one neat epigram summed up both the style of life and the aspirations of the upper echelons of Anglo-Jewry. 'There is only one race better than the Jews', he said, 'and that is the Derby.'

For the City bankers to acquire the outward appearances and habits of an English country gentleman was easy enough; obtaining the corresponding political power and social status proved a little more difficult. Influential sectors of Victorian society were still distinctly anti-semitic. Carlyle could quite cheerfully describe Disraeli as an 'accursed old Jew not worth his weight in cold bacon' and Trollope was undoubtedly reflecting a popular image of the Jew when he described his banker anti-hero of *The Way We Live Now* as a man 'who could make or mar any company by selling stock, and could make money dear or cheap as he pleased'. Even Queen Victoria, who was less prejudiced than many of her subjects, could turn down the Rothschild request for a peerage on the grounds that 'to make a Jew a peer is a step I could not consent to. It would be ill-taken and do the Government great harm.'

Even so these prejudices were not sufficiently strong to withstand sustained pressure from the Jews, for as Lord Macaulay pointed out:* 'In fact the Jews are not excluded from political power. They possess it; and as long as they are allowed to accumulate large fortunes, they must possess it.' Significantly it was in the City, where the power of money has always been

* 'Civil Disabilities of the Jews' in *Collected Essays*.

D

acknowledged, and in the legal profession that the barriers first crumbled. In 1833 Mr Francis Goldsmid of Lincoln's Inn became the first professing Jew to be called to the Bar and in 1855 Sir David Salomons became the first member of his faith to be elected Lord Mayor of London. Three years later, after a campaign that had lasted more than thirty years, Lionel Rothschild, Nathan Mayer's eldest son, set the seal on this achievement by taking his seat in the House of Commons. Only the House of Lords remained impregnable; but in 1885, when Nathaniel Mayer Rothschild finally obtained his long-desired peerage, even this bastion fell.

Such achievements were of course immensely gratifying to the entire community. That a Jew should become Lord Mayor or be raised to the peerage was a source of pleasure not only to those immediately concerned but to every Jew in the country. It provided visible proof that they had made it. But while the change of climate proved invigorating both to the Jews themselves and to the society into which they had belatedly been welcomed, there were also some entries on the debit side of the balance sheet.

By the turn of the century the Grand Dukes of Anglo-Jewry were beginning to lose their commercial zest. Seduced by the pleasures of Edwardian high society, the second generation of Rothschilds, Montagus and Samuels became more interested in cultivating their extensive gardens than in nourishing the businesses that had given them their wealth and influence. Commenting on the collapse of the great banking business of Overend and Gurney which went broke for £18 million in 1866, Bagehot wrote:* 'In the first place an hereditary business of great magnitude is dangerous. The management of such a business needs more than common industry and more than common ability. But there is no security at all that these will be regularly continued in the second generation.' Bagehot was talking about a Quaker business but the same principles hold good for any family firm, Quaker, Gentile or Jewish, as the comparative decline of the Rothschilds

* *Lombard Street.*

and the Samuels indicated. Lionel Rothschild and Sir Stuart Montagu Samuel, Lord Swaythling's nephew, became engaged in a lively rivalry to see who could grow the biggest and best rhododendrons and many a younger son made it quite clear that he was more interested in winning money on the race-track than earning it in the counting house. The bravery of Lionel Montagu, Lord Swaythling's youngest son, is still something of a legend in the family. When Lionel left school he was sent for by his father who, with his heavy beard and pontifical manner, was a distinctly intimidating figure. 'Lionel,' said the patriarch, 'I think the time has come for you to go into the bank.' 'Yes, father,' Lionel replied. 'But might I know what that involves?' 'Precisely the same as the rest of the family,' his father answered. 'Five per cent of the profits.' 'In that case,' said the intrepid Lionel, 'might I have two and a half per cent and leave at lunch-time?' Just what Lord Swaythling said to that is not recorded but presumably Lionel got his way for he later became both a partner in the bank and chairman of Tattersalls.

But the gardening and the race-going of the second generation should not be allowed to obscure the fact that in their time the Grand Dukes had been every bit as thrusting, opportunistic and generally go-getting as those whom they were trying to help were later to prove themselves. And just as the new arrivals were to exploit the opportunities presented by the growing mass market by moving on a large scale into retailing, tailoring and later property, so their predecessors had taken advantage of Britain's emergence, over the previous 150 years, as a trading nation of the first magnitude.

The stereotype of the Jew as the ubiquitous financier manipulating the levers of international trade in some dusty City counting house is so powerful that their contribution is often exaggerated. The late nineteenth-century German economist, Werner Sombart, claims that the Jews monopolized the business of stock-jobbing and bill-broking in England in the early eighteenth century and were pioneering loan contractors. This is not true. There were more Gentiles than Jews involved in the financing of the Napoleonic Wars, and the development of bill-broking as a modern technique for transferring money around the country owed as much to Quaker initiative as it did to Jewish.

Nor did the Jews play any part in the development of the network of country banks—the humble ancestors of today's giant clearing banks—that mushroomed up and down the country from the 1750s onward. Many of these little country banks were the creations of Quaker and non-conformist businessmen who had prospered by obeying John Wesley's injunction to 'make all you can, save all you can and give all you can'. The Barclays were grain merchants, as were the Gurneys from Norwich, while the Lloyds started out as Birmingham iron founders. All these men made their money in trade but saw an opportunity of further gain by financing the businessmen of the district. They issued notes, took mortgages as security for loans and eased their neighbours' financial worries by accepting bills of exchange which they often forwarded for discounting in the London money market. It was a risky business. Many of these banks were hopelessly undercapitalized, and collapsed the moment their panic-prone investors arrived at the front door of the bank to demand that their paper money be exchanged for gold. As such crises of confidence in a country almost continually at war frequently rocked the countryside, bank failures were correspondingly numerous, but those that did survive these shocks performed an economic function of great importance. They became the channel through which the vast store of capital locked up in the countryside flowed to finance both the Government's warlike adventures and private industry's peaceful enterprise.

To run a successful country bank one needed a strong local base and an intimate knowledge of the local businesses. The Jews had neither, for their skills were of an entirely different order. They were urban people with their roots not in the countryside nor in the provincial towns but in the great commercial centres of the Dutch empire. The Dutchmen whom Cromwell, in desperate need of funds to support the Protectorate, wooed were international merchants and traders who had already made huge fortunes in the diamond trade with India and in the West Indian sugar business. And it was as merchants, financiers and international money-lenders that the Jews first made their mark in England. There were Jews in London even before 1656 who survived and prospered largely because the Government found it convenient to turn a blind eye. Small as it was, the community had a reputation for wealth—one of the scare stories that circulated when the admission of the Jews became a public issue under Cromwell was that they were planning to buy St Paul's Cathedral and turn it into a synagogue; a plan that only failed, so it was said, because the authorities put up their price to £800,000. But whatever the resources of the resident community, they were eclipsed by the newcomers. The Dutch merchants who settled in tall, gracious houses around Finsbury Circus, just north of the City, were rich men by any standard. According to Professor Roth, a historian of the Jewish community, they brought some £1,500,000 in specie with them—capital which they employed so effectively that some fifty years later the twenty leading families were said to be worth some £5 million between them, of which some £2 million was invested in Government stock.

That they should choose to settle in London was to be expected. London was the headquarters of a Government with whom many of these Dutch merchants had established close links. The Glorious Revolution of 1688 may have been inspired by Englishmen and executed by Dutchmen, but it was mainly financed by the Jews. The cost of the expedition was largely met by an interest-free loan of 2 million crowns to William from a Dutch merchant named Francisco Lopez Suasso; and his troops and horses were fed with bread and forage provided by another Jewish financier, Isaac Pereira. In fact throughout the Wars of the Austrian and Spanish Succession, the enormously lucrative business of providing Britain's armies with supplies remained a largely Jewish

monopoly. It was so profitable that Marlborough's chief contractor, Solomon de Medina, who was knighted for his trouble,
was prepared to pay the duke an annuity of £5,000 a year for the
privilege—an arrangement which, when it came to light as the
result of the Government commission of inquiry, caused the duke
a good deal of embarrassment.

But the presence of a friendly Government in constant need of
cash was not London's only attraction. It was also a centre of
international trade whose importance rivalled that of Amsterdam.
Professor Plumb writes:*

> The early eighteenth century offered glorious opportunities
> for quick wealth. England's trade had expanded with great
> rapidity towards the end of the seventeenth century; not only
> was it brisk in exports, but the favourable trade balance
> stimulated the home market and home investments. There
> were insufficient outlets for capital investment and this gave
> rise to extravagant projects long before the South Sea Bubble.
> In consequence there was money, and money to spare, for
> exotics, and the consumption of tea, coffee, chocolate, new
> muslins and calicos from the East rose quickly. Men in com-
> merce or industry profited most and the gentry with high
> taxes and insecure rents least; and it was natural that the appe-
> tite of traders and manufacturers should be whetted.

In this climate the Jews could not fail to prosper. They were
already rich, were in a position to supply those Eastern exotics
for which the *nouveau-riche* housewives of London, Bristol and
other provincial cities were clamouring, and above all they were
skilled in the complex and mysterious business of international
trade. But it was not on diamonds and sugar that the legendary
fortunes were built. Most of the new arrivals may have started as
merchants, but like the merchant bankers who followed them
some hundred years later, they quickly saw that it was more
profitable to deal in money and credit than in goods. Dealing in

* *Sir Robert Walpole.*

precious metals had always been a traditional Jewish business, dating from their medieval money-lending days; so it was only natural that when the East India Company and the Bank of England needed agents to negotiate and supply their bullion needs they should turn to somebody like Moses Mocatta, who first set up shop as a merchant in Camomile Street in 1671. Once established, the business was handed down from father to son. It still exists, the oldest bullion broking business in England. And though it was taken over by Hambros bank in 1957 when the firm, after eight generations, had exhausted its supplies of young Mocattas and young Goldsmids, there is still one Mocatta, in the large and elegant shape of Mr Jock, in the business. Strictly speaking, Jock Mocatta is not a Mocatta at all as the family only lasted until 1751. But such is the family pride that the Lumbrozo partners, also Sephardic Jews, went to the trouble of taking out a Royal Licence to change their name. The firm still preserves, framed in a place of honour over the mantelpiece of its eighteenth-century Throgmorton Avenue offices, a letter of application from Isaac Goldsmid to the East India Company for the job of bullion broker. Isaac plainly knew his place and he asked for the job not so much on grounds of personal merit but because 'my father having had the honour of succeeding my grandfather in conjunction with Mr Mocatta … '

But bullion dealing, itself the reflection of the explosion that was taking place in international trade at the opening of the eighteenth century, was not the only avenue opening up for Jewish merchants anxious to make their way in a new and unfamiliar city. England was on the threshold of a financial revolution. The financial instruments that were to lubricate the workings of international trade and, under the pressure of almost constant war, to release the flood of capital that was dammed up in the countryside, were in the process of being forged. The Bank of England, the eventual cornerstone of the whole system, received its charter only six years before the opening of the century and even the Stock Exchange was no more than a couple of coffee shops in Change Alley, the narrow street that wound between Cornhill and Lombard Street, where merchants met in the mornings to exchange shares in the Bank of England, the East India Company and, at least until the Bubble burst, the South Sea Trading Company. The careful distinctions that the Stock Exchange draws today between jobber and broker did not exist: everybody bought and sold from everybody else, and though brokers liked to call themselves jobbers because they thought it sounded more respectable, the distinction was meaningless. Gambling was a national passion and the dealers of Change Alley were just as happy making bets among themselves as they were dealing on margin in South Sea stock. In 1696 Henry Shale promised to pay a friend five pounds if he kept off the bottle until Michaelmas and four years later Sir Stephen Evance laid ten to one in guineas that war would not break out in Europe by Christmas.

The atmosphere on Change Alley was one that the Jews found familiar and congenial. Even when they were still in Holland, the merchants of Amsterdam, anxious to deploy their trading fortunes to best advantage, had speculated on the London Exchange and it was natural that once they had arrived in England they should, despite the fact that the City authorities limited the number of Jewish brokers on the exchange to twelve, play an active part.

Of the twelve brokers none was more active than Samson Gideon, a financier and Stock Exchange speculator of a dexterity and skill that approached genius. Born in 1699, he came from a merchant family (his father had made a useful fortune in the Barbados) but like many of his contemporaries he was quick to see the attractions of a booming Stock Exchange, rushing upwards in an inflationary spiral. Gideon plunged into this volatile, fast-moving world with enthusiasm, dealing first in Government lottery tickets (a fund-raising device not unlike the modern Premium Bonds) and later in stocks and shares—the Jews were always particularly strong in the East India Company. Gideon made his mark by what Lucy Sutherland, the economic historian, describes* as 'his mastery in a new, and to his contemporaries, somewhat sinister craft, that of jobber in the rising market of stocks and shares and by qualities of mind and character that made him supreme in it'. These qualities not only made him a sizeable fortune (by the time he was thirty he had made himself half as much as a successful merchant could expect to amass in a lifetime) but it also brought him to the notice of the Government which was badly in need of such financial expertise.

During the early part of the eighteenth century going to war became an increasingly expensive business. As war in Europe became more frequent and widespread the armies became larger and more complex and correspondingly more costly. And as the cost of the armies rose so did the frequency with which the Government came to the money market for loans to keep the war machine working. Initially there was considerable competition among the City merchants to tender for these loans, for when the campaigns were going well and Government credit was good they often went to a premium which gave the 'stags'—the City term for speculators who apply for more stock than they can pay for—a juicy profit. Until the middle of the eighteenth century the Government reserved its loans for its friends. It was a typically eighteenth-century transaction. The merchants, the members of Parliament and the heads of City companies promised the Government financial and political support and in return the Government offered them the prospect of huge profits. As the Jews could not become either members of Parliament or heads of City companies, they had little to offer the Government and were therefore excluded from transactions of this kind.

But in 1742 this cosy system broke down. The War of the Austrian Succession had just begun and the Government's need for cash became so pressing it was forced to look outside the establishment for support. The man it turned to was Samson Gideon. He had no political influence but he and his friends did

* *Samson Gideon, an Eighteenth Century Jewish Financier.*

have sufficient money, most of it made on the Stock Exchange, to take up a substantial part of the loan. Three years later Gideon brought off the most spectacular coup of his career. In 1745 Bonnie Prince Charlie landed in Scotland and prepared to march south to London. When the news reached the capital there was panic in the City which the Bank of England, already heavily in debt to the Government, was quite unable to stem. The Government saw that unless something could be done quickly there would be such a run on the Bank that there was a very real danger it would collapse. In this emergency the Prime Minister, Pelham, turned to Gideon who promptly came to the rescue. With a consortium of City friends he raised a £1·7 million loan. At the time, with the Stuart cause apparently riding high, it must have seemed that Gideon had let patriotism get the better of common sense—and for several months afterwards Consols continued to plummet. The turning point came in April 1746 with the Prince's defeat at Culloden. The financial impact of the Hanoverians' victory was immediate. The price of the loan on the London market rocketed and Gideon and his friends benefited accordingly—but then he had taken the risk. From that point Gideon virtually abandoned his private business to become chief adviser to the Government—an activity that gave rise to a good deal of anti-semitic propaganda. Whatever his City rivals may have thought, however, Gideon's influence was wholly beneficial. 'His advice', writes Lucy Sutherland,* 'was always bold but never rash and though it was not his way to theorize and introduce generalizations that were not relevant to his immediate purpose, there shines through everything he wrote a clear grasp of the rising credit structure, a grasp of the functions both of the Bank and the money market in this structure, and a consummate mastery of all the day-to-day arithmetic of the financial world in which he moved.'

Gideon was the first of the Jewish loan contractors but he was by no means the last. And though it sometimes seemed so it was

* Op. cit.

never a Jewish monopoly. The lists of subscribers to Government loans show that the Jews as prominent stockbrokers, bullion dealers, bill brokers and merchants often took the largest stake, but the ordinary, true-blue mercantile bourgeoisie scrambled just as eagerly for a share in this lucrative business.

But though the profits were often great so were the risks, as the brothers Goldsmid discovered. The brothers Abraham and Benjamin were comparatively late arrivals on the scene, their father Aaron having come from Holland to set up as a London merchant some time in the 1740s. Working from a humble office in Leman Street, on the edge of London's East End, they had prospered not as merchants but as bill brokers, and by the opening of the Napoleonic wars they were already rich men with large houses and estates at Roehampton and Morden. Through their brother Asher, who joined the Mocatta's bullion broking business in 1787, they were connected to one of the richest and proudest families in Anglo-Jewry.

In 1800 bill broking was still a strange and little understood profession. The bill broker was the link between the emerging country banks and the financial centre of London. He bought the bills of exchange the country bankers had collected from their customers and sold them to the banks in London who were looking for good bills to discount. For this simple but essential service he charged the owner of the bill a commission for his services. The business was pioneered by a Quaker, Thomas Richardson, who was the London agent of the great bank of Overend and Gurney—and his success can be judged by the fact that by 1820 Richardson had a turnover of £20 million a year. But however Quaker its origins, bill broking was a classic middleman operation of a kind that the Jews have always found particularly congenial.

It was this bill-broking base that gave Abraham and Benjamin their opportunity to participate in the greatest money-raising exercise that the country had ever seen. During the eighteen years of the Napoleonic wars, Pitt and his successors raised from the

London money market over £400 million—about twice as much as had been called for by previous governments in the preceding ninety-five years. Though the pace was set by a non-Jewish firm, the Barings, the part played by Abraham and Benjamin was spectacular and dramatic. They took a large chunk of the £18 million that Pitt succeeded in raising in 1795; much of it they provided themselves but they underwrote still more. In 1809, the year of the ill-fated Walcheren expedition, Abraham took on a £14 million loan single-handed, on which the commission alone, irrespective of any profit they may have made in dealing in the market, was enormous; but Benjamin's name was missing from the list. The strain, as the price of the loans bucketed about, reflecting Britain's changing military fortunes, had already proved too much. Benjamin suffered badly from gout and depression and on April 15th he was found at Roehampton, hanging from a cord tied to a bar which he had had fixed to his bed to relieve the pains brought on by his disease. The jury returned a verdict of lunacy. But worse was to come. A couple of years after Benjamin's death, Abraham, in partnership with the Barings, took on a £13·4 million loan of which Abraham retained an £800,000 parcel for himself. It was a disastrous transaction. Sir Francis Baring, whose reputation had done much to bolster the price of the stock, died suddenly and on the money market the stock collapsed. To make matters worse, the East India Company which had placed £500,000 of Exchequer bills with the Goldsmids for negotiation became alarmed and asked for their money back. The City, which still resented the Goldsmid invasion of what it regarded as its own private preserve, was not disposed to come to Abraham's rescue and on September 28th, 1810, the financier was discovered lying dead, a smoking pistol in his hand. The jury returned a verdict similar to the one that had been passed two years earlier on his brother; 'Died by his own hand; but not in his senses at the time.'

The timing of Abraham's death was ironic, for the golden age of merchant banking was just about to dawn. With peace came unprecedented prosperity. And over the next seventy years, as trade expanded and Britain consolidated her imperial conquests, London became the financial capital of the world. Her bankers and financiers performed unprecedented feats. By developing the instruments of international credit, the merchant banks of London financed a good part of the world's trade; they provided the money which enabled defeated France to rebuild after Waterloo; by their support for Cavour they played an important part in the unification of Italy, and without their help Argentina would never have been able to build her *estancias* and her railways, her electricity supply or her tramways. They operated in every country and at every level. Everybody knows that without the Rothschilds' help Disraeli could never have bought the Suez Canal from under the noses of the French; much less well known is the fact that without the assistance of the Rothschilds, who took a mortgage on his house at Hughenden, Disraeli would have been in grave financial trouble. To entrepreneur and Government alike the merchant bankers supplied both development and working capital —a function which gave the great firms of the City, the Barings, the Rothschilds and the Hambros, an influence at least as great as any Government.

The City, a sentimental and often chauvinistic institution, is proud of these achievements; it likes to think of them as something that only British skill and British enterprise could have accomplished. What it sometimes forgets is that these coups were almost entirely conceived and carried out by foreigners—more often than not Jewish foreigners at that. 'Practically every acceptance house of old standing in this country', Sir Robert Kindersley of Lazards told the Macmillan Committee on Finance and Industry in 1931, 'commenced purely as merchants trading with foreign countries and a great many of them, I think, are of foreign origin.' Sir Robert thought correctly. Of the two dozen or so leading merchant banking houses founded in the first three-quarters of the nineteenth century, only two, Anthony Gibbs and Brown Shipley, which were started within two years of one another in 1808, were of British origin; the remainder were the creations of an assortment of Germans, Franco-Americans, and Danes who from the Napoleonic wars onwards arrived in increasing numbers.

That they chose this time to come to England was no accident. The war against Napoleon was an economic as well as a military one, and as the British Navy tightened the noose it had thrown round Napoleon's Europe, the continental merchants, already alarmed at the failure of the Bank of Amsterdam, and distressed at the prospect of finding themselves on the losing side, began to transfer themselves and their businesses to London. Henry J. Schroeder, who arrived from Hamburg in 1804, was the first of the new wave. A year later he was followed by the legendary Nathan Mayer Rothschild. Sent by his father Mayer Amschel, Nathan first set up as a textile dealer in Manchester. But his real task was not to buy and sell textiles but to find a safer and more profitable home for the funds of the Elector of Hesse, Mayer Amschel's patron and, with his mercenaries fighting all over Europe, reputedly the richest prince in Europe. Ten years later the Hambros arrived from Copenhagen where, so legend has it, the founding member, then called Hamburger, made a killing in black crape, having cornered the market after he was tipped off about the King of Denmark's death by a girlfriend who worked in the palace. In 1830 the Kleinworts came from Holstein—and the stream continued until the 1870s; only to revive again as the result of the growing persecution of the Jews in Nazi Germany in the 1930s. This later wave, which brought the Warburgs and the Japhets to London was, as one might expect, almost entirely Jewish but amongst the earlier arrivals Gentiles and Jews were to be found in almost exactly equal proportions. The leading members of the Jewish contingent were: Helbert Wagg, originally a bullion business, Rothschilds, Hambros, M. Samuel, founded by Marcus Samuel as an offshoot of his Shell oil empire, Erlangers, Samuel Montagu, Keysers and Lazards, who came from America via France and like the Hambros stopped being Jewish and acquired the patina of the English upper class almost as soon as they got here.

That the foreigners—and especially the Jews—should so quickly come to dominate the merchant banking scene is not really so surprising, for as the name implies it was a natural extension of their merchanting activities. As international merchants they had over the years built up a detailed and unrivalled knowledge of trading conditions throughout the world. Their horizons were far wider than those of the average English merchant who might know the score in Birmingham but who stood a very real risk of being short-changed in Hong Kong. To minimize this risk he turned to the merchant bankers. Through a network of international agents and correspondents they had made it their business to know which Bangkok trader was credit worthy and which was not; which Chinese silk dealer could be relied on to deliver on time and which could not. And as their reputation for this kind of expertise grew, the merchant bankers found that their reputation could be turned into hard cash. Instead of trading in Chinese silk or Australian wool themselves, they discovered that it was far simpler—and also far more profitable—to guarantee other people's transactions by accepting a bill of exchange.* The importer had to pay his bank their 2 per cent commission but then he slept easier at night knowing that if anything went wrong Hambros or Kleinworts had to foot the bill; as the banks had gone to a great deal of trouble to ensure the reliability of their information they rarely did.

But for all its importance the bill on London was no more than the bread and butter of the merchant bankers' trade; as the nineteenth century progressed governments as well as merchants turned to the merchant bankers of London for guidance and assistance. That the French, the Danes and the Austrians should

* A bill of exchange is nothing more than an I.O.U. Instead of paying on the nail an importer gives the exporter a bill of exchange, thus promising to pay within a stated time. The merchant bank merely guarantees the transaction. Once it has been accepted the exporter can recover his money by selling his bill to a discount house.

look to London and its bankers was no accident. England had emerged from the Napoleonic wars as financially the strongest country in Europe: while the franc, the kroner and the schilling tottered, the pound remained unshakably firm. England was the one country which was both rich and credit worthy. But before this wealth could be released and put to work, building French railways, compensating the slave owners of the West Indies for their loss and enabling the Danes to wage war against the Prussians, new financial techniques had to be devised. The British investor was more than anxious to invest his savings abroad but as long as his dividends were paid in foreign currency he remained naturally somewhat reluctant. It was a serious problem and it took the financial genius of Nathan Rothschild to solve it.

The Rothschilds are so encrusted with legend which their reticence has helped foster (no historian has ever been allowed to raid the archives at New Court, headquarters of the British bank) that it is extraordinarily difficult to disentangle fact from fiction. Nathan himself, gruff, uncouth and with a strong German-Yiddish accent, is an important part of the legend. The cartoons of the day show him, under his wide brimmed hat, as a portly figure with a short, *retroussé* nose, and above a receding chin (a traditional Rothschild feature which is still noticeable) rather fleshy, protruding lips. He was a man who from his vantage point by his pillar at the Royal Exchange could wipe millions off the price of a stock at the lift of his finger. And when he died, while appropriately enough attending the wedding of his eldest son and heir, Lionel, at Frankfurt (true to family tradition he married a cousin from the Naples branch), the news was announced by the arrival of a Rothschild pigeon bearing the simple message: 'Il est mort.' He left a fortune of between £5 million and £6 million and when the coffin was carried in procession from New Court to the cemetery of the Great Synagogue in Mile End, he was mourned not only by his four sons but by the Lord Mayor of London and his sheriffs and by the ambassadors of Austria, Russia, Prussia, Naples and Portugal. By 1836, the year of Nathan's death, the fame of the Rothschilds had spread far beyond the financial centres of Europe. Their power and influence was already a by-word in the ghettos of Russia and Poland. For the poor tailors and cobblers of Lodtz and Vilna the Rothschilds were a living example of what a Jew could do if he tried. Ghetto jokes about the Rothschilds are legion.

FIRST TEACHER: If I had Rothschild's money, I'd be richer than Rothschild.

SECOND TEACHER: What kind of crazy thing is that to say? If you had Rothschild's money, how could you be richer than Rothschild?

FIRST TEACHER: I'd do a little teaching on the side.

It was not only the wealth of the Rothschilds that so dazzled the City but the speed with which it had been acquired. When Nathan arrived in Manchester in 1804 with the £20,000 his father had given him to start up as a textile dealer he was, as far as anybody in England was concerned, an obscure and unlettered Jew from the Frankfurt ghetto. Eleven years later with the defeat of Napoleon he had become not only the dominant figure on the London Stock Exchange but he had official status as bullion broker to the Government of England—a position which he acquired *de facto* after he had succeeded with the help of his brother James in Paris in smuggling some £800,000 worth of gold, bought on spec from the East India Company, through the French lines to Wellington's armies fighting in the Peninsula. It was this coup plus Nathan's incredible skill as an operator on the London Stock Exchange, where he speculated with the money entrusted to him by the Elector of Hesse, that laid the foundations of the fortune of the House of Rothschild.*

* The famous story that Nathan made an enormous killing by using his private knowledge of Wellington's victory at Waterloo would seem to be untrue. Nathan certainly heard the news from his agents before word reached the Government, but it would seem, judging from the behaviour of Government stock which remained remarkably stable in the days just before and after the victory, that he made no great use of his knowledge. Nor did he keep the information to himself. As soon as he heard he hurried round to Downing Street and told the Prime Minister, Lord Liverpool, who, incidentally, did not at first believe it.

Even if Nathan had been operating by himself he would still be remembered as a great financier. But that was not the case. As his contemporaries were very well aware Nathan was not an isolated phenomenon. By the end of the first decade of the nineteenth century Nathan's brothers had fanned out from Mayer Amschel's house in Jew Street, Frankfurt, and established themselves throughout Europe. Jacob who later changed his name to James arrived in Paris in 1811, his brother Salomon travelled to Metternich's Austria in 1819, and eight years later Karl, the fourth son, after several years of acting as the family's courier, set up the Rothschild bank in Naples, while the youngest of the family, brother Amschel, remained behind in Frankfurt. The links between these brothers, fortified by the traditional closeness of Jewish family life, were very strong; so strong that they provided the framework for a banking business that was international rather than national in scope.

If one is searching for an explanation of why the Jews were so spectacularly successful as international bankers throughout the nineteenth century, then the existence of these family links, connecting one country to another, must be part of the answer. To be a successful international banker in the days when the financial press was in its infancy and communications infinitely less sophisticated than today, it was vital to know whom one could trust and whom one could not; which politician, trader or entrepreneur it was safe to back. In those days when bankers really did have the power to make or break a Government a banker was more than a dignified repository of financial expertise, skilled at advising his clients whether to float their loan at 6¾ or 7⅛ per cent: he had to be diplomat, foreign correspondent, politician and money man all at once. Theoretically this information could just as easily be provided by the bank's senior employees (and it often was) but for brother Nathan or brother Elias in London it was infinitely reassuring to know that brother Joseph or brother Isaac was managing the shop in Hong Kong or San Francisco.

The Rothschilds were not the only Jews to use the family as a kind of secret weapon. An infinitely variable network of sons, nephews, brothers and cousins linked the Seligmans in New York with the Seligmans in San Francisco, the Frankfurt Warburgs with the New York Warburgs and the Bombay and Hong Kong Sassoons with the Leadenhall Street branch. This system had, of course, its disadvantages. Not all members of the family were equally competent and some were too clever and ambitious — qualities which led to rows and divisions of an intensity of which only a tight-knit, self-conscious family is capable. When Elias Sassoon, founder of the E. D. Sassoon banking business, broke away from the family to set up a rival business in 1867, it was years before the family would talk to him. The Sassoons' biographer, Stanley Jackson, says:*

They remained outwardly polite to the rebel, but social contact virtually ceased after the secession, apart from letters about David Sassoon's benefactions and meetings at funerals or anniversary mourning services. For years to come, all the family births, Barmitzvahs and marriages would be acknowledged formally by letters and exchanges of gifts, rather in the fashion of distantly related kinsmen of royal blood.

No such dissensions marred the Rothschild partnership. And it was precisely because the relations between the five brothers were so close and so harmonious that the business could operate as one international concern with its tentacles stretching into every corner of Europe. It was this interdependence between the various branches of the Rothschild empire that gave the family their power and British investors their opportunity. Nathan, as I said earlier, was the first to realize that British money would only be forthcoming to finance a Europe hungry for capital if the interest on those investments could be paid in sterling. Once Rothschild branches had been set up in every important financial centre in Europe this became comparatively easy to arrange. Funds raised by Nathan on the London market would be

* *The Sassoons.*

channelled via Frankfurt, Vienna, Naples or Paris to whichever government required them; the dividends returning to London via the same network. In this way British capital flowed into and around Europe—long before the Common Market and such sophisticated devices as the Eurodollar, an invention of the American banks, were ever thought of. And such was the glamour of the Rothschild name with its massive reputation for honesty and integrity, that investors were only too happy to subscribe.

Other banks whose reputations were as prestigious as Rothschilds but whose expertise extended to other parts of the world followed Nathan's pioneering example. Schroeder's very first issue, in 1853, was a railway loan to Cuba; the Hambros, with their Scandinavian origins, made a speciality of Danish loans while the Barings became deeply involved in the financing of Argentinian railways: so deeply, in fact, that it took the concerted action of the City, led by the Bank of England, to rescue them from imminent collapse in 1890. But in 1890, as Barings tottered on the brink of disaster, the golden age of merchant banking had only a few more years to run. The outbreak of the First World War brought to an abrupt close a period of just on a hundred years when London had held sway as the financial capital of the world.

Chapter Four

The Survivors

In 1888 the *Banker's Magazine*, reflecting on the career of Sir Samuel Montagu could write:

> The Jews have shown a marked excellence in what can be called the commerce of imperceptibles. They have no particular superiority in the ordinary branches of trade; an Englishman is quite their equal in dealing with ordinary merchandise, in machine making and manufacturing. But the Jews excel on every Bourse in Europe; they have a preeminence out of all proportion to their numbers or even their wealth.

For this view there was some evidence because, though merchant banking was by no means a Jewish monopoly, many of the most thrusting financial houses of the time had been founded and were still being run by Jews. Rothschilds was at the height of its glory, simultaneously feared and admired; the banking business of M. Samuel was rapidly growing in importance as Marcus, its founder, converted with Rothschild assistance his Far Eastern trading empire into an international oil business powerful enough to challenge John D. Rockefeller himself; while that stern patriarch, Samuel Montagu, who first acquired his taste for foreign exchange dealing as a teenager among the sailors in the Liverpool docks, had established his reputation as the country's leading expert on bullion and foreign exchange. When the *Encyclopaedia*

Britannica wanted an article on foreign exchange it was Montagu who supplied it.

In 1880 all these businesses were recognizably Jewish for the simple reason that they still bore the personal imprint of their Jewish founders. Manned by members of the family, they were run almost as an extension of the family circle—the Family-in-the-City, as it were. Typically the heart of the business was the partners' room around which the members of the family sat, each in his appointed place. At Montagus until the 1920s even the foreign exchange switchboard was in the partners' room—symbolic of the fact that every decision down to the smallest silver order had to be taken by a partner. The distinction between the partners and the rest of the staff was clearly defined and rigidly drawn. 'If you wanted somebody on the staff', says Roland Franklin of Keyser Ullman, which was started in 1858 as an off-shoot of Samuel Montagu to provide a training ground for the junior members of the family, 'you simply yelled. Couldn't do that today. They'd leave.' For many years women were anathema at Keysers, and despite the arrival of a girl telephonist during the First World War letters continued to be transcribed by a couple of male stenographers. But while the staff could never hope to enter the magic circle, they were in some respect part of the family too, sharing the bank's disappointments and rejoicing in its successes. When in 1903 Samuel Montagu & Co. reached its fiftieth anniversary, it seemed only right and proper that the celebrations should take place not in some anonymous West End banqueting hall, the Edwardian equivalent of the Connaught Rooms, but at the banker's own home, 12 Kensington Palace Gardens. And the staff, some sixty all told who gathered round the U-shaped table, showed their appreciation by composing a poem, some twenty stanzas long, in praise of the founder. It began:

> In the year Eighteen hundred and fifty three
> In a vessel small called 'Leadenhall'
> Some pioneers put out to sea.

> With unlimited hopes and spirits bold,
> But not much cargo in the hold;
> Yet fairly equipped for a brave career,
> And determined a steady course to steer—
> And over their heads a flag there flew,
> With the superscription 'Montagu'

As long as the families remained in control these businesses naturally retained their Jewish characteristics: they were Jewish houses and recognized as such by the rest of the City. Lord Swaythling, for example, was particularly devout, keeping strictly to the letter of the law. Of his faith his daughter Lily wrote:* 'It mattered little ... whether there was beauty or even a living significance in a small enactment. It belonged to the system and he rejoiced in observing it, and guarded it with extreme jealousy from the attacks of his critics.' His rivals may not have taken such a strict view of their obligations but in most houses at least the formalities were observed. Everybody knew that at Rothschilds and Montagus the chances of a non-Jew sharing the mysteries of the partners' room were non-existent; that whatever the emergency a Jewish bank would do no business on the Sabbath and at the luncheon table the food would be invariably kosher.

Some vestiges of these practices are still to be found in the City. The Rothschilds still serve unleavened bread to their guests at Passover and at Keysers the original articles of association which stipulate that the business is to be closed on Jewish Holy Days are still extant—though not always observed. But in almost every other respect the Jewish banks that survive today are almost indistinguishable from their Gentile brethren. Almost but not quite. Rothschilds, Montagus, Warburgs and Keysers are still regarded (and regard themselves) as Jewish houses; identifiable not because of the Jewishness of their personnel (in every case except Keysers, Gentiles are in the majority on the board) or in the way that they conduct their business (Hill Samuel is every

* *Samuel Montagu, a Character Sketch.*

bit as thrusting as Warburg) but simply as a result of their continuing loyalty to the Jewish cause; a loyalty which was brought into sharp focus by Israel's Six Day War in 1967.

The Rothschilds, as paradigms of Anglo-Jewish achievement are still enormously respected, but they no longer lead the Jewish community in the old, authoritarian, nineteenth-century manner. Their influence is altogether subtler and less overt. Their leading place has been taken by a newer generation of self-made entrepreneurs of Russian and Polish origin for whom Judaism and Zionism are inextricably linked. 'How can you be a good Jew', asks Sir Isaac Wolfson of Great Universal Stores or Lord Sieff of Marks and Spencer, 'if you are not prepared wholeheartedly to identify and support Israel?' The outward manifestation of this change, which has been going on almost continuously since Chaim Weizmann first set foot in Manchester in 1904, came in 1962 when the key post of the presidency of the United Synagogue passed from the Honourable Ewen Montagu, a member of the old aristocracy, nephew of Lord Swaythling and a man cast in the Waley-Cohen mould,* to the distinctly unpatrician figure of Sir Isaac Wolfson, a man who began on the business ladder by selling cheap clocks in a Manchester market. Until recently the British Rothschilds' support for Israel has been lukewarm; unlike their French cousins who have poured thousands of pounds into Israel, building a luxurious housing estate and golf course at the seaside resort of Caesarea. In 1969 Baron Edmond arranged for an entire eighteenth-century salon, the pride of his grandfather's Paris mansion, to be transported bodily from France to Jerusalem where it was lovingly reassembled in the city's main museum. By contrast the British Rothschilds have preferred to stand in the wings, offering discreet advice and assistance when needed. Like everybody else the Rothschilds responded magnificently to the

---

* Mr Montagu, who retired as chairman of the Middlesex Sessions in August 1969, acquired a formidable reputation for outspokenness and eccentricity on the bench. His personal remarks about the barristers who appeared before him were, on occasions, so stinging that one barrister, much nettled, actually complained to the Bar Council.

crisis that the Six Day War provoked (an episode which I shall
describe in more detail in Chapter Ten), but it was entirely
characteristic that though their gift of £1 million (payable in cash,
within seven days) set the tone for the whole astonishing fund-
raising operation, the offer was made through an intermediary and
the money given anonymously. Unlike the Wolfsons and the
Sieffs, the Rothschilds stand apart from the Zionist fund-raising
machine, run on lines set by Marks and Spencer and organized
with awesome efficiency by the Joint Palestine Appeal. 'To get
wholly involved with the J.P.A. would not appeal to us very
much,' says Jacob Rothschild. 'My father and I felt just as involved with the Israelis' struggles during the Six Day War but we
do not care to say in public just how involved we felt.' It is not
the fear of anti-semitism that keeps the Rothschilds in the background: merely that they choose not to belong, as Jacob puts it,
to 'the active set'.

The same discretion distinguishes the Rothschilds' involvement
with Jewish business. 'I enjoy Jewish characteristics and like doing
business with Jewish people,' says Jacob. But it is a personal
preference; not the policy or the practice of the bank. From time
to time Rothschilds have stepped in in their capacity as unofficial
guardians of the Jewish community, custodians of its good name,
to offer guidance to Jewish businesses. It was, for example,
largely due to the Rothschild influence that Marks and Spencer
were advised after Lord Marks's death in 1964 to do the decent
thing and enfranchise their ordinary shareholders. The Marks and
Spencer directors had been much criticized by the City for
jealously keeping the control of what was, after all, a huge public
company in their own hands. This is no longer the case: now,
though it makes next to no difference in practice, power has
passed to the ordinary shareholders.

The Rothschild attitudes are the product of 165 years of
relatively painless and gentle assimilation. With some of their
newer, smaller rivals, however, socially and commercially less
securely established, the distinctions are sharper, the Jewishness

more obtrusive. Keyser Ullman is a case in point. As it has been
a feature of the City for just over one hundred years (it celebrated
its centenary in 1968) and is run by two old and much intermarried
families, it could hardly be described as an upstart. But it is only
recently, with the coming to power of an energetic third generation, that it has begun to make its mark as a modern merchant
bank. Before the war Keysers was not really a merchant bank at
all. It was a small, unambitious family partnership, well known in
the City but almost completely unknown outside the Square Mile.
'To be truthful', Charles Keyser told me shortly before he retired
as chairman to take up his first love, farming, 'we were pretty
stick in the mud.' Keysers did a certain amount of Scandinavian
business and was involved, like many other banks at the time, in
the financing of American railways, but these activities were
largely peripheral. Essentially Keysers was a discount house. And
like all discount houses it acted as a middleman, collecting spare
cash from the banks and other institutions and lending it out to the
Government in return for Government bonds and Treasury
bills. 'It was', says Charles Keyser, 'a very pleasant business to be
in.'

Under its young managing director, Roland Franklin, Keysers
is, as merchant banks go, in the second division—which is of
course one reason why it is trying so hard. The bank is something
of a rarity in the City in that the majority of its directors are
Jewish. It is not a conscious policy—a kind of reverse discrimina-
tion: simply that it is known as a predominantly Jewish house and
has therefore attracted a number of young and ambitious Jewish
boys, many of them like Sir Harold Samuel's son-in-law, Guy
Negar, with a property background, who were anxious for a
quasi-professional career. The pattern is nothing new. Every
Jewish mother, according to Jewish mythology, wants her boy
to take up a profession: jokes about My Son The Doctor or My
Son The Lawyer are innumerable. In this pantheon My Son The
Merchant Banker does not figure at all. The reason is quite
simple. There is still, however well disguised it may be, a good

deal of anti-semitism in the City—especially among merchant bankers who, considering their past, should know better. Arnold Weinstock's takeover of Associated Electrical Industries in the autumn of 1967 provoked an extremely unpleasant anti-semitic whispering campaign, directed against Weinstock personally, and I know of at least one highly distinguished merchant bank which politely handed one of its new recruits his cards on discovering that he was a Jew. 'If we had known we would never have hired you,' they said after he had asked for a day off for a Jewish holiday. The attraction of Keysers for the aspiring Jewish professional lies in the fact that there is no risk of him being exposed to this kind of humiliation.

Keysers makes no bones about being a Jewish business. In the course of gathering material for this book I have asked dozens of managing directors and chairmen of some of the largest companies in the land whether they regarded their firms as Jewish businesses. It was a question that most of them ducked in their various fashions; the conversation often veering off into a laborious head-counting exercise designed to discover how many Jewish directors there were on the board or plunging us both into a steamy metaphysical discussion about the nature of the Jew. Roland Franklin employed none of these stratagems. 'There is no doubt about it,' he said. What is more, he added, he had found that in his own Jewishness there was a distinct commercial advantage. In the last five years Keysers in its struggle to expand has taken on a whole string of clients which, as it cheerfully admits, the senior banks would think twice about before taking on: either because they were too small or because they were insufficiently grand. It is, for example, difficult to imagine Rothschilds or Montagus acting for Cyril Shack, a former Kilburn greengrocer, who sixteen years ago founded a company called Phonographic and with his own savings, and some money borrowed from his brother, built up a juke-box and one-armed bandit empire big enough to challenge (unsuccessfully as it happens) Billy Butlin's holiday camp kingdom. The fact that

Shack is a Jew was not, of course, the main reason why Keysers accepted his offer to handle the bid. But it was not entirely irrelevant. 'I can assess a Jewish businessman far more accurately than I can a non-Jewish one,' Franklin says. 'Just as a matter of record, every Jew we have backed has been a success and every non-Jew has been a failure. We tend to go for the up-and-coming and the up-and-coming tend to go for us.' 'Of course', Franklin conceded, 'that has not necessarily anything to do with the difference between the Jews and the non-Jews; merely our ability to pick them.'

In tenaciously preserving its particular Jewish character, Keysers is, as I have already said, something of a rarity among merchant banks. But in demonstrating a continuing ability to survive and renew itself, adapting to changed circumstances and conditions, it is less singular. It is a characteristic that Rothschilds, where the ethos is now more professional and less familial than it used to be, has displayed *in excelsis*.

At New Court the family, after going through a lean period during the 'thirties and 'forties, is still in control. Rothschilds is the only bank in the City which is still a private partnership and it is an indication of the continuing magic of the Rothschild name that when in 1968 they wished, in order to give their bright up-and-comers a better chance of promotion, to increase the number of partners from ten to twenty, the Board of Trade passed a special law to allow them to do so. The dispensation which fifty years ago would have been granted on the nod from a friendly Cabinet Minister was by no means automatic: according to Jacob Rothschild, the heir to the Rothschild title and the most active of the younger generation, there was a good deal of discreet lobbying by the Rothschilds before the Board of Trade relented. It is not just for sentimental reasons (though these play, I suspect, a surprisingly large part) that the Rothschilds choose to remain such a charming anachronism. There are for those that can afford them substantial advantages as well. A partnership means that not only is the Rothschild succession unquestioned but that, even more important, there are no prying shareholders poking their fingers into the bank's accounts and demanding to know why last year's profits were not as large as they were led to expect. The Rothschilds remain splendidly impervious to all criticism. 'As long as it continues to work we see no reason to change it,' says Jacob Rothschild.

But that is not to say that the Rothschild business itself has not changed. Being private and traditionally reticent the transformation has not been accompanied by the fanfares blown by their noisier rivals—some of whom actually employ public relations men. But it is nonetheless extensive. In the Rothschild internal telephone directory the partners are dignified by the title Mr; everybody else has to make do with a plain surname. At the top of the list are the Rothschilds themselves: Mr Edmund, the head of the bank;* Mr Leo, who looks after the banking side; Mr Evelyn, who is responsible for investment and administration and the Hon. Mr Jacob, who is in charge of the finance business, both foreign and domestic. But the four Rothschilds are not the only 'Mr's on the list; there are, if one excludes the French Rothschilds who became partners when links were re-established with the French bank in the early 'sixties ('up until then we used to meet socially but when we did we usually did not talk business'), another nine names: all of them professional men and none of them Jewish. In the last ten years the Rothschilds have brought in outside talent, recruited entirely on merit. Jewish circles were deeply shocked when the Rothschilds broke with tradition in 1960, appointing David Colville, a former treasurer to Lloyds Bank, to a partnership. It was a double break: not only was he a joint-stock man (not previously a fertile hunting ground for merchant banking talent), but he was also a non-Jew. Since then Rothschilds, following the example set by Sir Siegmund Warburg,

* The head of the family, Lord Rothschild, has no connection with the bank. He is a distinguished Cambridge zoologist and biochemist and is chairman of Shell Research. Science as well as finance is a Rothschild speciality. Lord Rothschild's sister, the Hon. Mrs Lane, is a world authority on fleas.

have been as catholic (if that is the right word) in their choice as anybody, bringing in barristers, accountants and even financial journalists. And it is these men, hard, success-orientated professionals, who, just as much as the family, set the style and determine the success of the Rothschild business.

It is a business that bears little resemblance to that of even thirty years ago. The name retains its charisma, but down in the market-place Rothschilds have to fight for business just as hard as anyone else—perhaps even harder. In some respects the glamour of the name is a disadvantage. Like many other merchant bankers between the wars the Rothschilds tended to turn up their noses at domestic business which is today the mainstay of any merchant banker's activity. Now his success is measured by the City and by the financial press not so much by the number of international loans he floats as by the success and number of the new issues he floats for British companies and, most important of all, the number of takeover battles he wins. To achieve a successful takeover victory is the ultimate test of a merchant banker's virility.

Before the war, so Jacob Rothschild believes, ambitious, merger-hungry companies, often led by men whose own origins were pretty humble, tended to ignore Rothschilds. 'We were really too grand to act for such people,' says Jacob. And as the Rothschilds themselves admit, the bank did little to encourage them. Until Jacob himself came down from Oxford with a First in P.P.E., the bank did not possess a finance department. 'When we started we were doing practically no domestic business at all. It was a side of the business we had not developed and we started it because we reckoned that we were not as competitive as we ought to have been.' It is an indication both of the importance that the bankers attach to this side of the business and to the change that has come over Rothschilds itself that the bank is surprisingly sensitive, considering the self-confidence that comes from generations of pre-eminence and success, to any suggestion that the Rothschild commercial record is perhaps slightly less splendid than the name would warrant. Jacob Rothschild countered this charge, somewhat defensively I thought, by pointing out that of all the British banks, Rothschilds is by far the biggest and most active in Europe—which is, after all, traditional Rothschild country. 'I expect you don't want to hear about it,' Jacob said. 'No journalist ever seems to be interested in what we are doing in Europe.' He then proceeded to reel off a whole list of massive Eurobond loans which the bank had floated for such international companies as Shell (the biggest ever), Philips, Rio Tinto Zinc, a company with traditional Rothschild connections, A.K.U., the Dutch chemical and fibres firm, and de Beers—not to mention the financing, together with Warburgs, of the Trans-alpine pipeline. Having finished this list, Jacob turned to Roth-schilds' British business, gently pointing out, in the politest possible way, that in the last five years the bank had acted for Allied Breweries in their merger talks with Unilever (which if the Monopolies Commission had allowed it would have been the biggest merger in British industrial history); had played the part of midwife in the National Provincial–Westminster link up, and had been retained by the Industrial Reorganization Corporation to handle its controversial bid for the engineering firm of Brown Bailey. Shortly after I saw Jacob, Rothschilds was to become entangled in the biggest City row of the 1960s—being retained by Saul Steinberg's Leasco to handle its ultimately successful bid for Robert Maxwell's Pergamon Press. Though much mud was flung in the course of the battle, it was generally agreed that the Roths-child team, led by Jacob, proved that they could mix it with the best of them.

Rothschilds is a classic case of a family business which, though its reflexes may from time to time have slowed, has prospered; partly by its ability to produce in each generation at least one member of the family with genuine ability and partly by its willingness to take on gifted outsiders and give them jobs of real responsibility and power. But this process, in the City as else-where, does not take place in a vacuum. The external stimulus of competition is also needed; Professor Toynbee's theory of challenge and response is just as applicable to the comparatively narrow field of industry and commerce as it is to the rise and fall of nations and civilizations. In this case the stimulus was provided, not just for Rothschilds but for the City as a whole, by the arrival of a whole crop of thrusting, ambitious newcomers, unencumbered by generations of merchant banking tradition. On the whole the Jews, the inheritors of an earlier tradition, have played, at least numerically, a comparatively small part in the City's post-war revival; certainly nothing to compare with their impact in the early years of the nineteenth century.

Many of the famous names have disappeared altogether as the driving force of the founder faded and the sons made way for new and more aggressive entrepreneurs who though self-made were, with the notable exception of Sir Siegmund Warburg, not Jewish. Looked down on by the rest of the City as 'West End bankers' (a reference to the fact that many of them had their headquarters not in the City at all but in the West End), men like the late Lionel Fraser of Schroeder Wagg and Philip Hill have made an impact on the City which has been felt by Jewish and non-Jewish firms alike. Neither had a traditional City background. 'The City meant precious little to me,' Lionel Fraser has said, 'for I was completely without background and connection. It was just somewhere to scrape a living.' Fraser started in the City at sixteen as a clerk in the Jewish firm of Helbert Wagg and ended up as chairman not only of Wagg but of Schroeders, taken over in 1962, as well; while Philip Hill started life as the son of a Torquay cattle auctioneer.

One of the most spectacular casualties occurred in 1968 when Philip Hill, which had already absorbed the venerable firm of Erlangers, took over M. Samuel, the bank which Marcus Samuel founded as an adjunct of his Shell empire and one of the main props of the Bearsted fortune. The Philip Hill attack was led by a young, highly aggressive, former Welsh Guards Officer, called Kenneth Keith, who despite the immaculate suits and the half-moon glasses is far from being a merchant banker in the traditional mould. An accountant by training, his sardonic tongue and tough manner have made him many admirers—and not a few enemies. Nobody was very surprised when, after a brief but bitter board-room battle in the weeks following the M. Samuel takeover, Keith emerged victorious. And though the family name still adorns the title of the City's second largest merchant bank the Samuels no longer play an influential part in the business.

But influence cannot be measured by numbers alone. Sometimes a man appears who by sheer originality of thought and force of personality exercises a power and influence out of all proportion to the size of his business or his position. Siegmund George Warburg, knighted in 1966, is such a man.

Though Warburg, since his arrival from Nazi Germany in 1938, has built up one of the City's most successful and respected banks (though respect was not the first emotion Siegmund Warburg's activities evoked) from nothing at all, it would be hardly accurate to describe Warburg as self-made in the sense that Samuel Montagu or Marcus Samuel were self-made. Warburg has become a banker but was born an aristocrat, a member of one of the most distinguished Jewish families. In common with many other German refugees who escaped from Hitler, and in contrast to the poor ghetto Jews of Russia and Poland who fled from Tsarist persecution some fifty years before Hitler's pogrom began, the Warburgs played a distinguished part in German society, moving in the highest circles. The family first appeared in Germany from Italy some time in the seventeenth century and by the 1920s the Hamburg bank of M. M. Warburg, founded in 1798, was among the most powerful and influential in Germany, close to such huge industrial concerns as Siemens and advising the Government itself. The young Siegmund, though still a trainee with the bank, was on first-name terms with many of Germany's leading politicians, among them Baron von Neurath, Germany's Foreign Minister. And it was his friendship with von Neurath that inadvertently led to Warburg's hurried departure from Germany. The Foreign Minister was impressed by the young Warburg and

F

used to call him into his office to discuss the affairs of the world. One day after Hitler had been in power only a matter of weeks Warburg was paying one of his normal calls on the Foreign Minister.

'Well, my dear young man,' asked the Foreign Minister, 'what have you to tell me about events in foreign countries?'

Warburg who had already heard rumours of Nazi arrests replied: 'I don't want to talk about events in foreign countries today. I want to talk about events in this country. We are at the beginning of a revolution.'

When von Neurath said: 'I can't tell you anything,' Warburg quoted Paragraph 18 of the Constitution at him. Paragraph 18, he pointed out, empowered the Minister to intervene if he felt that the Constitution was being abused. Von Neurath listened and then said: 'I am not considered very reliable.'

It was at this point that Warburg realized the full seriousness of the situation. If von Neurath, the Foreign Minister, was not considered reliable, what chance was there for him, a Jew? Warburg hurried home and told his wife to pack. They were, he said, going to England.

Warburg himself is a highly cultured, reticent man with a fine drawn, oblong face in which his eyes are so deep set that they seem to be entirely surrounded by dark rings. He is thin, walks along the corridors of the bank with a pronounced stoop and has a shy, nervous smile that flashes on and off with alarming suddenness. The son of a South German farmer (by no means all the Warburgs are bankers—they have produced distinguished artists, politicians and publishers), Warburg originally had academic and political ambitions. Philosophy, history and, rather more surprisingly, graphology are still major passions. Despite twenty years of British merchant banking he remains very much a Central European figure who retains the—to the English—discomforting habit of saying exactly what he thinks. He still speaks with a heavy German accent, makes no effort to conceal his German Jewish origins and combines a German formality of manner, often

pausing for minutes at a time before answering a question carefully and precisely, with a particular brand of nervous dynamism.
He is, so his staff say, a great worrier. He is also, at least to outsiders, extremely reticent; a reticence that shows itself in his
instinctive dislike of the personal publicity that his spectacular
achievements in the City have naturally generated. He grants
interviews only on condition that he is never directly quoted,
and insists, in a vain attempt to divert the limelight from himself,
that it is all a team effort. Merchant bankers, he says, are not the
romantic, piratical figures of City legend but rather are skilled,
professional technicians like surgeons and doctors—most effective
when working silently and unobtrusively behind the scenes.

Warburg's insistence on team work is not just a smoke-screen
thrown up by a man who has carried his distaste for personal glory
so far that he appears on the bank's note-paper simply as a director, ranking below the seventeen executive directors. Warburg
did not become a merchant banker until a year after the war ended:
he had spent the war organizing, through a concern called the
New Trading Company, barter deals designed solely to enable
German refugees to extract their money from Nazi Germany. In
1946, the year Siegmund Warburg opened shop, merchant banking was still essentially a money-lending business, run on un-
professional family lines. The old-boy network, always a feature
of City life, was still very much in operation. But it was also a
time when British industry was beginning to look outwards,
becoming increasingly receptive to outside ideas and outside help.
By gathering together a collection of professional men, mostly
accountants and distinguished ex-civil servants like Sir James
Helmore and later Sir Eric Roll, former head of the Department
of Economic Affairs, Warburg was able to break what was for a
merchant banker entirely new ground. Hitherto merchant
bankers had regarded Britain's industrial companies from afar,
only becoming involved when private companies decided to go
public or when public companies came to the market for more
cash. Even then the banks acted mostly as technical advisers,

helping with the financial intricacies of the money raising operation. Warburg's men, by contrast, showed none of the traditional
bankers' reluctance to get their hands dirty. Travelling up and
down the country and working what the City regarded as
indecently long hours (Warburgs is one of the few banks where
the top men are still at their desks late on Friday afternoon), the
Warburg emissaries got under the skin of British industry,
advising companies on personnel and organization policy and
telling them how best to strengthen their international links.
They even penetrated local government ('It was always regarded
as not exactly *haute banque*,' says the Warburg man who master-
minded the deal), working out with Sir Harry Page, treasurer of
the Manchester Corporation, a new form of negotiable local
authority bond. It may not have been *haute banque* but, as Warburgs
have discovered, it has been an agreeably profitable business.

Useful and profitable as these excursions have been, Warburgs'
reputation really rests on the part it played in a series of dramatic
and bitterly contested takeovers in the late 'fifties. One reason for
the bitterness was the appearance of the Americans in force,
threatening large and important sections of British industry and
in the process arousing the City's always latent xenophobia; in
1958, after a battle which raised emotions in the City and elsewhere to fever pitch, Reynolds Metal, in partnership with Tube
Investments, bought British Aluminium; in 1959 Roy Thomson,
an ebullient Canadian, almost unknown in Britain, bought for
£4½ million Lord Kemsley's newspaper empire, the pride of which
was the staid and conservative *Sunday Times* and in 1960 anti-
Americanism flared again when Ford of Detroit acquired full
control of Ford of Dagenham—a business which it already largely
controlled and managed. On each occasion Warburgs played the
anti-establishment role, acting, successfully in each case, for the
attacking outsider. In the City these Warburg victories were not
well received. The part that Warburgs had played in the Great
Aluminium War, in which the leading banks of Lazards, Hambros,
Morgan Grenfell, M. Samuel and Samuel Montagu suffered a

public and humiliating defeat, was particularly resented—it
seemed to confirm their impression that Siegmund Warburg was
an outsider who somehow did not play the game according to
the rules. It was even suggested, in certain circles, that as a
foreigner and a Jew, Warburg's sense of the national interest was
not quite as strong as perhaps it might be. It was an indication of
the distance travelled that in the controversy it was forgotten that
many of the City's most revered insititutions had origins just as
Jewish and just as foreign.

Chapter Five

The Escape from the Ghetto

> He will not, if he can help it, if I may say so, be a hewer of
> wood and drawer of water. He will not be at the bottom if
> he can help it, and generally he will help it. He has suffi-
> cient power in him not to go down.
>
> Samuel Mather, superintendent of the
> Tower Hamlets division of the London
> School Board in evidence to the Royal
> Commission on Alien Immigration, 1903.

The careers of the children of the East End ghetto whom we left
at the end of Chapter Two on the threshold of their climb are in
marked contrast to those of their protectors and sponsors. Even
if the opportunities had existed, few of them, at least at first, were
equipped to become City bankers and financiers. Violently up-
rooted from the small towns of Eastern Europe, economically they
were still only a step away from the Middle Ages. As two outside
observers writing at the turn of the century remarked: 'The newly
arrived Russo-Jewish immigrant is in all essentials a medieval
product.' And though they fast lost these characteristics the most
that they could hope for at the time was that they would be
allowed to continue in their traditional trades.

It was in the little workshops of the East End backstreets that
the majority of the pogrom victims first found work. The tailors
and the bootmakers were mostly in Whitechapel, clustered in the

alleys that branched out from the Commercial Road, with another outpost just south of that main artery. The cabinet makers,
on the other hand, settled a little farther north on the borders
between Whitechapel and Bethnal Green. If they were lucky the
refugees ended up in proper, custom-built workshops at the backs
of the houses, with skylights and decent ventilation. But most did
not. As the employers were small men who had themselves only
arrived a few years before, most of them could not afford proper
workshops and used instead the rooms of their own houses. 'The
small employer', wrote Beatrice Potter* (later Webb), who got to
know and understand the East End tailor better than most,
'seldom knows the distinction between the workshop and the
living room; if he himself sleeps and eats in a separate room, some
of his workers will take their rest on a shake-down between the
presser's table, the machines and scattered heaps of garments.
And this living and working in one room intensifies the evil of
the percentage of persons per acre which is characteristic of this
district.'

These intensely squalid conditions did not in fact last very long.
They began to disappear round about 1910 when the tailors,
organized by trade union leaders and encouraged by such diverse
talents as George Bernard Shaw, Ernest Bevin and the Cadbury-
owned *Daily News*, succeeded after a series of strikes in getting
the employers to grant them a twelve-hour day with two meal
breaks—a concession the illegal unions had forced from some
employers in London, Sheffield and Aberdeen as long ago as the
reign of Queen Anne. Even so, the hardships that the immigrants
suffered at that time were so great that they are still over a time-
span of more than sixty years vividly remembered.

Like thousands of others, Sam Goldstein started in the workshop of a brother who having left Poland some ten years before
had saved enough to become a master tailor himself. Sam,
together with the boy who wheeled the pieces of cloth on a
barrow from the City warehouse to the East End workshop, was

* In *Life and Labour of the People of London.*

later to found one of the first rag trade companies to go public, but in 1905 he had no money and was working a fifteen- or sixteen-hour day. In the slack periods he earned as little as six shillings a week—about half what he was paying for his Burcross Street lodging. 'I used to get up to go to work at six o'clock in the morning. We had an hour's break at lunch time but we often worked until midnight or one in the morning. The workshop was small with a big fire, lit by gas jets, for the irons. The lodging-house keeper used to leave a kipper for my supper but I was so hungry that I often did not feel like eating it. But because it was so hot and sweaty, I used to buy a bottle of soda water and mix it with a glass of milk. After I had drunk it I would wash under the cold tap in the yard and when I woke up in the morning I was so stiff that I couldn't move my body.'

The conditions may have been wretched, the pay barely above subsistence and the hours inhumanly long but at least it was work —and what is more it was work of a type for which the fleeing Russians and Poles were by temperament and background almost ideally suited. The Russian and Polish authorities, as I showed in Chapter Two, had gone to great lengths to divert the Jews from the mainstream of economic life. Barred from the professions, the higher echelons of the army and the civil service and forbidden to hold land, they were forced to struggle for their livings among the foothills of the economy: they were either traders, like Sam Goldstein's father who was a horse dealer in a small town near Warsaw, liquor salesmen, drapers or shoemakers. The alcohol was bought from the farmers, but the shoes and the clothes they made themselves in the backstreet workshops of the towns of the Pale: towns like Lodtz, Kiev and Vilna—a town which had such a large Jewish population that it was known throughout the Jewish community as the Jerusalem of Lithuania.

At first sight they would seem to be ill-equipped to make their way in the England of the 1880s. They suffered the customary disadvantages of the refugee. One or two managed to bring their savings with them. 'I have seen a cheque for £1,000 on one of these persons drawn on a Russian bank,' said Thomas Hawkey, a customs officer whose job it was to board the boats as they came into the Thames and to inspect the immigrants. But on average they had no more than twenty German marks—and a large number, around a quarter, had nothing at all. Language was another problem, creating difficulties on both sides. If few of the new arrivals could speak English, even fewer of the native English, including policemen of H Division, which in those days covered most of the Whitechapel, Wapping and Mile End, could manage even a word of Yiddish. It was a point that interested the Royal Commissioners. 'When you are arresting these people or are concerned with them, I suppose they talk to one another in their own language?' the Commissioners asked the inspector in charge of H Division. 'Yes,' he replied. 'And you as police officers cannot understand what they say?' 'No.' 'That would be a great difficulty in your way?' 'That is a great difficulty.'

The language barrier only served to emphasize the 'foreignness' of the Jews. Nearly every observer of the East End, whether friendly or hostile, remarks on this, and though the reaction may seem odd now, accustomed (though not perhaps reconciled) as we are to the presence of over a million West Indians and Pakistanis, there is no doubt that the Jews did strike even the most sympathetic, including many of their assimilated co-religionists, as a profoundly alien people. Throughout the violent controversy caused by their arrival, they were invariably referred to as 'The Alien Immigrant' and though this became a synonym for racial prejudice it was at that time a not inaccurate description.

Everything about them was strange, their language, their clothes, their customs and their religion. Long after they arrived the immigrants continued to be conspicuous if for no other reason because they continued to wear Eastern European dress, the men in kaftans, tall, polished boots and the ringlets of the orthodox Jew; the women with their heads covered in brightly coloured scarves. 'Owing to the presence of the Jews,' Charles Booth wrote,* 'parts of Whitechapel and St George's give the impression of a foreign town; women with olive complexions and dark bearded men in Russian-Polish dress … ' Once off the streets and inside the tiny synagogues that sprang up wherever a community settled, the illusion of being in a foreign country became almost overwhelming. Certainly that is how it struck Beatrice Potter.†

> Here, early in the morning or late at night, the devout members meet to receive the morning and evening prayers, or to decipher the sacred books of the Talmud. And it is a curious and touching sight to enter one of the poorer and more wretched of these places on a Sabbath morning. Probably the one you will choose will be situated in a small alley or narrow court, or it may be built out into a backyard. To reach the entrance you stumble over broken pavements and household debris; possibly you pick your way over the rickety bridge connecting it with the cottage property fronting the street. From the outside it appears a long wooden building surmounted by a skylight, very similar in construction to an ordinary sweater's workshop. You enter; the heat and odour convince you that the skylight is not used for ventilation. From behind the trellis of the ladies' gallery you see at the far end of the room the richly curtained Ark of the Covenant wherein are laid, attired in gorgeous vestments, the sacred scrolls of the Law. Slightly elevated on a platform in the midst of the congregation stands the reader or minister, surrounded by the seven who are called up to the reading of the Law from among the congregation. Scarves of white cashmere or silk, softly bordered and fringed, are thrown across the shoulders of the men, and relieve the dusty hue and disguise the Western cut of the clothes they wear. A low, monotonous, but musical toned recital of Hebrew prayers, each man pray-

* *Life and Labour of the People of London.*
† Op. cit.

ing for himself to the God of his fathers, rises from the congregation, whilst the reader intones, with somewhat louder
voice, the recognized portion of the Pentateuch. Add to this
the rhythmical cadence of numerous voices, the swaying to
and fro of the bodies of the worshippers—expressive of the
words of personal adoration: 'All my bones exclaim Oh
Lord, who is like unto Thee!'—and you may imagine yourself in a far-off Eastern land. But you are roused from your
dreams. Your eye wanders from the men, who form the
congregation, to the small body of women who watch behind the trellis. Here, certainly you have the Western world,
in the bright coloured ostrich feathers, large bustles, and
tight fitting coats of cotton velvet or brocaded satinette. At
last you step out, stifled by the heat and dazed by the strange
contrast of the old world memories of a majestic religion and
the squalid vulgarity of an East End Slum.

The East End was certainly squalid but at the same time it was
intensely active and vigorous: there was nothing passive about it
or its inhabitants. And what gave it its momentum was the
character of the immigrants themselves. They suffered, as I have
already said, from many disadvantages, but against this must be
set the intensity of the Jews' desire to overcome them. Most were
willing to slave in the sweatshops for a piece of black bread and
a few shillings a week, but few were prepared to do it a moment
longer than was absolutely necessary. The ambition of the majority
was to become master of their own sweatshop—and thus of their
fate.

Obviously it would be ridiculous to suggest that every apprentice tailor was a budding Sir Isaac Wolfson of Great Universal
Stores or a Sir John Cohen of Tesco, but all the same there *were*
differences in attitude between the Jewish immigrant and the
native English worker; differences sufficiently strong to stand the
weight of a generalization. Jacob Fine who started in a Sheaba
Street workshop behind Truman's brewery went on to spend

forty years of his life in the uphill task of trying to organize his fellow garment workers said:

> The English worker went along very slowly: he had to have his protein, his pint of beer and his fish and chips. The Jewish worker was an immigrant. He had to be ambitious to survive and he had to fight for himself. The top workers, the ones who had been in the workshop the longest and were the most skilled, engaged the under-workers. The ambition of the under-workers was to become a top worker; that of a top worker to become a master; and that of a master to become a manufacturer.

One of Charles Booth's investigators, Hubert Llewellyn Smith, observing the same scene from a rather different standpoint, reached a similar conclusion, though being a Victorian civil servant he put it more elegantly, when he wrote:*

> The economic weakness and strength of Individualism form the economic strength and weakness of the East London Jewish community. Each for himself, unrestrained by the instincts of combination, pushes himself upward in the industrial scale. His standard of life readily adapts itself to his improved condition at every step. We have here all the conditions of the economist satisfied: mobility perfect, competition unremitting, modifying conditions almost absent; pursuit of gain an all powerful motive; combination practically inoperative.

Here, said the Victorians, was surely the perfect personification of Ricardo's Economic Man.

Nearly, but not quite. Where the immigrant did not fit into the Ricardian mould was in his ability, itself a carry-over from his *shtetl* days, to adjust his standard of living to suit the circumstances. What astonished observers of the East End scene was the elasticity (a word they constantly used to describe the pheno-

* Quoted in *The Jewish Immigrant in England, 1870–1914.*

menon) of the Jews' standard of living: the Jews behaved as if
they had never heard of Malthus's iron law of subsistence. They
may have eventually climbed higher than the beer-swilling, fish-
and-chip eating British workmen but in the process they were
prepared to sink much lower. Of course there were some who
found their miseries too hard to bear: one, Samuel Levy, pleaded
with the Royal Commissioners to send him home. But the majority
coped. Though grindingly poor they did not form, as Arnold
White the anti-alien agitator had said they would, a whole new
class of paupers—a liability to honest Christian rate-payers.

So elastic was their standard of living that the Jews scarcely
troubled the Poor Law Guardians in the parishes of the East End
at all. Officials of the Jewish Board of Guardians, who made a
special inquiry at the request of a somewhat apprehensive Local
Government Board, were surprised to learn that of the 1,772
paupers in Mile End only nine in 1897 were foreigners; in Whitechapel, which had no less than 20,420 paupers, the proportion of
foreigners was even lower: there the Guardians could only find
twenty Jewish paupers—and this after the tide of immigration
had been running at full spate for some fifteen years. Throughout
the East End—in Bethnal Green, Hackney, St George's and
Shoreditch—it was the same story. The Mile End Guardians who
were asked to explain these figures said:

It will thus be seen that the abiding of foreigners in large
numbers does not necessarily cause an increase in pauperism,
but a general low rate of payment to wage earners in the
trades in which such foreigners obtain employment. This
affects the British workman to a considerable extent as,
generally speaking, his ideal of life is higher and consequently
more expensive than is the case with his congenes [sic] of
other lands, to whom love of home and its surroundings has
no meaning in the sense which the expression is understood
by an Englishman, as many of them accommodate themselves
to conditions disgusting and wretched in the extreme.

They may not have realized it at the time but in many respects the Jews were lucky and their arrival in England could not have been better timed. Though the economic historians generally agree that by 1880 England had passed the zenith of her industrial power and was being rapidly overhauled by Germany and, to a lesser extent, France, they also agree that in the last twenty to thirty years of the nineteenth century the face of England was changing more rapidly than ever before. The population was growing at an unprecedented speed. 'The elemental factor which conditioned so much English history in the nineteenth century', writes Professor Peter Mathias,* 'was the inexorable rise in population: in the number of mouths to be fed.' When the nineteenth century opened, the population of England, Scotland and Wales was barely 10 million; by mid-century the figure had doubled and by 1911 the population was four times greater than it had been 110 years before. Nor were these extra 30 million people spread evenly across the face of the land: the vast majority poured into the towns, changing the face of London, Manchester, Birmingham, Leeds and Glasgow. London grew vastly—from one million in 1800 to over 7½ million in 1911. But it was in the provincial towns, the manufacturing centres of the Midlands and the North, that the growth was really dramatic. In 1800 London was the only city in the country with a population of more than 100,000 and only fifteen cities had more than 20,000 inhabitants. By 1891 no less than twenty-three had topped the 100,000 mark and 185 had reached the 20,000 level.

This growth and concentration of population would in itself have been enough to change the habits of the British shopkeepers, for the snapping of the links with the countryside called for an entirely different style of retailing and marketing. A community of some 500 or even 5,000 people could easily be supplied each day with fresh farm eggs from the surrounding villages; but catering for 50,000 or 500,000 was a very different matter.

What made the opportunities really dazzling was the dramatic

* *The First Industrial Nation. An economic history of Britain, 1700–1914.*

change in the economic climate which occurred in the last thirty
years of the nineteenth century. Between 1873 and 1896, for
reasons that the economic historians are still arguing about, prices
fell by some 40 per cent—the first major change in a climb that
had lasted without any significant interruption for nearly 900
years. It was known as the Great Depression—a collapse that was
to remain until the 1930s quite unprecedented in Britain's
economic history. But whereas the working classes were the main
sufferers of the 1931 debacle, the Great Depression of the 1880s
actually worked to their advantage. Though prices fell, wages
remained more or less steady with the happy result that the real
income of the average British household increased dramatically:
in the last thirty years of the nineteenth century the ordinary
British housewife saw her husband's income rise by some
62 per cent.

The consequences of these demographic and economic changes
were far-reaching. It was no accident that it was during this
period that the grocery business flourished and that the first chain
stores and multiples took shape, catering for a developing and
increasingly affluent mass market. Apart from one or two isolated
examples the immigrant Jews were still too low on the economic
ladder to take advantage of these developments. Their chance
came later. The pioneering grocers were Scotsmen, Quakers and
other non-conformists. John Sainsbury, the son of a West
Country ornament maker, opened his first shop in Drury Lane
in 1869 (the only Jewish blood in the business being his daughter-
in-law, Mabel Van den Bergh, of the Dutch margarine family
which later joined hands with Unilever); Thomas Lipton, the
ebullient Scotsman who founded Allied Suppliers and who once
offered Queen Victoria a five-ton cheese as a sales ploy, started in
1871, while up in Nottingham Jesse Boot was applying to the
chemists' business the robust, mass-marketing techniques that
were to make his name a household word.

When the Jews arrived these entrepreneurs had been hard at
work for at least ten years providing tea, sago and bars of soap

for the masses. There was, however, one area into which they had not penetrated and on which the Jews quickly made an impact all of their own. In this they were helped by two technological innovations. In 1851 an American named Isaac Merrit Singer introduced the sewing machine. The importance of this invention was immediately recognized, but its significance was misinterpreted. 'The astonishing velocity of the new sewing machine', *The Economist* observed, 'will extinguish the race of tailors.' Nothing of the kind happened: in 1880 there still were, according to Sir John Clapham, no less than 160,000 of them all busily stitching away. Instead of wiping them out, the sewing machine helped the tailors to survive and prosper.

The second technological change came seven years later when a Leeds clothing manufacturer, John Barran (a distant ancestor of the present managing director of Shell), adapted the bandsaw of a local metal works for his own business; instead of cutting out suits one by one with a pair of scissors, John Barran's workers were able to turn out the pieces by the half-dozen and the dozen — an invention that led to a fortune for himself, a baronetcy and a career in politics for his son, and work and comparative prosperity for the thousands of Jewish garment workers in Leeds.

Barran was a new figure in the clothing business; a wholesaler who did no tailoring himself: he merely bought the cloth from the wool merchants across the Pennines in Bradford, cut it up into the appropriate pieces and then handed it out to the immigrants working in their homes or in small workshops for making up into suits. The results were remarkable. Until the 1860s or thereabouts a suit took one man, sitting cross-legged at his table several days to make and was a luxury item costing £6 or £7 — a price no working man could afford. But when the wholesalers began to organize the industry on semi-mass-production lines, a 45s. brand-new suit became a possibility.

Not all the wholesalers were in Leeds and not all of them used John Barran's bandsaw. But most sprang up in the early 1860s and most were Gentile — although nearly all of them relied on Jewish workers for their invariably sweated labour. The wholesalers turned to the Jews for two very good reasons: they were cheaper because they were hungry and unorganized, and they were faster because they were prepared to split up the work. The English tailor was highly unionized and used to regular hours. He saw himself as a craftsman and the idea of handing over any part of the garment he was working on to anybody else was abhorrent. It was *his* coat from start to finish—from the cutting of the broadcloth to the stitching of the final buttonhole. And though the new sewing machines boosted his output he still apparently could not, as the factory manager of Charles Barker, a High Holborn firm of tailors, explained in his evidence to the Royal Commission, keep pace with the increasing flood of work from the wholesalers:

> The English tailor seems quite unable to take to the system of sub-division of labour; he likes to make an article throughout; but even were this system possible in our business it would be impossible to find more than an infinitesimal number of English tailors trained or capable of being trained to it. The ready-made trade, as we term it now, is entirely the work of foreign Jews ... The English tailor would take one hour to put in one pocket and the Jew tailor, with subdivision, puts in four in twenty minutes.

From the very beginning subdivision was the predominant characteristic of the Jewish garment trade. As John Burnett, the percipient Board of Trade official who made a special study of the sweating system in the East End in the late 1880s, observed: 'The cheaper branches of the trade have been completely cut up into sections ... Instead of a complete tailor we now have men who make only coats or waistcoats or trousers. Nor does sub-division stop here. We have cutters, basters, machinists, pressers, fellers, buttonhole workers and general workers brought in to bear in the construction of a coat.' This subdividing habit was both the trade's strength and its weakness. Firms grew amoeba-fashion, splitting up and reproducing themselves when they reached a

G

certain size. An immigrant would join as a 'greener' (the Yiddish term for an apprentice tailor) often paying the worker immediately above him a premium for the privilege of sweeping the floor or making the tea. Then he would gradually ascend the rigidly defined hierarchy of the workshop, and as he climbed, so would his pay. For the first three months he would earn virtually nothing at all; for the next six he would be lucky to be earning 4s. or 5s. for an 'indefinite' day and after a year, depending on how high he had climbed, he could be earning between 6s. and 10s. for a day lasting thirteen to fourteen hours. It was not much, but then not much was needed. A workshop could be equipped for under £5 — the heavy, 16 lb. flat iron for the presser could be bought for 5s. and a treadle sewing machine for £2 or £3.

The low cost of entry was a feature peculiar to the clothing trade.* Between 1881 and 1901 the numbers employed in tailoring rose by over 100,000 — from 160,000 to 260,000 — but the manufacturing units remained pitifully small. Shortly after the turn of the century Beatrice Potter calculated that 80 per cent of East End trade was made up of workshops employing under 10 people.

The wholesalers took every advantage of this situation — playing off one workshop against another. John Burnett, the Board of Trade man, told a Parliamentary Select Committee:†

Every time the sweater takes work out further reductions are attempted ... when a man goes to take work out, he is told that he can have another order for the same kind of coats if he likes to take them at 3d. or 6d. a coat less. If he is indisposed to take them he is told that Samuel Abrahams or Moses Isaacs, or some other man in the trade, will make them at that price and in that way he is left with little alternative.

* It had once been true of boots and shoes — another Jewish trade — but after the introduction of the Blake machines in 1860 which stitched the soles to the uppers, the business became increasingly mechanized; the amount of start-up capital needed rose; the factories became bigger and the proportion of Jews, except in the very cheapest end of the trade, declined.
† *Report to the Board of Trade on the Sweating System in the East End of London.*

The fashion trade was a very seasonal business and the pressures were worst in the slack time that was ushered in each autumn by the Lord Mayor's Show. The East Enders did not join in the jollity of that peculiar City festival, for the day after the Lord Mayor rolled down Ludgate Hill in his gilded coach with livery-men and the halberd bearers of the Honourable Artillery Company in their Cromwellian uniform in attendance the trade died; the greeners were laid off and only the most skilled workers were kept on to make up the samples for the coming spring season. For most of the winter the greeners and the underworkers eked out a living as costermongers and orange sellers in the streets around Petticoat Lane, coming back again to the workshops when trade picked up in the spring. For the small masters it was a worrying time since their livelihood in the coming year depended on their skill in negotiating with the wholesalers during the winter. Sometimes the wholesalers would advertise for samples but just as often the masters would buy cloth on their own account and make up samples on spec. 'A lot of bargaining went on,' Jacob Fine, the trade union organizer recalls, 'a manufacturer would hesitate, reluctant to accept a sample. "Right," said the tailor, reconciled to cutting his margins still further, "I'll do you six repeats for 5s." They cut each other's throats.'

But even when spring came and the trade picked up again, the work, even for the skilled men, was far from regular—they were lucky if they worked four and a half days a week. The under-workers fared even worse. For them the week did not start until Wednesday lunchtime. But from then until work stopped on Saturday morning the pressure was intense, with the sewing machines clacking away non-stop for thirty-six hours. 'We used to work 16, 17, 18 hours a day,' said Lewis Lyons, general secretary of the United Garment Workers (a mainly Jewish union), explaining the background to the great Jewish tailors' strike of 1889. 'And on Thursday morning we used to go in at 6 o'clock and not leave until Friday night or sometimes we went in on a Saturday.' The immigrants, almost without exception, were rigidly orthodox but when an order was pressing even the dictates of the Sabbath were set aside.

If life was hard for the men, it was even harsher for the women. The Jewish workshops employed very few women and when they did they were given the dirtiest and most degrading jobs. The pay was correspondingly poor. 'Earnings', Beatrice Potter reported,* 'can never exceed 1s. 6d. and frequently fall below 1s. for 12 hours' work.' More often than not the women were not employed in the workshops at all but sweated on their own at home, taking the work to and from the factory themselves. Mrs Turnhouse, a lady of fifty-eight, who lived by herself making trousers on a Singer machine which she had bought on hire purchase, was one such woman. Each pair of trousers took her more than an hour to make. On one of his expeditions into the East End, the novelist John Galsworthy, who was as interested in the condition of the working classes as he was in the moneyed middle classes of the Bayswater Road, met Mrs Turnhouse and reported the following conversation:†

GALSWORTHY. How much are you paid?

MRS T. Twopence a pair.

G. How much do you earn in a week then?

MRS T. Oh four shillings, perhaps five, sometimes six.

G. And what do you pay for your room?

MRS T. Two shilling a week.

G. Are you telling me that you are living on between two shillings and four shillings a week?

MRS T. Oh yes, my dear.

G. But what do you live on?

MRS T. Well, I haven't got a very good appetite and sometimes I go without.

G. TO MRS. T's

LANDLADY. She doesn't really go without food for a whole day does she?

---

* Op. cit.   † Quoted in *The Needle is Threaded*.

LANDLADY. Yes she does. Sometimes I take her a cup of tea but she goes without nothing to eat.

The interview proved too much for Galsworthy and he left in tears.

The ordinary worker's lot was undeniably harsh, but for the most part the employers were equally hard pressed. Competition had pared their profit margins almost to vanishing point. The prices, as John Burnett pointed out, varied widely—from 15s. for a high-quality job to 9d.; on which, Burnett dryly observed, 'little profit can be expected'. On a coat costing 1s. 2½d., Burnett calculated that a sweater was left with 3½d. to pay for the rent, the machines, the fires for the irons and the other bits and pieces needed to keep the workshop going. The economic borderline between the masters and their workers was so narrow that the stereotype of the sweater, as portrayed by Herbert Evans, an assistant inspector of factories, was largely a figment of his imagination. According to Evans's evidence to the Royal Commission: 'the taskmaster and sweater is an unprincipled, loathsome individual whose tyrannical methods and disposition are only equalled by his complete ignorance and open defiance of everything that is normal and humane ... of baleful practices he is the monopolist ... his disposition is exemplified by the hideous way he shrieks at his workers.'

The sweater probably did drive his men hard but only because he himself was equally driven. If anybody was to blame it was the contracting wholesaler, not the sweater. It was Beatrice Potter who analysed the situation more eloquently and probably more accurately than anybody. She wrote:*

Without a constant supply of destitute foreigners and of wives to supplement their irregular earnings the low class tailoring trade would cease to exist ... No one profits by this extreme form of sweating except the most grinding whole-sale house, and the unknown landlord who secures through

* Op. cit.

the transformation of backyard and living room into work-shop, a double rent. The real 'sweater' therefore, has a threefold personality—an ignorant consumer, a grinding and fraudulent wholesale or retail shop trader, a rack renting landlord; in some instances we might add a driving labour contractor. This is the body of the sweater; the soul is the evil spirit of the age, unrestrained competition.

The Jewish tailor in London was predominantly a ladies' man. Before the Jews arrived ladies' suits, or mantles as they were known in the trade, were imported from Germany; but by 1900 these imports had virtually ceased, and from then until the 1920s when the rag trade moved its headquarters to the streets around the Middlesex Hospital just north of Oxford Circus, it was the East End that dominated the cheaper end of the blouse and mantle business. And it was in the backstreets around Petticoat Lane that many of today's rag trade tycoons first learnt their trade. To give just one example, Louis Mintz, one of the very few men to have built up a rag trade empire of any size (his company Selincourt was, after a rather patchy trading record, worth £3·9 million in 1970), started in this way in a small attic in Plummers' Row—a street no wider than Mintz's present office just off Oxford Circus. Mintz's father was not really a businessman, and though the lace that he sold on his Petticoat Lane stall brought in enough to keep the family alive, it was Mintz's eldest sister who gave the business the push that it needed. After she had taught herself blouse making she persuaded the rest of the family to follow her example: father Mintz learnt how to cut out blouses and the girls would make them up. It was not a very sophisticated or com-plicated business; the patterns were cut out of newspaper and if the wholesaler for whom they worked asked for a blouse that was a little larger than normal, they used the same pattern but left a margin all the way round.

Conditions in Leeds, where as late as 1939 one-third of the in-sured population was still employed in the clothing trade, were never quite as bad as they were in London. The Jewish work-shops were larger—a man with a dozen employees would be a big man in London but a small one in Leeds—and the trade was less seasonal and more regular. If London was the headquarters of the volatile, fashion-prone mantle business then Leeds was the centre of the altogether more sober and more profitable world of the three-piece, working man's suit. For every cloth cap there was to be a cheap but impeccably tailored made-to-measure cloth suit.

'We conceived it', Sir Montague Burton, who is widely but wrongly regarded as the pioneer of this idea, once said, 'as a complete operation. And it was based on the conviction that the majority of males in the British Isles were conscious of their own uniqueness and thus very loath to consider themselves as average men, even for the purpose of buying clothes.' Though Burton subsequently became by far the largest purveyor of suits to the masses (at the height of his expansion in the 1930s he was opening one shop every week) the first steps were taken by the non-Jewish owners of the large wholesale factories, which by the 1880s were cutting up suits to be made up in the Jewish workshops of Leeds in their hundreds and thousands.

When Montague Burton was still serving behind the counter in his little shop in Chesterfield, bought for a hundred pounds that he had borrowed from a relative; while Moses Jacobsen, the founder of Newcastle's Jackson the Tailor was still struggling with his brother in an unprepossessing shop in Clayton Street; and while Simon Lyons, who was later to sell his Alexandre business to Sir Brian Mountain's United Drapery for £2 million, was still a foreman cutter with a Leeds tailor called Paul Hibbs (now part of Sir Isaac Wolfson's G.U.S. empire), two non-Jewish manufacturers in Leeds, W. Blackburn and J. Hepworth, were firmly entrenched in the retail business on their own account, selling hundreds, if not thousands of made-to-measure suits through their own shops in the north-east. Exactly who was first is difficult to tell as they both claim this distinction but, what is more important, they and Sir Henry Price, another non-Jewish

Leeds businessman who started his own Fifty Shilling Tailors shortly afterwards, set an entirely new pattern for the trade which spelt prosperity for themselves and extinction for the traditional Jewish workshop on which they had relied.

Gradually suit making became not a workshop but a factory business. Among the grimy rows of terraced houses on the out-skirts of Leeds there rose what were initially little more than vast sheds filled with row upon row of sewing machines, manned, if that is the word, for the first time by girls. The whole process was run and organized on factory lines, the only difference being that the end product was an individual item made specially to measure for Mr Bloggs of Sunderland or Mr Higgins of Hartlepool. It may sound wildly uneconomic, a factory manager's nightmare, but the truth is that once the system of processing the orders from the shops was properly organized there were, as Stanley Burton, Sir Montague's eldest son, explained to me, considerable commercial advantages. In the first place, he said, it increased the turnover of the shops. Instead of measuring the customer and then hanging about while he tried on half-a-dozen suits, he simply ran a tape measure up his leg and round his middle, entered the result of his researches on a special card which he then posted off to the factory. The customer was told that his suit would be ready in ten days and the assistant was free to deal with the next man. The factory too benefited from this system; instead of holding vast stocks of ready-to-wear suits which were expensive to store and even more costly to finance, all the factory need hold in its ware-houses were the bales of cloth which could be pulled off the shelf and made up on demand.

The refinement and exploitation of this system was, with the eminent exception of Sir Henry Price, largely a Jewish achieve-ment. To quote Beatrice Potter again. Referring to the East End sweater she said:* 'His earnings are scanty ... But the chances of the trade are open to him; with indefatigable energy and with a certain measure of organizing power he may press forward into

* Op. cit.

the ranks of the large employers, and if he be successful day by day, year by year, his profit increases and his labour decreases relatively to the wage and labour of his hands.' This was just as true of Sir Montague Burton, of Moses Jacobsen and Simon Lyons as it was of the men Beatrice Potter was observing and describing. All of them had made the vital jump into the retail end of the business when still very young, all were as good salesmen as they were manufacturers and all had by the time that they died entered the ranks of the large employers. The largest of them all was Sir Montague Burton who, when he died of a heart attack at a lunch for his own employees in 1952, left a fortune of £750,000 and an organization which embraced some 600 stores (at one time he had no less than five in Oxford Street alone) and which employed directly and indirectly over 120,000 people. It was described quite simply and unequivocally as 'The World's largest tailoring organization'. Though attempts were made to copy it in Canada, where a firm called Tip Top Tailoring was started up, there was until Burton itself moved into France in 1964 nothing quite like it anywhere else in the world.

Sir Montague was a small man with a fringe of jet black hair round his bald head—'there are no brains above five foot five,' was one of his favourite sayings—and he ran his empire bene-volently but with a distinct touch of personal autocracy—a trait which nearly brought the business crashing down in disaster. Against all advice Sir Montague had bought forward in the commodity markets a huge amount of wool—some 13 million pounds of it—at very high prices in the expectation that the price would go still higher. It did not and the resulting shortage of cash, which occurred when Burtons had to meet its commitments, was so acute that the business was only saved by a rescue operation mounted by the company's bankers, Kleinwort Benson. The bankers reorganized the company, bought Moses Jacobsen's Jackson the Tailor for £2 million and put Moses's son Lionel, a brilliant wool buyer, and his brother Sydney in charge of the combined operation, which they continued to run until 1969.

But though Sir Montague's judgment may on occasion have been erratic he was in his heyday a brilliant organizer and an equally successful property dealer. By the time Burton had, with the help of a small Leeds clothing manufacturer called Ellis Hurwitz, graduated from his Chesterfield shop, property was becoming just as much part of the tailoring business as button-holes and sewing machines. For it was not only the Jewish work-shop that was threatened by the new factory system: the tailor's shop was changing too. It was no longer the hallowed sanctum where a gentleman could consult his tailor in a cubicle resembling the confessional. It had been downgraded to become merely a sales point for the factory.

Competition for good shop sites became intense, as did the rivalry between Burton's and Price's. Corner sites were, for obvious reasons, particularly prized. On one occasion Sir Montague bought three out of the four shops on a corner in Mansfield —more than he really needed—just so that he could freeze out Sir Henry. One of the most conspicuous casualties in this personal war was the public house which frequently offered corner sites. 'I reckon that I've closed more pubs than the whole temperance movement put together,' Burton used to boast.

Good sites, however, were only the first step in the unceasing battle for sales. 'You can't sell a suit unless you can get a man in the shop,' Burton used to say. 'Therefore we must have maximum display.' Throughout the 1920s and the 1930s all sorts of gimmicks were employed to lure customers into the shops. Sir Henry Price's were deliberately rather flashy affairs. The shop fronts were chromium plated and decked out in neon lights and often there stood in the windows two figures, one very fat and one very thin, and below them a legend which read: 'No extra charge.' The Burton stores were, by contrast, much more sober. The exteriors were ponderous and heavy and came in four different styles: Empire stone for the prestige stores in Oxford Circus; granite facing for the slightly smaller West End emporiums, terracotta and a treatment called Marshall Tweedy, named after the architect, for the suburbs. The interiors were wood-panelled and thickly carpeted—deliberately designed to give the customer the impression that he was not in a shop at all but rather a member of some sort of club. Even the neon sign which topped the store was styled so as to appear as dignified as possible. The whole object of the exercise was, so Stanley Burton says, to attract the customer but at the same time to inspire a feeling of confidence and trust. 'As we did not cut an inch of cloth until we had received a cash deposit from the customer we had to look as much like a bank as possible so that people would trust us with their money,' he explains.

In many ways Sir Montague was a more sophisticated operator than his chief rival. He had as keen an eye for a neat property deal as he had for a well-cut suit. Whenever he came to London he used invariably to walk up Oxford Street as far as Oxford Circus eyeing the buildings. 'That business', he used to say of Selfridges long before it was taken over by Charles Clore, 'is worth £10 million.' He never bought Selfridges but he did in 1947 buy one of its main rivals, Peter Robinson, which occupied a superb site, fronting Oxford Circus itself. It was one of the best deals he ever did. Even though he originally intended to turn the whole of the ground floor into a massive men's wear store—an idea which never materialized—the building was far too big even for Burton's ambitions. But by selling the freehold to the Prudential Insurance Company, leasing the store back himself and then subletting the upper floors to the Iraq Petroleum Company he acquired the entire building, in effect, for nothing. It was an early example of a technique that has now become famous.

It was a principle that Burton had already been applying for many years on a smaller scale. Unlike many other retailers Burton's stores were never single-storey affairs. The shop occupied the ground floor but the upper storeys were let off: sometimes to other chains, sometimes to individuals but more often than not to billiard hall companies. It was not such a madcap idea as it sounds. Billiards was a very popular game amongst young people in the 1920s. And to have a stream of youngsters constantly passing the Burton windows on their way upstairs to pot the red was a prospect that Sir Montague found distinctly pleasing. In the 1930s he even bought a billiard company of his own, Bright Billiard Halls Ltd, but the boom was already on the wane and the experiment was not a success — gradually the billiard rooms emptied, the companies folded and above Burton stores today there are sometimes dancing schools, sometimes labour exchanges but more often than not nothing but empty space.

For over forty years Sir Montague and Sir Henry dominated the mass tailoring business. The early pioneers like Hepworths, who had allowed the newcomers to concentrate on the cheaper end of the market, had been left far behind and enterprising characters like Simon Lyons of Alexandre and Moses Jacobsen of Jackson the Tailor ('The House that Value Built') were, though successful, too small to make much impact on the national scene. But in 1952–3 the situation was suddenly transformed by a series of events that shot a number of quite minor characters into unexpected prominence. Perhaps the most surprising figure of all was a sad-eyed, one-legged man called Joseph Collier who in the 1940s was running a successful but somewhat obscure drapery business in the Elephant and Castle. 'I am', he used to say proudly before the business was badly damaged by flying bombs during the war, 'the largest knicker manufacturer in South-East London.' In 1944 Collier jumped from being the owner of a bombed-out drapery shop to become the boss of United Drapery Stores, a medium-sized clothing and credit trading business with a rather dubious and chequered trading history. In the early 1930s United Drapery Stores, after a series of misfortunes most of them connected with the failure of Glaves, its Oxford Street store, was in the eminently respectable hands of the Eagle Star Insurance Company which, in an unusual step for an insurance company, had moved in after foreclosing on the mortgage it had held on Glaves. The first job confronting Eagle Star's Sir Edward Mountain was to clear the £400,000 worth of debts that United

Drapery had accumulated, but once this was done Sir Edward, after an abortive attempt to sell the company shortly before the war, decided to make the best of a bad job and set out in search of new management; a quest which eventually led him to the Elephant and Castle and Joseph Collier.

For the boss of a large insurance company Sir Edward was an unusually aggressive and entrepreneurial character.* Immediately after the war ended he set out on an ambitious shopping expedition. The first stage started in 1946 with the acquisition of Arding and Hobbs, the Clapham department store, and ended in 1953 with the purchase of Sir Henry Price's Fifty Shilling Tailors.

By 1953 much of Sir Henry's early fire had died down. He had moved south to a farmhouse in Sussex, leaving the day-to-day running of the business in Leeds in the hands of two lieutenants who, as it proved, had little of Sir Henry's flair. The property portfolio was magnificent but the business itself lacked management and was in a sadly run-down condition. It was to solve this problem that, two years later in 1955, Collier turned to Bernard Lyons, the heir to his father's Alexandre business. 'Bernard,' he said one winter evening over a late night whisky in the Queen's Hotel at Leeds, 'I need help. I can't run this business by myself. I've only got one knee but if I had two I would go down on both of them.' It was a tempting offer and one that young Bernard found difficult to resist. 'We didn't need any part of United Drapery but compared with them we were a small company and I was restless,' Lyons recalls. In the event Alexandre was sold to U.D.S. for £2 million and Bernard Lyons, a much more managerial figure than his father, took over the running of Sir Henry's former empire. The name of Fifty Shilling Tailors disappeared from the High Streets to be replaced by that of Collier himself. Collier died in 1967 and United Drapery is now in the hands of

* His first question on meeting Collier was: 'Are you a self-made man, Collier?' 'Yes,' Collier replied. 'That's all I wanted to know. You can come and help me run United Drapery.'

his former partner Jack Sampson and the two Lyons brothers from Leeds. Between them they have had more success in managing U.D.S. than the Jacobsens have had at Burtons. In the last five years U.D.S. has made two attempts to take over Burtons and, but for the Monopolies Commission, its second attempt in 1967 would have succeeded: a prospect that would have made Sir Montague and Sir Henry surely turn over in their respective graves.

The building of the great tailoring multiples like Montague Burton was the immigrant Jews' most characteristic and spectacular achievement. But though, for reasons I have already explained, tailoring remained the staple trade, the Jews were not slow to channel their mass-marketing skills in other directions. There were many incentives for them to do so. Tailoring was for many a profoundly unattractive occupation: the conditions were depressing, the wages low and the future uncertain. To many young immigrants the prospect of a lifetime in their father's backstreet workshop was infinitely discouraging. And what may have been good enough for their fathers certainly was not good enough for them. An English education had widened their horizons and they looked around for alternatives. They did not have to look very far. The inter-war period in which they grew up was one of slump and depression. But it was also, paradoxically, the time when Britain, turning in on herself after a hundred years of outward-looking Imperial expansion, began to develop her consumer industries. The trend towards mass-market retailing had got under way before the First World War, but it was not until the 1920s that the enormous purchasing power of the British working classes, whose real wages actually rose throughout the years of the Depression, began to be fully tapped.

In 1918 the furniture trades, the electrical goods business, the radio industry and the cinema were still in their infancy. Vacuum cleaners, electric irons and radio sets only made their appearance in the late 1920s. And it is, I think, no accident that so many Jewish entrepreneurs chose these areas in which to expand. Their background and their commercial training, first in the ghettoes of Eastern Europe and later in the East End and elsewhere, made them particularly sensitive to the needs of the burgeoning mass market; they knew almost instinctively what their customers wanted. Moreover, they were needs that they could supply without any great outlay of capital. Just as it took only a few pounds to equip a tailor's workshop, so the setting up of a small radio shop, a furniture store or a scrap metal business was equally inexpensive, and the opportunities were infinitely greater. Just how the children of the immigrants seized those opportunities, and what use they made of them we shall now see.

Chapter Six

Sir Isaac Wolfson

I am no legend or anything like that. I am a respectable Jew. I worked with all my fingers. That's my secret.

Sir Isaac Wolfson in an interview with the Israeli paper, *Maariv*, in April 1966.

Sir Isaac Wolfson is of course mistaken. He *is* a legend. And one that is compounded by almost everything about him: the size of the business he controls, the manner by which this extraordinary agglomeration of around 250 companies has been put together, his spectacular philanthropy and, not least, the peculiar character of the man himself with its strange combination of almost manic ebullience and obsessional secrecy.

Wolfson is a highly complex and paradoxical figure. In many ways he is the most public of men, appearing at numerous functions both in England and Israel (which he visits regularly about twice a year) in his role as philanthropist, benefactor and energetic supporter of the Jewish cause. His name appears on the portals of innumerable schools and scientific institutions which have been supported or frequently, created, by his charitable foundation; there is even an Oxford college named after him. But the spotlight of public attention has been carefully directed to illuminate Wolfson the philanthropist, not Wolfson the businessman. Information about his charitable work is not hard to

Pub. by J. Fairburn Broadway Ludgate hill July 14 1829

N. Sharpshooter, fec.

THE MAN WOT KNOWS HOW TO DRIVE A BARGAIN.

1. A contemporary cartoon of Nathan Mayer Rothschild, founder of the London Branch of Rothschilds.

2. Samuel Montagu, the first Lord Swaythling, taken about 1900.

3. The morning-room at Tring Park as it was in 1890. Home of Baron Lionel Rothschild, this 3,500-acre estate was bought for over £250,000.

A BENEVOLENT JEW.
taken on the ROYAL EXCHANGE.

Drawn Etch'd & Pub.^d by Dighton, Charing Cross, Decr 1802.

4. Abraham Goldsmid (1756–1810), one of the founding members of B. and A.
Goldsmid, merchant bankers and loan contractors.

THE CHEAP TAILOR AND HIS WORKMEN.

5. (*above*) A contemporary cartoon illustrating popular feeling about the notorious conditions in the sweat shops of the East End.

6. (*left*) Portrait of a Jewish tailor in the East End.

7. (*below*) The great migration: Jews leaving Russia after the pogroms of 1881.

come by: digging out facts as distinct from gossip and rumour, about his business career, particularly the early years, is an altogether more difficult and demanding exercise. Apart from the *Maariv* interview, quoted above, he has not to the best of my knowledge given a full-scale interview since 1943 when an enterprising *Daily Express* reporter collared him at his Worcestershire home, publishing the next day a highly coloured interview whose consequences were little short of disastrous. To protect himself from such intrusions Wolfson has surrounded himself with a group of intensely loyal, highly paid aides—one of whose functions has been to shelter their master from the prying eyes of the world outside. As one of his directors said to me: 'He likes to shroud himself in mystery so that it is impossible for any one man to understand what he is up to. A lot of people know a little bit, but nobody, except of course I.W. himself, knows the lot. It is characteristic of wealthy men who have made their own way that they don't like people to know what they are really worth.'

The secrecy is important because until very recently it has served to mask not only the size of Wolfson's own fortune but also, more seriously, the true extent of his commercial influence and power. Several years ago the *Sunday Express* published a feature article on Wolfson, illustrating it with a cartoon showing him as a puppet master. He was portrayed standing behind a composite high street, his companies dangling from his fingers like puppets on a string. What the cartoon was rather crudely trying to convey was the idea of Wolfson as the anonymous but all-powerful force behind the high street. It was a not altogether inaccurate picture.

Part of the mystery arose from the circumstances in which the Wolfson empire grew. The main strides were taken in a series of largely private deals during the war and in the years immediately after when people had other things besides Isaac Wolfson to occupy their minds. But it must also be said that Wolfson was not exactly prodigal, much to the annoyance of the *Investor's Chronicle* which throughout the 'forties and 'fifties clamoured for more

H

disclosure, in the information that he gave his shareholders about the progress and nature of their company. And it was only gradually that people began to realize that Wolfson's Great Universal Stores was Western Europe's largest mail order chain. But his activities did not stop there. With some 2,200 shops and stores he was also by far the largest retailer in the land. Though it was impossible to guess the fact from the names on the shop-fronts, by the late 'fifties, when a series of dramatic takeover bids brought Wolfson inexorably into the public eye, he had under his hand 2 per cent of the country's shoe shops, 5 per cent of Britain's furniture business, an important stake in both men's and ladies' tailoring, a whole string of clothing factories, plus an embryonic supermarket chain, a house-building company and a travel agency; not to mention important interests in Canada, South Africa, Holland, France and Israel. Altogether, it was estimated that by the early 'sixties one-quarter of all the families in the country were customers of Mr Wolfson.

But that was only the public side of his activities. Right from the beginning Great Universal Stores has not been Wolfson's exclusive interest. Through two financial trusts, Drages and General Guarantee Corporation, he had an undisclosed stake in many other businesses as well. One of the most remarkable features of the Wolfson career is that in the course of some fifty years he has built up not one empire but two: one of them, Great Universal Stores and its satellites, public, and one, represented by his two trusts which were amalgamated in 1962, largely private. Drages was admittedly a public company but share-holders had little information about what it consisted of or what it was doing.

When he joined Great Universal Stores as a young buyer in 1930, shortly before it went public he asked the directors to sign an agreement whereby it was understood that he was not obliged to give G.U.S. his full attention. Long before he joined G.U.S. Wolfson had been active on his own account and very early in his life, while still a travelling salesman for his father's Glasgow mirror framing business, he had grasped, perhaps better than anybody else, one important and basic fact: that one of the best ways to make money was to lend it. 'Isaac never insisted on cash,' a man who dealt with him at that time recalls, 'he would say: "You don't have to pay for it. I will take a bill." And thus I learnt in those very early days what a bill of exchange was.' At that time he was taking bills off everybody: not just bills of exchange which were secured against the goods he sold, but straightforward I.O.U.s, otherwise known as bills of accommodation. As Wolfson's interests grew, so too did his money-lending, so that in the course of time he became the private banker to a whole host of businessmen who found that it was easier, more convenient, though not necessarily cheaper, to raise money from Wolfson rather than going to a bank. 'I. W. invariably demands a 50 per cent stake in the deal,' says Alec Colman, the property developer who has on occasion borrowed as much as £5 million from Wolfson. 'You get no bargains from Isaac. But at least you get a decision the same day. I'd go to the joint stock banks if they moved that quickly but unfortunately they don't.' Over the years Wolfson, mainly through his General Guarantee Corporation, has had his finger in almost every conceivable pie. He provided the one million pounds necessary to put Michel Gotla's red minicabs on the road—the ones that so angered London's taxi drivers that they held a mass meeting in Hyde Park to protest —and he also supplied the working capital to finance the hire purchase side of John Bloom's ill-fated washing machine empire. And it was Wolfson's reluctance to go through with an eleventh-hour refinancing deal that was one of the factors that brought the entire edifice crashing down in the spring of 1964.

Wolfson is not only an important businessman, he is also an important Jew. Unlike some he makes no attempt to play down or conceal his Jewishness: quite the reverse. He glories in his faith and welcomes the obligations and responsibilities that it brings. He practises his religion with such messianic intensity that he has little in common with those older-established members of the community who argue that Judaism is just another religion. Wolfson's concept of his faith is quite different: rooted in the Old Testament and reinforced by the memories of the fanatical orthodoxy of the East European medieval *shtetl* it is altogether fiercer, and, in the last resort, exclusive. Wolfson comes from a devout and strictly orthodox family. His father Solomon, an immigrant from Bialystock in White Russia (the same town incidentally from which Michael Marks, the founder of Marks and Spencer, fled), was not—though he worked hard at his furniture business to support his family of three sons and eight daughters—according to his middle son, Isaac, 'a great businessman'. Solomon Wolfson inherited an older tradition which, according to the practice of Jewish life in the East European ghetto, laid down that the first duty of the father was not to work but study the Talmud and become learned in the intricacies of The Law. Businessmen and successful traders were respected in the *shtetl* but it was the scholars, not the businessmen, who were accorded the honoured place in the synagogue on the Sabbath. And in the most traditional households it was the mother who did the bread-winning while the father stayed at home with his books. The pressures of earning a living in the slums of Glasgow at the turn of the century prevented Solomon Wolfson from devoting as much time to his studies as he would have liked but there was no doubt in which direction his inclinations lay. 'I know I am no good at business,' he is supposed to have told a friend. 'But never mind. I have a son who is a financial genius.' 'How old is your son?' the friend asked. 'Isaac is nine,' the proud father replied.

It was at his father's table that Wolfson learnt what it meant to be a Jew. And the lessons have never been forgotten. Again unlike some, his family life—he has been married to his wife Edith, the daughter of a wealthy cinema proprietor who started life in Stoke Newington—for more than forty-five years—is of an irreproachable rectitude. He neither smokes nor drinks, preferring either milk or Coca Cola, and is regularly at his desk at eight o'clock in the morning. He lives comfortably but considering his

wealth by no means lavishly. He has a villa in Israel, next door to
the Weizmann Institute, and has lived in the same nineteen-room
flat at 74 Portland Place for over forty years, but these are about
the extent of his possessions. He owns no yachts, country houses,
strings of racehorses or any other of the playthings customarily
associated with the newly rich. He claims to be able to live on
a shilling a day (like royalty he never carries money himself which
sometimes leads to embarrassment among his executives who
provide the small change and are reimbursed at the end of the
month), and has given away the bulk of his £40 million fortune
to his foundation. 'No man should keep more than £100,000,' he
once told a friend. 'That's enough for any man. The rest should
go to charity.' Apart from the business, charity, which is in a
complicated way bound up with his religious duties (see Chapter
Ten), is Wolfson's main obsession. 'It is', he says, 'my only vice.'

It has often been said that the obligations of a traditional Jew
are so demanding that to keep them all is almost a full-time
occupation. In Wolfson's case this is obviously not true. But he
takes them extremely seriously. When he appeared briefly before
the Lynskey Tribunal in 1948 (to give evidence about some minor
dealings with one of the central figures, Sidney Stanley) he
insisted, as orthodox Jews do, on taking the oath with his head
covered and when, shortly after he was made a baronet, taking
the title Sir Isaac Wolfson of Marylebone, for philanthropic
services in 1962, he and his wife dined with the Queen and the
Duke of Edinburgh at Windsor Castle, the Royal Household took
good care to provide food that was strictly kosher.

Wolfson has always been a devout Jew, but his Zionism is of
a more recent date. Up to about 1948 he was too busy building
the business to devote much time or money to the Zionist cause,
but after discreet and gentle pressure from Israel (now Lord) Sieff
of Marks and Spencer, who explained that a businessman of his
standing in the community could not really remain on the side-
lines, Wolfson's attitude changed. His first recorded donation to
the Joint Palestine Appeal was in 1949 when the *Jewish Chronicle*

reported that a meeting of the furniture and timber trades committee of the J.P.A. was held at his house. The target was
£150,000. 'After Mrs Rebecca Sieff and Mr Israel Sieff had
spoken', the newspaper said, 'Messrs Charles and Isaac Wolfson
contributed £24,000. Other donations followed.' Since that time
Wolfson has been one of Israel's most fervent supporters. His
name is regularly to be found at the head of many charitable lists
and over the last twenty years he has contributed both from his
personal fortune and through his foundations in England and
Israel millions of pounds. In 1966 he told *Maariv* that up to that
time he had contributed about £6 million to Israel as against £10
million to mainly non-Jewish charities in England. Since then
Israel has fought the Six Day War and there is every indication
that the sums earmarked for Israel have increased appreciably.

It was this combination of wealth and piety that in December
1962 made Wolfson, who was already the head man of the Great
Portland Street Synagogue (which he had rebuilt after the war
and which is unkindly known in the community as 'St Isaac's'),
seem the natural and indeed the inevitable choice as president of
the United Synagogue. The United Synagogue, the headquarters
of orthodox Jewry, is far and away the most powerful Anglo-
Jewish religious institution. And correspondingly its president
exercises enormous influence—in many ways greater than that
enjoyed by the Chief Rabbi. The president of the United Synagogue is by custom the lay leader of the community—a position
that has no equivalent in the Church of England—and as such
it is his duty to set the tone and to a certain extent to determine
the character of the entire community. The United Synagogue has
long looked to its businessmen for leaders. But until Wolfson's
appointment they were invariably drawn from the ranks of the
assimilated, anglicized aristocracy: the Rothschilds, the Montagus and the Waley-Cohens. Wolfson's arrival denoted, as the
Jewish Chronicle observed, a turning point in the evolution of the
Anglo-Jewish community. 'The United Synagogue's lay leadership', it remarked, 'has traditionally been the preserve of the

patrician families of Anglo-Jewry ... Sir Isaac Wolfson's election marks, in the first place, the changing structure of the community and the rise and acceptance of the children and grandchildren of the fertilizing waves of emigration from Eastern Europe.'

Wolfson's election was naturally welcomed by many: the community was glad that such a rich and powerful man was prepared to speak for them. But at the same time the change of leadership brought to the surface the tensions that had been present ever since the first immigrants from Eastern Europe landed eighty years before.

Many of the difficulties were internal ones, revolving round the customs and practices of the Jewish faith. As I have already said, the old leaders of the community who prided themselves quite justifiably on their culture and learning took a fairly relaxed, liberal view of their religion, regarding the traditional orthodoxies of Isaac Wolfson and his fellow immigrants not, as he did, as the repository of all that was best in Judaism but more as a throwback to the intolerances of the Middle Ages. And they were somewhat disturbed that the leadership of the community should pass to a man who, whatever his other qualities, possessed none of their cultural traditions. Two years after Wolfson's appointment these differences were brought out into the open by a dispute which split Anglo-Jewry into a number of warring factions—and the resulting publicity caused the community, always nervous about attracting attention, intense discomfort and embarrassment.

At the centre of the row was a modest, scholarly rabbi called Dr Louis Jacobs who had suggested that a literal interpretation of the Talmud was no longer relevant: it should, he argued, be a guide book, not a rule book. There was nothing very radical about these opinions—both the Reform and the Liberal Synagogues had been taking a similar line for many years. Even so they proved sufficiently obnoxious both to the Chief Rabbi and to his lay partner Sir Isaac Wolfson, that Jacobs was prevented first from taking up his appointment as the principal of the Jews' College, the leading seminary for young rabbis, and then when this route was barred, from returning to the pulpit of his former synagogue. The decision caused a storm of protest. There were noisy meetings at Woburn Square, home of the United Synagogue, and the *Jewish Chronicle*, which took the liberal side, published letters protesting about 'the deplorable state of medieval orthodoxy'. The older families adopted a particularly strong line, with much of the protest emanating from the New West End Synagogue where many of them worshipped. And the subsequent attempt by the council of the United Synagogue to dismiss the New West End's board of management only served to exacerbate the dispute still further.

But Wolfson's election raised more than just internal religious problems: with his arrival as the official head of the British community the dilemma about the image they should present to the outside world was brought sharply into focus. This question of image, of how the Jews are regarded and thought of by the outside world, is not just a problem that the community's public relations men worry about: one way or another it is the personal concern of practically every one of the 400,000 Jews in the country.

Even more than most minority groups, the Jews remain an acutely self-conscious community, painfully sensitive to outside, Gentile opinion. They worry, perhaps unduly, about what people say and think about them. In view of their history such sensitivity is explicable and understandable but it is sometimes carried to excess, leading to an obsession with their own problems and neuroses to the exclusion of everybody else's. It is particularly noticeable when colour questions are discussed. 'God has been good to the Jews,' Louis Saipe, the official spokesman of Leeds Jewry, said to me shortly after there had been some racial trouble in the city, 'he has brought some coloured people here, so that people forgot about the Jews.'

The Jews are schizophrenic about many things: they desire to be an integral part of Gentile society and yet they wish to remain apart; they identify passionately with Israel and yet they are undoubtedly sincere when they profess loyalty to England; they seek out Jewish achievement wherever they can find it but are frequently resentful when anybody else does so, accusing them of anti-semitism. The Jews, one sometimes feels, love to be loved but hate to be noticed.

But it is perhaps in their attitudes to their businessmen that this fundamental duality emerges most clearly. The Jews have always suffered for their reputation as businessmen and financiers. For centuries the stock portrait of the Jew, as painted by the Gentiles, was of the grasping, usurious Shylock figure who made nothing but money—invariably at somebody else's expense. And for this reason they tend to be, as I have discovered in gathering material for this book, extremely wary when the subject of their economic activities is raised. Any question, no matter how carefully or tactfully put, is greeted with instant suspicion. In a way they tend to reinforce the stereotype merely by denying its existence. 'We are not all millionaires, as you know,' said the public relations man at the Jewish Board of Deputies when I told him of the nature of my inquiry. 'I wouldn't advise you to go on with it: it could give a very wrong, a very dangerous impression.'

And yet the Jews are enormously proud of the achievements of their businessmen—especially those like the Rothschilds, the Marks and the Sieffs whose reputation extends far beyond the comparatively narrow confines of the Jewish community. The Marks and Spencer family enjoys massive prestige in Jewish circles not just because they are good Jews but because the business commands such universal respect—even gratitude.

Sir Isaac Wolfson is not of this company. Great Universal Stores does not enjoy the place in the public's affections that Marks and Spencer does. And it is a sign of the growing self-confidence of the Jewish community that they should choose as their leader a man who in some respects seems to confirm rather than dispel the stereotype of Jewish economic man. Wolfson is often described as the master trader—the Emperor of the High Street, the *Sunday Times* called him in 1961. But in fact his

considerable skills as a trader and a salesman are equalled if not outshone by his extraordinary financial talents, for Wolfson is above
all a dealer for whom business proceeds not in a smooth, carefully ordered and planned programme but in a series of dramatic
and fundamentally opportunistic leaps: the take-off point being
the individual deal. In later life Wolfson has rationalized his success by saying that his business has grown by his ability to identify
and then to supply the needs of the increasingly affluent working
classes: to provide them with cheap, readily accessible clothing,
shoes, furniture and even housing. 'David,' he told a friend with
whom he was staying at Monte Carlo shortly after the war ended,
'this is a new world we have come into, the old world is shat-
tered. The working man has come into his own. It's that market
I'm going for and nobody realizes yet. I'm going to let them have
everything at the cheapest possible prices. But no shoddy stuff ...
There is going to be a day when this company will make £40
million.' And indeed that is the background against which the
business has prospered.

But the driving force is much simpler, cruder and more personal than that. It is the excitement of the chase, the thrill of doing
a deal and the knowledge that a bargain has been struck, that has
given Wolfson most of his excitement—and profit. 'Striking a
good bargain is a kind of national sport with these heroes, rather
like shooting and fox hunting is with the Tory squires,' says
a very senior (non-Jewish) merchant banker who has worked
closely both with Wolfson and Charles Clore for many years.
Wolfson, for all his native Glaswegian shrewdness, is not a cold,
calculating man who stands apart from the battle, his upper lip
set firm, carefully analysing the profit and loss account. He wades
right into the middle, engaging all his emotions—a process that
is as wearing for his opponents as it is for him. For Wolfson every
deal contains drama and the bigger it is, the greater the his-
trionics. In 1943, in the middle of the war, Wolfson pulled off
one of the first and most important coups of his career, buying for
£1·2 million Jays and Campbells, the furniture chain of some 160

stores which belonged to Sir Julien Cahn, a keen cricketing fan who used to take a team out to the West Indies each year and who was knighted for building almshouses in Nottingham. 'We are', said Wolfson after finally closing the deal, 'on our way to becoming the Sears Roebuck of Great Britain.' The step was undoubtedly large and important but it was only taken after much havering. To escape the bombing Wolfson had at that time moved his headquarters to Worcester, where he lived on the outskirts in a large house which had belonged to the managing director of Kays of Worcester, a company which he had acquired a couple of years previously. During the negotiations for Kays, Wolfson, an associate recalls, used to march up and down, haranguing his lieutenants. At one moment he would be all euphoria. 'It is a fantastic deal,' he would say, 'The best thing that could ever happen to G.U.S.; it's going to make all our fortunes.' But the very next moment, much to the consternation and bewilderment of his friends, the mood had changed and he would appear to be in black despair. 'What do I want with a load of old rubbish like that. It's going to ruin the company.' Wolfson's moods changed so often and so fast that his friends did not know what to say or what to advise. But in a sense they were unimportant. In the last resort it was Wolfson himself who made up his own mind— alone. 'He took no one into his confidence,' says a man who worked with him throughout the 'forties and 'fifties, 'not even his lawyer. I.W. was always very close. He took damn good care never to tell anybody what he was up to. When talking on the phone he would answer questions but never give out any information himself.' His associates sometimes bravely tried to give advice but it was often, at least in the early days, ignored. On one occasion his attention was drawn to the obvious lack of management in one of his potential purchases.

'What about the management, Isaac?'

'God will help us,' Wolfson replied.

'Perhaps God is busy, Isaac.'

This individuality, this passion to hold all the reins in his own hand, did not always work to his advantage. It gained him deals but it also lost them. Perhaps the most famous missed opportunity occurred in 1953 when it emerged that Sir Henry Price's Fifty Shilling Tailors was up for sale. By 1953 Price, preoccupied with his second wife whom he had just married, was beginning to lose interest in tailoring, becoming involved in property dealing. He had originally promised that if the business ever came up for sale, it would be offered first to Sir Edward Mountain, whose Eagle Star insurance company had previously acquired the ailing United Drapery chain. However, despite this promise Price entered into secret negotiations with Wolfson whom he had met by chance when they were travelling on the same ship to South Africa. Mountain's first inkling that the prize was slipping from his grasp was when he picked up the *Daily Express* and was astonished to read that the Fifty Shilling Tailors were on the point of being sold to Wolfson. He was so convinced that he had lost the battle that he and his son Brian decided to do nothing at all: instead they went off to watch a Test Match at Lord's. It was while they were watching the cricket that a message from Price, carried by Sir Edward Beddington Behrens, arrived. Price and Wolfson had apparently had a row, Wolfson having reduced his original offer. 'Would Sir Edward be so kind as to come down to Haywards Heath to talk over a proposition?' Mountain lost no time. Abandoning the match he leapt into a car and hurried down to Sussex, where it was agreed that they should have a week to prepare their bid while the accountants went over the figures. The offer was duly made and when they arrived the following week to hear the verdict they were greeted by Sir Henry telling them: 'I have a letter from Wolfson in my pocket but I am not going to open it. I have decided to accept your offer.' If he had opened it, he would have been placed in an embarrassing dilemma for the letter was to inform him that Wolfson had reconsidered the matter and had decided to negotiate on the basis of his original offer.

Where Wolfson leapt many less adventurous men would have

hesitated. He took risks, piling up debts and straining the resources of his master company almost to breaking point, that appalled and alarmed the City's fainter hearts. Throughout the 'fifties Wolfson's operations were regarded with the gravest suspicion and many people expected, and some even hoped, that his empire would come crashing down at any moment. In October 1946 the *Investor's Chronicle* expressed a general view when it wrote: 'The ordinary shares inevitably attract interest as the equity of a company with a large stake in retail distribution but at the present stage they are not a suitable holding for the long term.'

Wolfson survived these crises to prove the *Investor's Chronicle* and his other critics wrong. His company is among the largest and most profitable in the country—the only retailing concern to rate in the top twenty. In one sense Wolfson is typical only of himself—after all nobody else built up Great Universal Stores, and his two brothers, Charles and Sam, have displayed none of the same energy and flair. But in another sense Wolfson stands not for Jewry as a whole, which is as complicated and diverse in its talents as any other society, but for a particular generation of Jews, a special group of people who because of the circumstances in which they found themselves flourished at a particular point in time. It is for that reason that Wolfson's career is instructive and illuminating.

The physical presence is remarkable; a short, stocky, somewhat red-faced man, now in his seventies, with a mane of white hair, set off by thick black eyebrows, giving him, as Goronwy Rees has noted, a startling resemblance to Spencer Tracy in his old age. He talks in the rich accents of his native Glasgow, firing off opinions, figures and injunctions to buy his shares like tracer bullets, often grasping the lapel of his listener to emphasize a point. He is, so those who have been exposed to the Wolfson barrage say, a talker of almost hypnotic power. An associate recalled a train journey he once spent with him travelling from Birmingham to Sheffield during the war. Wolfson, bored by the journey, began to talk to him, but when he saw that he was absorbed in his own thoughts he turned his attentions to a very junior employee who happened to be travelling with him, and started to weave a fantasy around a favourite theme: how to be a millionaire. 'And there you will be', he said to the astonished junior, 'stepping off of your yacht at Monte Carlo. And people will turn and say who is that man … ' As the story proceeded, becoming more and more elaborate as Wolfson warmed to his theme, the man became more and more goggle-eyed. By the end of the journey he was so transfixed that, so Wolfson's travelling companion said, he had to be helped from the carriage. Somewhat embarrassed by this episode he turned to Wolfson as they left the station and said: 'What did you do that for? You know he will never make it.' Wolfson replied: 'But you wouldn't talk to me.'

Wolfson has the gifts of a born salesman: his knack of getting under his victim's skin, exploiting his weaknesses and magnifying his desires. And throughout his life the pitch has remained remarkably consistent. 'He will build you up, creating an enormous fantasy about yourself,' says Jim Slater, one of the most energetic of the new-style, financial entrepreneurs who have emerged in the last ten years and to whom in 1969 Wolfson sold his investment company, Drages. The negotiations over the Drages sale lasted twelve weeks at the end of which everybody, except Wolfson himself, was exhausted. During the negotiations Wolfson told Slater a story that with minor variations was identical to the fantasy he had created on the Birmingham–Sheffield train over twenty-five years before. 'There is an opera house', Wolfson said, 'completely full of glittering people. An orchestra is playing. It is the Israel Philharmonic, and the tickets are a hundred guineas a time. You don't mind because it goes to charity. Everybody turns—who is that they ask? It is Jim Slater, the great industrialist.' On this occasion Wolfson failed to weave his customary spell. 'But I am a great industrialist,' replied a rather injured Slater.

That Wolfson should still be employing these stratagems is in a way only to be expected for it was as a salesman for his father's furniture business that Wolfson first set out on his career with a weekly wage, so legend has it, of only five shillings a week. The furniture business, like tailoring, was one of the staple industries of the Jewish community in Glasgow, for it required little capital and, since they were dealing with such basic items as cheap tables and chairs for the working-class families of the Gorbals and Langside, only rudimentary skill. By the time Wolfson was into his teens there was already a sizeable Jewish population in Glasgow, as there was in other large provincial towns such as Leeds and Manchester. In each case the pattern of settlement was much the same, with the Jews moving like the present-day West Indians and Pakistanis, into the poorest areas of the town. Just as the poor Jews arriving in London made for the East End, so the Manchester Jews clustered round the bottom of Cheetham Hill, Leeds Jewry settled in the notorious dank hollow known as the Leylands (a Jewish corruption of Low Lands) at the bottom of Chapeltown Road, and the Glaswegian Jews found themselves in the Gorbals along the docks in Langside, only to move up the hill to the middle-class district of Pollokshields when they became relatively more prosperous. The Wolfsons lived in Camphill avenue, Langside, in the middle of the Jewish district. Like the East End, it was what the sociologists call a face-to-face society. In other words, everybody knew everybody else. And as they were all in the same economic boat it stood to reason that everybody also knew everybody else's business. 'It was', says a man who was also in the furniture business and had many dealings with the Wolfsons, 'a poor community. Nobody had any money and everybody needed everybody else's help.'

It was into this tight community that the fourteen-year-old Wolfson plunged after leaving Queen's Park School. And it was during this time that he formed links and friendships that were to last him all his life. Many of his closest associates, both in the business and outside it, are not only Jews but also Scotsmen: the clannishness of the one group reinforcing exactly the same trait in the other. Wolfson still goes on holiday with the boys with whom he grew up next door in Camphill Avenue and many of his deals have been arranged and supervized by a man he has known since he was a child and who lived only a couple of blocks away. The almost claustrophobic closeness of the links that bind the Wolfson organization is one reason why it is so impenetrable.

As his aptitude for figures was beginning to show long before he left school, there was some talk of his training to be an accountant, but it was an expensive course, the Wolfsons were not well off—though Solomon was rich enough to send his son to a fee-paying school—and his father needed help with the business. And so Wolfson, after a brief stint making picture frames, became his father's salesman. He was, by all accounts, quite extraordinarily good at it. 'My father', says the same man I quoted earlier, 'was always conscious that when Isaac left he had bought more than he needed. He had a very persuasive manner: he kept reminding you that his father had a family of eleven children to support.' There are other testaments to Wolfson's sales skill. 'He could sell you a five-pound note for six pounds or even refrigerators to Eskimos,' says a man who ran a Newcastle furniture business and bought much of the Wolfson furniture. They were in the main simple, unsophisticated items designed for the poorest working-class homes: an upholstered seven-piece suite of furniture consisting of a couch, two armchairs and four dining-chairs sold for £3 10s. the lot. 'He used to come round begging us to take his stuff. He would never take no for an answer. We once ordered six dozen sets from him. He was in such a hurry to get them to us that he did not wait for a covered wagon from Glasgow but he put them straight on an open truck. As a result when the stuff arrived it was all ruined.'

In those early days he travelled widely throughout Scotland, especially in Caithness, Sunderland and Fife, and in the North of England. But Scotland and his father's business was to prove too small a theatre for his ambitions and in 1920 he went south to

8. (*above*) A portrait of Sir Isaac Wolfson taken at the age of thirty-four before his rise to fame and fortune.

9. (*right*) Sir John Cohen's favourite photograph of himself.

0. (*below*) Sir Montague Burton and his wife celebrating their silver wedding in 1934 on board the R.M.S. *Empress of Britain*.

1. (*below right*) Simon Marks (*left*) and Israel Sieff as young men in Manchester.

12. (*left*) Marks and Spencer's branch in the Stretford Road, Manchester, as it was in 1896.

13. (*below left*) Tesco in the pre-supermarket age.

14. (*right*) Finch's Army Stores, the site of Sir Montague Burton's first shop in Chesterfield.

15. (*below right*) Thirty years' later: a corner site in South London.

16. J. Lyons's 'Nippies' stand by – ready to serve 8,000 people at a Masonic lunch at Olympia, August 1925.

London where he found lodgings in the Central Hotel, Aldgate —a popular centre for Jewish commercial travellers and one which impressed Wolfson by virtue of the fact that there was a telephone in every bedroom. It was soon after he arrived in London that he set up in Old Street, just off the City Road in Clerkenwell, where he started a business selling clocks, mirrors, upholstery covers—and even pianos. It was also about this time that he married Edith Specterman, the daughter of Ralph Specterman, who as the proprietor of a string of small suburban cinemas was already a comparatively rich man. It was Ralph Specterman who provided the backing for Wolfson's earliest business adventures. However, for the next ten years Wolfson remained a successful but essentially small-time trader, selling clocks and mirrors and on his own account developing an embryonic private banking business by discounting other people's bills. 'He was always glad to do so, always providing, of course, that you traded with him. His customers were thus tied up in a whole network of obligations,' says a man who did a lot of business with him at this time.

However, it was not until 1930 that his main chance arrived— and it came, as these things often do, unheralded and quite by accident. One day George Rose, a director of a mail order company which had recently added the adjective 'Great' to the name Universal Stores, was walking round a trade exhibition in Manchester's City Hall inspecting the stands. At one of them, attended by a man who struck him as smart and good looking, his attention was attracted by a particularly fancy clock. As Great Universal Stores sold a lot of clocks Rose was sufficiently interested to ask the stallholder how much it was. Wolfson, for that is who the salesman was, replied with a couple of questions of his own.

'Are you in the trade? How many do you want to buy?'

'500,' Rose replied.

Wolfson was for a moment taken a little aback, for this was a large order.

I

'For that quantity I would take fifteen shillings a clock,' he replied after a moment's thought.

'Right,' said Rose, 'it's a deal.'

It was only after the deal had been done that Wolfson asked the identity of the buyer, and when he was handed Rose's business card he asked: 'Do you want anything else? Can I come and see you?'

'By all means,' said Rose, who had been impressed by the young salesman, 'I was just going to ask you round.'

The two men went out to lunch for which Rose paid, Wolfson volunteering the information that he never carried any cash on himself. Afterwards he was taken on a tour of the G.U.S. Devonshire Street factory. It was an imposing five-storey affair of some 275,000 square feet with an impressive portico. The building was topped by a cupola from which there streamed a banner bearing the proud legend: 'Established 1900'. 'Mr Rose,' said Wolfson after the tour had finished, 'I think I could be very useful to you.' Rose agreed and shortly afterwards Wolfson joined the Great Universal Stores as its chief buyer. The contract of employment was not entirely conventional: Wolfson agreed that instead of a salary he should take an option on a parcel of G.U.S. shares and take a share of the profits. In the light of what happened over the next twelve months this seemed to have been a rash and foolhardy step.

Somehow or other the impression has been created that the G.U.S. of 1930 was an insignificant, run-down affair whose fortunes began to prosper only after Wolfson had taken over the reins as joint managing director some time in 1932. It is true that the company hit a bad patch, due to the slump, immediately after going public in July 1931—moving from a record profit of £410,374 to a loss of some £54,964 in 1933. But that is to do G.U.S. an injustice. At the time of going public it was a very substantial business with assets of nearly £600,000 and, with a dividend covered some nineteen times, apparently in the pink of financial health. When the profits, which had risen from £110,000 in 1929 to over £400,000, were disclosed, the 1,000 employees, so the *Investor's Chronicle* reported, immediately put in for a substantial pay rise—a claim which added to the company's later financial embarrassment.

This company was the creation of three brothers, Abraham, George and Jack Rose, who had shortened their name from Rosenson and had come from Lithuania to Manchester shortly before the turn of the century. The Rose family, whose father was a furniture dealer with fourteen children, was a large one. The origins of the business were extremely modest; it started as a general dealing and merchanting concern which was carried on from the attic of the family home. They dealt in almost anything they could lay their hands on for which there was a demand: one of Abraham's biggest lines was gramophone records which be bought cheaply and sold in large quantities; blankets were another staple of the G.U.S. business. But it was not until they stumbled into mail order that Universal Stores began to gather speed.

The first steps taken in the early 1920s were experimental and tentative. Nobody, least of all the Roses, realized that they were in the process of creating an industry that today has a turnover of £382 million and accounts for around 4 per cent of all retail sales. The Roses' involvement grew out of their interest in advertising. In 1910 this, too, was a pretty embryonic business but the Roses were ardent readers of the popular newspapers and they could not help noticing that stores like Catesbys in the Tottenham Court Road and H. Samuel, the jewellers, frequently took large spaces in the newspapers to advertise their linoleum and watches. George Rose, who was responsible for the sales end of the operation, was fired by their example. 'These people are always advertising,' he thought, 'it must pay.' And he set about to discover suppliers from whom he could buy clocks and watches at a price that would enable him to undercut the H. Samuel product which was being offered at 50s. Rose searched about until he found a wholesale jeweller who was prepared to sell him a similar clock for 22s. 6d.—a margin which allowed him both to undercut the Samuel price by 5s. and pay the necessary £3 per column inch for advertisements in such papers as the *News of the World* and the *Irish Weekly Independent*. 'I chose the Irish', says Rose disarmingly, 'because I thought they were an ignorant lot who would fall for it.'

By the early 1920s the Roses were advertising extensively a whole range of goods. Some idea of the scope of the business can be gauged from the original articles of association which were drawn up when Universal Stores (Manchester) Ltd was registered on March 16th, 1917. Articles of association are customarily widely drawn to cover every contingency, but even so the Roses were unusually thorough. The object of the company is, they declared:

> to carry on in connection with the said business or as distinct and separate businesses of dealers, factors and general merchants selling and disposing of watches, clocks and every kind of fancy goods, ladies and gentlemen's clothing, waterproof garments, boots, shoes, gloves, hats and every description of hosiery, drapery and kindred sundries connected with the drapery trade. Bags, trunks, cases constructed of leather, wood cane, fibre or any other materials, household furniture, household utensils, iron-mongery, bedding, carpets, rugs, linoleum, pictures, crockery, musical instruments, ornaments and household linen. Sports outfitters, games, toys, children's carriages, office and warehouse furniture, dress pieces and woollen clothes or any other business which may seem to the company capable of being conveniently carried on in connection with the above or calculated directly or indirectly to enhance the value or render more profitable any part of the company's property.

The Roses had been advertising for some years when suddenly the penny dropped. Why not, the Roses thought, instead of advertising each item singly as they had been doing, collect all their advertisements together, paste them into a book and then

circulate the collection to their customers in the form of a catalogue. This is exactly what they did and though the result was,
compared to the modern mail order catalogue weighing several
pounds and containing hundreds of glossy photographs, a pretty
crude affair of some hundred pages and measuring some four
inches by six inches (Wolfson still keeps an early G.U.S. catalogue in his desk), it was put together with a certain amount of
flair. So as to obtain maximum impact George Rose insisted that
there should be no more than one advertisement to a page. The
catalogue was then circulated to the customers who had replied
to the original newspaper advertisement and thus the Roses built
up their mailing list—the essential weapon of any successful mail
order house.

Once it was established the Roses began to refine the system,
making it yet more attractive to their working-class customers.
Credit trading had long been a feature of the North Country
retailing scene. The usual system was for companies like Alexander
Sloan, a firm which was later bought by Wolfson, to employ
tallymen, familiar figures in any working-class district, who
travelled round delivering the goods and at the same time collecting the weekly instalments from the householders. It was an
early and more personal form of hire purchase. The Roses adapted
this system to their own needs. They invited their customers to
join what was in effect both a club and a lottery. Each week the
members paid in their subscription—usually no more than a shilling—and at the end of it they drew lots to see who would take
delivery of their goods first. The attraction was obvious: the
lucky customer drawing the Number One ticket could take
delivery immediately even if he had only paid one shilling while
those at the bottom of the draw had to wait, even though they
may have had a credit of several pounds. To drum up business
still further the Roses invited their own customers to distribute
catalogues, giving them as an incentive a discount of 2s. in the
pound on all the goods they bought themselves. With variations
it is a technique that is still used today. Though the system was

designed to ease the financial problems of the customers, it was
also of great advantage to G.U.S. The danger of any high volume,
mass-market operation is that if the business builds up too fast
and the customers pay too slowly, the company runs out of the
working capital needed to finance the stocks. It is a fate that has
overtaken many an enthusiastic but imprudent business. The
chief beauty of the credit club method was the money came
rolling in, even before the goods had left the warehouse.

Just how and why G.U.S. came unstuck immediately after
Wolfson's arrival and its successful public flotation (the issue was
over-subscribed with applicants for large blocks of shares receiv-
ing only about 20 per cent of what they had asked for) is to this
day not entirely clear. Part of the answer was that the Roses
were over-enthusiastic and financially inexperienced, for they
capitalized not only their assets but a large chunk of their current
profits as well. Also their stock control, essential in a business such
as theirs, was not as tight as it might have been. And when profits
tumbled during the financial crisis of 1931-2, they could only pay
the guaranteed dividend to their shareholders by digging into
their own pockets; an exercise which is rumoured to have cost
them some £94,000. The organization of the company had
already been badly stretched by Abraham's decision to move the
headquarters to London and set up a furniture factory in Wembley, and their troubles increased when the factory burnt down in
a fire which gutted the building. The combination of these misfortunes proved too much for Abraham who was already a sick
man and he died shortly afterwards.

Wolfson, commuting between his home in London and the
business in Manchester, had never made any secret of his ambitions, and the collapse of the share price in the first half of 1932
when it fell from its issue price of 20s. to 8s. 3d. gave him the
opportunity he needed. As the price plummeted Wolfson exercised
his options. In 1932, the same year that he became joint managing
director with George Rose (Rose resigned this position two years
later) Wolfson acquired from Abraham a 40 per cent stake in the

company—a stake which cost him, so it is said, around £250,000.
Part of the money came from his father-in-law but the bulk was
raised from a stockbroker friend, Sir Archibald Mitchelson,
'whose monocle', the *Investor's Chronicle* observed, 'set off a manner
of old world courtesy'. Sir Archibald had 'supreme faith' in
'I.W.' and his confidence was later rewarded when, after the death
of Abraham's successor, Major-General Sir Philip Nash, he
became chairman of G.U.S. In 1945 Sir Archibald died and Wolfson took his rightful place as chairman of a company that in the
preceding fifteen years he had rationalized and expanded out of
all recognition.

Wolfson spent his first eighteen months in power streamlining
and rationalizing the badly shaken G.U.S. Under his guidance
the business made a quick, even spectacular recovery. The losses
of 1932 were converted the following year into a profit of
£333,536—a figure which was not to be improved until well after
the war was over. The truly remarkable feature about this
recovery was that it took place in the midst of the Depression
which, it might be thought, would have hit businesses like G.U.S.,
directly dependent on the prosperity of their customers, particularly hard. In fact the retail trade not only emerged unscathed but
actually improved its position throughout the 'thirties. 'The new
light industries', says A. J. P. Taylor in his *English History, 1914–
1945*, 'were little affected by the Depression, sustained no doubt
by the fact that the general level of wages hardly fell. The service
industries actually increased their employment figures throughout
the Depression and when, with recovery, general employment
rose by about ten per cent, employment, in these industries rose
by forty per cent.' Taylor's point is reinforced by the fact that the
foundation of Wolfson's Great Universal Stores, Simon Marks's
Marks and Spencer, Jack Cohen's Tesco and Joseph Collier's
United Drapery Stores were all laid in this period.

G.U.S. provided the foundations but it was Wolfson himself
who laid the bricks above them. The first ones were small and
comparatively unimportant: much more significant was the

manner and timing of their acquisition. Even before he gained control of G.U.S. Wolfson had been buying companies on his own account and enthusiastically singing their praises to his friends and characteristically urging them to buy their shares. One such company was Lyeesi, a small furniture business which he bought in 1928. But it was not until 1934 that he made his first purchase on behalf of G.U.S.—a process that was to continue to gather uninterrupted momentum for the next twenty years. It was in this year that Wolfson bought Midland and Hackney, an amalgamation of two small furniture businesses which up until then had operated separately with moderate success in the East End and Leicester. The reasoning behind the Midland and Hackney deal is interesting, for it provides a valuable insight into the way the Wolfson mind was working at that time. At first sight it did not look a particularly promising deal. The company's profits were small and its debts considerable. But here lies the clue: it was precisely because its hire purchase debts were so large — about £100,000 — that Wolfson found the company so attractive. The debts, like the company's property, were part of its assets and he realized that if only they could be collected he would have in his hands the most valuable of all commodities: cash — cash that could be used in the days before share exchanges became fashionable for further takeovers. No sooner had he acquired the company than he set about releasing the cash by collecting the debts and mortgaging off the property. This is an early example of a now famous technique and one that Wolfson was to use over and over again in the coming years.

Not all the companies that he acquired at this time were slotted into G.U.S. Some, like Drages, he bought off his own bat, with the help of a million-pound debenture, raised for him by Sir Edward Beddington Behrens, the City financier. It was often difficult for outsiders to discern exactly where I.W.'s private empire stopped and his public one began, and this later led to some controversy and confusion. In 1943, when it became clear that Wolfson and his family had made a profit of nearly £60,000 from selling privately acquired companies to G.U.S., the *Investor's Chronicle* commented sternly: 'Certainly few shareholders of the company can have received the last annual report with its reference to these deals and few outside can have studied the published comments in that report without being led to reflect on the duties and responsibilities of directors and the companies on whose boards they sit.' Although G.U.S. acquired the right to use Drages' name for trading purposes in 1943 (it had been turned from a furniture retailing group into an investment company, providing cash for G.U.S. in 1941), Drages was never part of the G.U.S. empire—though at one time Wolfson did attempt to incorporate it. Like Midland and Hackney, Drages' initial attraction was as a provider of cash.

Like G.U.S., Drages was one of the first of the credit traders, though it was a furniture business not a mail order house. It was started in 1908 by Sir Benjamin Drage (originally Cohen), a highly colourful figure whose mother, after cutting her commercial teeth selling shoes on credit in the Whitechapel High Road, went on to found John Blundell's, another credit business which eventually ended up as part of Joseph Collier's United Drapery chain. Sir Benjamin had a most engaging style of trading, designed, so he said, to appeal to the Common Man. His shop fronts were plastered with bright neon signs featuring 'Mr Everyman and Mr Drage.' His credit terms were loudly and widely advertised. 'The Drage way of furnishing out of income', he shouted, 'places within the reach of all the opportunity of a well-furnished home.' To judge both from the profits of the company and the number of plain vans that were to be seen dashing about the country delivering Drages' economical three-piece suites, it was an appeal to which a very large number of people responded. Between 1923 and 1925, the year before the company went public, profits rose from £71,569 to £146,000. But as war approached the public lost much of its *esprit* (the prospect of imminent invasion did not after all encourage people to lash out on new furniture, no matter how convenient the terms) and the business faltered. It lost money in 1937, the year Wolfson acquired it, and again in 1938. Between January 1st, 1938 and September 3rd, when it finally stopped trading 'because of the international situation and the consequent restraint in trade', the company lost a further £44,346. Drages was, at the time of the sale, short of working capital and was finding it difficult to repay money it had borrowed from Debenhams, the department store group. But though the company's trading position was extremely unhappy, its assets were substantial. It had properties valued in the balance sheet at £122,945 and hire purchase contracts and other debtors of no less than £859,062 14s. 11d. This was the plum in Drages' pie and one which Wolfson lost no time in extracting. 'I.W.', says Sir Edward Beddington Behrens in his somewhat disappointing autobiography, *Look Back, Look Forward*, 'knew the value of the large volume of hire purchase contracts and how to collect the arrears, and the idea was to purchase and gradually liquidate the business.' The Drages stores in Holborn and Manchester were sold off (the Manchester one to an enterprising company called British and Colonial run by two brothers, Henry and Alfred Cohen, which ironically Wolfson was later to acquire) and the collection of the hire purchase debts began, following the same pattern as the Midland and Hackney operation four years before.

It would be wrong to give the impression, however, that all Wolfson was interested in was the acquisition of unhappy companies that could be bought cheaply and then stripped of their assets. He welcomed the cash that such operations provided but he was just as interested in widening G.U.S.'s base by acquiring companies that either complemented its activities or fitted in snugly alongside. In 1938, as the threat of war became more and more apparent, suitable companies were not hard to find. Many entrepreneurs, like David Sloan, a shrewd hard-headed Scotsman whose father had started one of Scotland's tallyman's businesses with a capital of £500, were unhappy at the turn events were taking on the continent and were eager to sell. The arrival of

Wolfson, who was offering some £800,000 for the company, seemed to Sloan little short of providential. Alexander Sloan was not the only company Wolfson bought at this time: by ploughing back G.U.S. profits and at the same time raising fixed interest capital by floating debentures in the market, Wolfson found the money to pay not only for Sloan but for a crop of other similar businesses as well. There was of course nothing especially novel in using the money-raising potential of a public company such as G.U.S. to finance further takeovers: what was remarkable was the timing and vigour of the operation. It was at first sight an odd moment to choose to be thinking about expansion; at a time when nearly everybody else was putting up the shutters in preparation for war, Wolfson was to be seen boldly striding about the market place accumulating bricks for his mansion. But his reasoning was logical enough. If Hitler won the war there would be no G.U.S. anyway: if he lost the opportunities would be enormous. Wolfson, who at forty-eight was too old to go to war, had nothing to lose and everything to gain. But though this may seem obvious enough now, at the time it required considerable courage and imagination.

Many of Wolfson's most important acquisitions were made between 1940 and 1945. Some idea of the size of the strides he was making in this period can be gained from the figures. When Wolfson assumed control in 1932 the assets of G.U.S. totalled £686,541; by 1938, the year in which the figures for the group were consolidated for the first time, they had risen to £1,982,671; but it was in the next ten years that the really dramatic growth occurred. By 1948 when Wolfson proudly described G.U.S. at the Lynskey Tribunal as 'the Ark of Free Enterprise' the assets of the group exceeded £16 million. There are a number of reasons why the building of the ark proceeded so rapidly. Contemplating this phenomenon in 1948, the *Investor's Chronicle* observed: 'The really spectacular expansion of G.U.S.'s scope has been made possible because of the fluidity of conditions during the war years and since.' And this is certainly part of the answer.

Many of Wolfson's rivals faced with appalling difficulties and hedged about with wartime restrictions lost heart and sold up— often at a price which was fair enough at the time but which did not reflect the real peacetime value of the business. The purchase of Sir Julien Cahn's Jays and Campbell's in 1943, Wolfson's biggest wartime acquisition, is a case in point. Sir Julien was an old man when he sold, but it was not old age that prompted the sale, but a realization of just how strict wartime regulations were. Throughout the war, in an attempt to prevent retailers from cashing in on the shortages, profits were rigidly controlled by Government decree. In the case of the furniture companies the level of permitted profit was set at 42·86 per cent—no more, no less. And any company which the Board of Trade discovered exceeding that limit was heavily jumped upon. These strict controls and the penalties attached to them left proprietors like Sir Julien very vulnerable, exposed to the misdoings of their staff. No matter how strict the supervision it was impossible to keep a watch on everybody all the time. In 1943 Jays and Campbells, like practically every other firm in the business, was dealing mainly in second-hand furniture—and it was this situation, offering temptations to profit-hungry store managers, that gave rise to much of the trouble. One of the commonest dodges was for the local managers to buy a second-hand piece for, say, £15 but enter it into the books at £10—pocketing the difference for themselves. The difficulty came when they had to sell it again, for in order to show any profit at all to the store (as opposed to themselves) they had to mark it up above the permitted limit. Jays and Campbells, through no fault of Sir Julien's, was caught a number of times in this way. Between April and November 1943, so Hugh Dalton, then President of the Board of Trade, revealed in the House of Commons, Jays and Campbells was convicted for five offences under the Goods and Services Price Control Act, paying fines which ranged between £50 and £2,470. All this proved too much for the unhappy Sir Julien and it was one of the factors that prompted the sale of the business to Wolfson.

But these were not the only strains imposed by war. As business became tougher so cracks appeared in the board rooms of a number of family firms — cracks which in the prosperity of peacetime could have probably been pasted over. This is what happened at British and Colonial, an enterprising and prosperous concern which was one of the very few retailers to extend its empire beyond the United Kingdom. In 1945, the year in which it was sold to Wolfson for just on a million pounds, it had seventy-five shops trading under the Woodhouse and Cavendish banner (names which incidentally Wolfson has not only retained but used for many of his other stores) and another ninety in Canada. But though the business was energetically run by two brothers, Henry and Alfred Cohen, its control was shared with another fourteen members of the family who found it difficult to agree among themselves. Rumours that the board of British and Colonial was not a united one began to circulate in the trade, which is proverbially gossipy, eventually reaching Wolfson's ears. It did not take long for him to discover just how disenchanted the Cohen brothers had become and after a protracted haggle the sale was concluded.

The British and Colonial was a good deal for Wolfson and shared an important common factor with many that he negotiated at the time. The company's chief asset was the bricks and mortar of its stores. It had large emporiums in prime sites like Oxford Street, New Oxford Street and High Street, Kensington — all valued in the balance sheet at pre-war prices. And it was on the basis of those prices that the deal was negotiated. As long as the war lasted the values of the buildings remained residual but the moment it ended their value, enhanced by the twin effects of the natural demand and the shortages created by the bombing, soared astronomically. The chief beneficiaries, as I shall show in Chapter Nine, were the property developers but Wolfson was in property too and the bonanza did not pass him by. The revaluation of his stores not only swelled his assets, a fact that was reflected in the price of his shares, making them more attractive as a takeover weapon, but they also provided him, a keen exponent and pioneer of the sale and lease-back technique, with a valuable source of cash. The money was raised by selling off the freehold of the stores to a pension fund, a life insurance company and other institutions from whom he would then take a medium- or long-term lease. The lumps of cash which resulted from this ingenious exercise were then either ploughed back into the company to supplement its working capital or used in combination with the shares to acquire yet more companies. By the end of the war Wolfson was reaping the benefits of size and was prepared to pay well for businesses which were of little value when considered by themselves but acquired an additional attraction when integrated into the G.U.S. empire. In 1948, for example, Wolfson bought Smart Brothers, the furniture group, for one million pounds — about three times its market value. But what the share price did not reflect was the value of Smarts as part of a much larger group; nor, rather more surprisingly, did it take into account the group's property potential — a feature which did not, however, escape Wolfson's attention. Shortly after the deal had gone through Smarts' shops were sold off at a profit of some £130,000.

There is, as I have tried to show, no one simple explanation for Wolfson's astonishing success. Many factors contributed to the building of the ark: Wolfson's own highly individual and distinctive talents as a trader and a financier; his appreciation and, even more, his anticipation of the needs of the public; his ability to produce profit out of the most unpromising of situations and his skill at turning the particular conditions of the day to his own special advantage. And if these achievements have sometimes been greeted with not quite the enthusiasm they perhaps deserve it is partly because it is difficult to acquire an organization of such size and ramifications without stepping on a large number of toes, and partly because Wolfson is the product of an era when the obligations of private enterprise to acknowledge the public were not as clear or as heavy as they are today. Wolfson is now in the process of handing over the reins to his son, Leonard, the private side of his empire has now been sold and the acquisitive phase which lasted for nearly thirty years is drawing to a close. In the 1950s and the 1960s G.U.S. continued to grow, but the pace was less headlong and the style less individual.

Chapter Seven

Sir John Cohen

To Sir John Cohen of Tesco cut-throat competition is what supermarketeering is all about. 'Bulk buying and bulk selling is our object,' he said to me, 'with the emphasis on more promotion and cut prices.' It is this philosophy, symbolized by the Tesco knight, Sir Save-a-lot who rides into battle, his sword ready to slash prices, that enabled Cohen first to escape from the family tailoring business which he hated, to break out of the East End ghetto in which he grew up, and later to found a business which has played a large part in changing the face of Britain's high street and has in the process made him a millionaire about twelve times over.

Cohen is the very epitome of the Jew as a trader: the market boy made good, the classic rags to riches story of the Jewish myth. He has none of the sophisticated financial skills of a Wolfson nor yet the dedicated, high-minded idealism of a Marks or a Sieff. His achievement has been simpler and more direct—but in a way no less significant. By applying with complete single-mindedness the trading principle he first learnt nearly fifty years ago in the markets of the Caledonian Road, shouting the odds from his barrow, he has built one of the most successful and aggressive retail chains in the country. But though it has made the rare transition from a one-man business to a modern, computer-driven corporation and is now huge and immensely complex—in 1969 it had a turnover of

144

£186 million, making it the largest supermarket chain in the country—the business retains a warmth and a brassy directness that stems from' the personality of its founder. In many ways Cohen (and I mean this in no derogatory sense) is still a barrow boy— and proud of it.

Despite his £12 million, one of the biggest post-war fortunes to be made in Britain, Cohen remains an essentially friendly and uncomplicated man who enjoys talking about himself, his business and his family. He lives in a well-appointed but essentially modest ground-floor flat overlooking Regent's Park, owns but one racehorse, Tesco Girl, gives generously but not spectacularly to Jewish and other charities, is president of a couple of synagogues, has financed an old people's home in Israel and enjoys reading the racing pages of the *Daily Mirror*. His frequent appearances on television, where he is invariably presented playing his favourite role of shopper's champion and friend, have made him, with his battered, prizefighter's face (his nose was broken in a market scrap) and his gravelly, Cockney accent, one of the best-known retailers in the land. To the general public Jack (or John as he now prefers to be called) Cohen is Sir Save-a-lot: to his family and to the trade he is still 'Uncle Jack'. It says a great deal for his approachability that he is the only millionaire—indeed the only businessman of any tax bracket—that I have interviewed in bed. The appointment was made several days in advance and when I arrived at his flat, one rainy Saturday morning, the door was opened by a maid. 'I have come to see Mr Cohen,' (he had not then been knighted) I explained. 'Oh, I'm afraid he is sick in bed,' she said, and hurried away to consult. Minutes later I was led into the bedroom where Cohen was sitting up in bed, wearing dark glasses to protect his eyes from an infection he had caught while watching racing at Ascot the previous day. 'Well,' he said, putting down the paper he was reading, 'and what can I do for you ... ?'

Jack Cohen, like the business he controls, is very much a product of the Jewish East End of the 1920s. It was here that he scored his

K

first business successes and it was here too, first in Rutland Street where he was born and went to school, and later in the street markets of Hackney and the Caledonian Road, that his attitudes were formed. Cohen became a street trader more out of necessity than choice. For a traditional Jewish household like the Cohens, street trading was not a prestigious occupation. To be a tailor, even a relatively unsuccessful one, like Cohen's father, meant that the family had a certain standing—even though its reputation did not extend far beyond Rutland Street. But to go on to the streets was a retrograde step—a throwback to the days of Israel Zangwill's *Schnorrer*.* 'It was the worst thing you could do in those days,' Cohen recalled. 'Anyone who saw me there thought I was a beggar.'

Cohen left school when he was twelve to join the rest of the family in the workshop and for a while the young Cohen dutifully served his master tailor's apprenticeship: carrying the bales of cloth from the City warehouses which supplied the East End outworkers at the beginning of the week and returning on the Friday with the finished garments. But for the war Cohen might never have made the break. In 1917 Cohen joined what was then still called the Royal Flying Corps for, as the primitive biplanes were made of canvas which was stitched together by hand, tailors were needed almost as badly as mechanics. He had an adventurous time on the way to Egypt (his troop carrier being torpedoed off Alexandria) and later found himself with Allenby on Mount Carmel when Haifa was captured. But along with these excitements he was exposed for the first time to anti-semitism. 'I was peeling potatoes and doing all sorts of odd jobs. Mixing with people and fighting some of them I didn't like: a name like Cohen seemed to be like poison to some of them. Some of them thought that Jewish people had horns, you know. I had many a tussle with a sailor but I always held my own—I tried anyway.'

It was while he was in the Middle East that Cohen's determination not to rejoin the family business crystallized. Sitting in his

* The Yiddish for 'beggar'.

Air Force tent in the desert he used to worry about his future. 'I often used to wonder to myself when I was in the Forces, when we were quietly sitting down, what I was going to do with myself when I got back. And I couldn't figure it out at all.' In February 1919 Cohen, who had picked up a fever, was invalided out and returned to his father's house in the East End. But not to work. Armed with a thirty-pound gratuity he went straight to the local Labour Exchange where he signed on, being paid a pound a week. And for some time he wandered aimlessly about, taking on casual jobs and looking for work.

It was his brother-in-law, Morry Isaacs who had married his sister Ray, who gave him the lead he was looking for. Isaacs, who died on the day the Second World War broke out, was a very tall, imposing man with a passion for trotting horses which he kept in a stable behind the family house in Alfred Street, Bow. He was already a well-known figure in the East End. And though he could neither read nor write, he was an immensely effective street trader. He started working the street markets before the First World War, selling what are known in the trade as 'white goods'; Isaacs specialized in lace curtains which he sold in pairs. But his big break, the entry into the food business, came quite by chance —coupled with a bit of foresight on his wife's part. One day a load of Walls sausages fell into the Thames where they lay for some time as nobody, except for Mrs Isaacs, thought they were worth recovering. She was, however, a determined lady. She fished them out, found them good, and sold them off in the High Street, Walthamstow.

In many respects the working classes were better off in 1924 than they had ever been: until the Great Depression prices remained more or less stable while the cost of living actually fell. But as the average industrial wage was still only three pounds a week, many of those who crowded the inner suburbs of London, squashed between the centre and the burgeoning commuter dormitories that were springing up around the stations of the Southern Railway and around the rapidly expanding tube system in the north, found that they could not afford the carefully maintained prices of the grocer on the corner. Even Sainsbury's, catering for a largely middle-class and lower middle-class clientele, was too expensive. For the necessities like tea and sugar they went instead to the street markets, many of them survivals from the eighteenth century, that ringed London. And where they went, traders like the Cohen family followed.

Cohen first thought of trading when Morry Isaacs told him of the tons of unwanted Naafi goods that, now that the war was over, were pouring back into England and accumulating in embarrassingly large quantities in warehouses all over London. They were veritable Aladdin's caves, filled to the ceiling with powdered milk and Maconachie's fish paste, tins of jam, toothpaste, metal polish, shoe polish, button sticks and blanco—all the things needed to supply the expeditionary force to France and of course equally handy for the penny-pinching housewives of Hackney and Walthamstow, Dartford and Hammersmith. 'You know all these goods are coming back to England from France,' Isaacs said. 'Why don't you try and buy some?' Which is exactly what Cohen did. 'I thought I would have a go. I think I bought a few pounds' worth and I went out to my local market—it was only about five minutes away—and I took these goods and put them on a barrow. I'd never opened my mouth in my life before—not in any selling way. But a few people came round and I started talking. I took four pounds that morning—in profit. And that interested me very much indeed.' Thus, as the hagiographers at the *Daily Express* would put it, Cohen set out that morning in 1919 on the road to fame and fortune.

He was, however, not alone in his travels. It was a journey in which the whole family—brothers, sisters, brothers-in-law and later nephews and cousins—were involved: each, at least in the beginning, encouraging and supporting the other. One way and another they were all working the markets. There was Cohen himself who eventually became the axis around which all the others revolved; there was Morry Isaacs; there was Dave Gold who was to become Cohen's great rival at the Hammersmith market (they were forever letting down the tyres of each other's lorries) and who had married one of Morry Isaacs' sisters; and there were Cohen's two nephews, Morry's son Sidney and Mossy Vanger whose father, also a tailor from Rutland Street, had married Cohen's sister Olive. Two of these men, Morry's son Sidney, who changed his name to Ingram, and Mossy Vanger, went on to found supermarkets of their own. Ingram started Anthony Jackson (later sold to Garfield Weston's Fine Fare) and Vanger started Elmo, which after a complicated chain of events became part of Cohen's Tesco when Victor Value was taken over in 1968. But of them all it was Cohen who came out on top.

This eminence was not achieved overnight. His success is now so evident and his red-and-green stores are so ubiquitous that it is often forgotten that it took Cohen nearly forty-five years of aggressive buying and hard pitching to emerge as a major figure on the retailing scene. And it was not until the last ten years or so, with the arrival of his sons-in-law (neither of whom, incidentally had a grocery background), that Tesco forged ahead of its rivals. In the 1920s Cohen was just another street trader, covering the same beat and offering much the same goods as his brothers-in-law.

Like the others Cohen, though brought up in an orthodox household, worked seven days a week. Street trading was a tough, competitive business and to survive, let alone to make a profit, a trader had to man his stall all day, every day. It was thus virtually impossible for an ambitious Jew to succeed in business while at the same time observing the strict rules and regulations imposed by his religion—which among the 613 injunctions requires that he should do no business (or indeed work of any kind) from sundown on Friday to sundown on Saturday. But like many others Cohen chose to ignore this dictate. 'If you wanted to get on, you could not leave Saturday out,' he says. Cohen would spend Sunday visiting his suppliers. He dealt mainly in seconds, discontinued lines and damaged goods—buying them from City firms who were anxious to get rid of them and willing to sell them cheaply: it was only later that Cohen moved into such staples as tea and sugar. On Sunday night, helped by his nephews, he would load up his horse-drawn cart with its oil-lit Blanchard lamps and very early on the following morning, before it was light, he would set out for the markets.

The routine hardly varied from one week to the next. On Monday it was the Hammersmith Market; on Tuesday, Well Street, Hackney; Wednesday, Chatsworth Road, Homerton; Thursday, Queen's Road, Upton Park; Friday, Castle Market, Islington and on Saturday, Frith Street, Croydon. Often he would not arrive back at his house in Gore Road, Hackney, where his wife, Cissie, was waiting for him, until well after midnight. 'I used to come home with money in every pocket', he says, 'and we used to be up half the night, counting it.'

It was not easily earned. Competition for the best pitch in the market was intense and the rule was: first man there had his pick. But even among the rough and tumble of the market a certain discipline prevailed. At first light the market men, Cohen among them, used to line up crouching on their marks rather like the drivers at the start of the motor race at Le Mans. At a given signal the men would sprint across the market, the first man home getting the best place. Cohen was by no means the biggest or fastest man there but he used his brains to overcome the dis-advantage. When the signal was given everybody rushed across the cobbles; everybody but Cohen that is. He remained on the line motionless—and threw his cap instead. As it travelled faster than even the strongest could run, Cohen frequently had the best place in the market.

Getting a good pitch was the easist part of the day's work: attracting customers was much more difficult. It was done with a combination of hard price-cutting and fast talking. Cohen, like everybody else, was a price-cutter not because, as the Fascists fondly imagined, he was anxious to do the Gentile shopkeepers down but because his goods were much the same as those on the stall next door.* And the only way he could compete was to buy more shrewdly and sell more competitively than his next-door neighbour. He is still, fifty years later, applying the same basic lessons that he learned in the Hackney markets.

But price-cutting was not the only stratagem employed, for the goods had not only to be priced right—they also had to be advertised. As all that was needed was a fast tongue and a quick wit, Cohen and his friends became highly expert in the art of attracting a crowd and then getting it to buy. Sidney Ingram, Cohen's nephew, was particularly good at this and his expertise was widely admired. Even when he had become the owner of Anthony Jackson, a large supermarket chain, he could not resist slipping down himself on the opening day of one of his stores to address the crowds. His favourite opening gambit was: 'I have been sent here by Sir Anthony Jackson ... ' In his market days, his technique was rather more personal. He once sold a torch to a man who then complained that it didn't work.

INGRAM. When did you buy it?
MAN. Just now.
INGRAM. What do you expect. It's only intended to work in the dark.

And the man went away quite satisfied.

Even after 1929 when he moved away from the markets and into shops of his own Cohen went to great trouble to preserve as far as he possibly could the atmosphere and conditions of the market-place. At first the shops had no fronts at all, opening straight out on to the pavement. Cohen was not the only man to trade in this way. Geoffrey Kaye, chairman of the Pricerite chain, remembers that it was so cold that he had to keep dipping

* Price-cutting was one of the sticks the Fascists used to beat the Jews. Addressing a grocers' meeting in the East End in 1936, Mr Raven Thompson, one of Sir Oswald Mosley's lieutenants, said: 'We have got to face the fact that the Jews had an entirely different standard of moral values from the Englishman's. The Jew was a man who was prepared to buy up bankrupt stocks—possibly from a member of his own family—and he opened a cut-price shop, traded for a few months, and then off he went.'

his fingers into a bowl of hot water so that the customers' change would not fall from his numbed fingers.* It was only in the 'forties that Cohen installed doors and roller shutters which opened up to reveal the cans piled in high pyramids, and proper windows and doors were not a feature of the Tesco stores until about 1950. The whole object was to maintain an atmosphere of constant hustle, bustle and excitement. At the far end of the shop there was often a rostrum on which the manager stood to conduct mock auctions. 'It was a means of getting the thing going and getting the public interested,' Cohen says. 'We used to auction tins of peaches. We would start at 5s. and then when the public got interested we would bring the price down. It went like this: "5s., 4s., 3s. 6d., 3s., 2s. 6d.—gone to the lady in the pink hat." That was our type of trading and it went down like hot cakes.'

Cohen did not start out with the intention of being a shop-keeper—and he became one almost by accident, after being a wholesaler, supplying other market men with canned goods, sardines and tea—especially tea. Tea, then as now, was one of the great mass-market commodities, which everybody needed and bought. To Cohen this was but one of its attractions; the other was the margins. The conventional grocers sold their tea at 1s. 6d. a pound—a price which gave them a very useful profit. Cohen who was (as he still is) more interested in low margins and high turnover saw his opportunity. He made a deal with a long-sighted tea merchanting firm, called Tyde and Stockwell. They were to supply the tea, he told the proprietor, T. E. Stockwell, and he would sell it on to the market men. The price: 1s. a pound. Cohen's hunch proved correct, and Tesco Tea (named after Stockwell's initials and the first two letters of Cohen's own name) was much in demand. If there was any single turning point in Cohen's long career this was it, for it was the popularity of Tesco Tea that enabled Cohen to climb out of the rut. As he controlled the supply, he could dictate the terms to his customers. Between

* Cohen had a hand in starting Pricerite too. He was one of the first suppliers to the founder, Michael Kaye, and until 1955 had a 50 per cent share in the business.

1924 and 1929 Cohen financed a number of traders, undertaking to supply them with goods and taking in return 50 per cent of the business and a corresponding share of the profits. However the venture, though sound in theory, was not wholly successful. Though Cohen appreciated the extra profit, he did not relish running other people's businesses for them, which is what it eventually amounted to. 'My customers were not very strong payers,' he explained. 'They didn't pay their accounts properly. I used to do my own book-keeping, served them myself, went to the market. But even when I came home from some social function I would find these fellows waiting for me.' But it was 1930, when one of his customers refused point blank to pay Cohen his 50 per cent share, that Cohen realized that he would probably be better off running shops himself.

He could not have chosen a better time to make the move. London was expanding fast, with housing estates springing up on what had five years before been green fields. The rash of semi-detacheds had spread up the Northern Line through Hendon and Burnt Oak to Edgware and fanned out sideways through Neasden, Kingsbury, Harrow Weald and Pinner, engulfing ancient villages in the process. Each village had its own artery, the shopping street, and as the housing estates spread these too were transformed by the developers, who built long, brick arcades to house the shops. As the Depression approached the developers, anxious lest their newly built arcades should prove to be white elephants, energetically wooed the shopkeepers, offering them all kinds of inducements to move in and set the ball rolling. They knew that shopkeepers were cautious folk who preferred to move only after somebody else had taken the plunge. Very often Jack Cohen was that somebody else, for he was only just beginning his career as a shopkeeper and had little to lose. Cohen knew most of the estate agents but with one, a man called Edward Lotery, he was particularly friendly. 'I used to go out with him and see what he'd got,' Cohen recalls. 'I used to like the look of it—I had vision—I used to feel this is all right, people living here, living there and they'll come in. We'll draw them. We used to give out handbills in the district and we used to make it come alive. We still make it come alive.' But the prospect of making Burnt Oak live was not the only attraction. So eager were Lotery and the other developers for Cohen's custom that they offered to lend the capital or even pay for the shopfitting themselves. Cohen was delighted. 'They made me a multiple in no time,' he says. 'I became a multiple not because I wanted to but because the pressure was on all the time—people were offering us shops that were empty. "Come in here and I'll give you six months' free rent," they said. "I'll give you £300 to fit it all up and make a parade for us." And we did.'

Cohen was of course not the only retailer whom the developers wooed: much bigger and grander chains than his, among them Woolworths and Marks and Spencer, also benefited. But he was one of the first to spot the coming self-service boom. It was the Express Dairy which actually pioneered self-service, opening its first Premier supermarket in Edgware in 1938. But, as so often happens with genuine pioneers, the Express Dairy, which in the autumn of 1969 was taken over after a bitter fight by Maxwell Joseph's Grand Metropolitan Hotels, failed to reap its just reward.

In view of what happened later it is perhaps ironic that initially Cohen was unimpressed by the supermarket idea. In 1932, shortly after he had moved into shops, he went to America where he was shown round by Max Zimmerman, one of the great pioneers of the American supermarket business. In those days the super-markets were not the glossy monsters that they are today. The operators set up shop in the unlikeliest places—disused churches and old halls—simply laying out the goods in the nave and fitting turnstiles at the west end. At the time it did not strike Cohen as a vision of the future. A former associate recalls hearing Cohen describe what he had seen and then asking him: 'Do you think we will ever have self-service in this country?' Cohen thought for a moment and then replied, 'No. Self-service won't work here. The women would never stand for it.'

By the time the war was over Cohen had changed his mind—

though it took another visit to America and considerable pressure from his son-in-law, Hyman Kreitman, who actually left the firm for a brief spell in property after a row with his father-in-law, before he was finally persuaded. He still hankered after the classic bash-em-over-the-head style of market trading which he knew best and which he had practised with such elan. Self-service was a much cooler operation requiring more scientific and sophisticated techniques of persuasion. If Cohen had been left to himself it is possible that he would never have made the switch and his doubts were reinforced by the failure, shortly before his second American visit, of his first self-service experiment at a small store in St Albans. But he was ultimately persuaded to try again—with results that are now evident for all to see.

The Tesco of today is a thoroughly modern business, scrupulously controlled and highly sophisticated. It has to be, for the job of keeping millions of customers a year supplied with £186 million worth of everything from canned peaches to disposable nappies is not a simple one. It is not enough to know how many people in Croydon are buying Tesco chocolate: the men at the Tesco headquarters at Cheshunt, if they are to run the business efficiently, have to be told how many prefer fruit and nut, how many like plain and how many buy only the squashy kind that comes in boxes. It is a problem, common to all large retailers, that is duplicated in thousands of different ways, in hundreds of separate stores, right across the entire range. And to help them untangle such complexities Tesco has turned to the experts: it has hired consultants to mechanize the warehouses; has recruited a whole army of works study and operational research men to design transport and other systems and it has brought in a £300,000 computer which sits mysteriously clicking away in its air-conditioned room at Cheshunt, connected by landlines to the warehouses, keeping a continuous tally on the goods that flow out of the warehouses in such numbers that they have to be refilled every one and a half weeks. The whole business is a good example of

what is often called, at those expensive and improving courses
that British middle managers seem to spend a large part of their
time attending, scientific management.

The takeover by Tesco in November 1968 of the ailing Victor
Value chain, also run by a family called Cohen (but no relation),
provides an excellent opportunity to watch the computerized
Tesco steam-roller in action. Victor Value's East End origins
were similar to Tesco's. But while Cohen had succeeded, with the
help of his two sons-in-law, in making the difficult transition from
a one-man business to a corporate empire, the Victor Value Cohens
seem in the course of their climb out of the East End to have lost
their way. For a number of reasons the shops did not prove to be
crowd pullers on the Tesco scale and the trouble was compounded
when Victor Value backed the wrong side in the Great Trading
Stamp War which shook the high streets in the mid 'sixties,
rousing the ire of Lord Sainsbury in the process.* Victor Value's
system of cost control was not as highly, nor as carefully,
organized as Tesco's and, as turnover fell, a seemingly helpless
Victor Value moved in the autumn of 1968 inexorably into the red.

The opportunity of snapping up the extra outlets presented a
temptation that Cohen found irresistible. It was not the first time
the company had been on the takeover trail. In the preceding five
years it had mopped up a whole string of grocery and other food
and catering businesses, many of them Jewish, which had prospered in the early 'fifties when, with the supermarket boom
gathering speed, it had been difficult not to make money. But as
competition hotted up and the founding proprietors who had
made their pile ran both out of steam and, even more frequently,

* Lord Sainsbury, with some assistance from the John Lewis Partnership, waged
a vigorous campaign against trading stamps, taking large advertisements in the
newspapers to explain that in the long run the customer would have to pay the price.
There was some truth in this charge as the weaker shops like Victor Value found
that the stamps did not put up sales sufficiently to offset the cost. Lord Sainsbury's
advice, however, was not wholly disinterested although Sainsbury's appeal has
always been more on quality than price. And stamps, after all, are no more than
a sophisticated variant on price-cutting techniques that firms like Tesco have been
employing for years.

of professional managers competent enough to succeed them,
these businesses faltered; eventually being snapped up by the
large chains.

The Victor Value name has now disappeared from the high
street, though if you look carefully at some of Tesco's shiny
façades, the faint outlines of the name can still be seen; a ghostly
reminder of the carnivorous nature of big business. Once the
financial details were settled, the mechanics of the Tesco takeover
were planned and organized with the precision of a high-class
military operation: the brigade in attack. Shortly after the takeover
in the autumn of 1968 I was taken on a tour of the battlefield by
Hyman Kreitman, who shortly before had been promoted from
managing director to joint chairman in preparation for Cohen's
retirement. Kreitman, although his origins as the youngest son
of an East End ladies' shoemaking business are almost as humble as
Cohen's own, is a very different, altogether more wary character
than his father-in-law. Smooth, soft spoken, highly articulate and
unwaveringly courteous, he is the very model of a modern
professional manager—as much an administrator as an entrepreneur. In a different context he would make a very good
management consultant.

Phase One of the takeover began on July 9th, with the Tesco
men moving in on some sixty stores simultaneously after the
store had closed on the Saturday night. Working throughout the
week-end they assessed all the stock, removed all the Victor Value
labels, replacing them with Tesco stickers, reshuffled the goods
on the shelves, putting the fastest moving lines at the front, and
changed the trading stamps from Sperry and Hutchinson's pink to
Green Shield's green. The Victor Value signs were torn down
('As a name it appeared not to have a great deal of merit,' Kreitman dryly observed) and in their place rose the letters of the Tesco
trademark, four foot high and brilliant red. By the following
Tuesday the transformed shops were open again for business,
their windows plastered with posters, their banner headlines
announcing introductory cut-price bargains, which, they said,

could never be repeated and were available for one week only. The operation was, so Kreitman says, immensely successful. The weekly turnover at one new town store rose from between £7,000 and £8,000 a week to between £17,000 and £18,000 and by the end of the first month, so the slide-rule men at Cheshunt calculated, the whole Victor Value chain was back in the black.

The razzamatazz of a Tesco opening is as much part of the Tesco style as the flow charts of the operational research men and the tabulated print-outs from the computer. For beneath its glossy managerial surface the business remains true to its East End huckster origins, run by a man for whom the memories of those days, nearly fifty years ago now, remain as vivid as if it were yesterday. 'We have brought the market to the high street,' is one of Jack Cohen's favourite and most repeated phrases. 'Our shops are still markets with roofs on.' And even though competition has become perhaps a little more genteel than it was in the Hammersmith Market of the 1920s, it still remains vigorous, uninhibited and intensely personal.

Chapter Eight

The Family in Business

> 'I always think that though we may have our heads in the clouds our feet are always very firmly embedded in the ground.'
>
> 'Some people think we are too bloody good to be true.'
>
> 'One of the terrible disadvantages of working for Marks and Spencer is that you are the butt of everybody's complaints. It's rather like being a tax man.'
>
> Marks and Spencer's executives.
>
> 'Union fait la force.'
>
> The Gluckstein family motto.

When Lord Marks died in 1964 after a sudden heart attack in the office after lunch, there was no dispute about who should succeed him; it was accepted as the natural order of things that his friend and partner, Lord Sieff, should step into the vacant chair, and when three years later the time came for Lord Sieff to retire, it seemed equally inevitable that his younger brother Edward should succeed him. And when his turn comes to retire it seems equally certain that his son Marcus, the present joint managing director, will take his place. Thus the principles on which M. & S. was built are guarded and handed down from generation to generation.

The ethos that surrounds a family business can be extraordinarily powerful and seductive: the family is the firm and the firm is the

159

family, the success of one reinforcing the power and glory of the other. And when that family happens to be Jewish, where family pride and tradition is particularly strong, the process is often doubly potent. But for all its attractions it is a double-edged weapon. At its best it is an ideal mechanism for preserving and handing down the principles, the ideals and the ideas of the founding father to be reinterpreted by each successive generation. Sometimes this sense of family is so strong that it permeates not just the firm, as it does at M. & S. where portraits of Lord Marks and Lord Sieff hang in every store, but a whole town. In St Helens the Pilkingtons who control Britain's largest private company have held sway developing their successful glassmaking business since 1826, while at Street in Somerset the influence of the shoe-making, Quaker-born Clarks, now in their fifth generation, is so all-pervasive that until recently the town boasted only one pub, specially built for visitors. Until quite recently it was customary for all the work-people to attend family prayers in the works before the day's shoemaking began.

But there is another side to this coin. Successful families often regard their firms as being as much part of their personal property as their houses, their motor cars and their other possessions and this proprietorial state of mind often leads to a confusion of the interests of the family with those of the firm. They are, however, not always identical. It is a rare family that can throw up geniuses, or even men of quite ordinary, straightforward ability, generation after generation. The laws of genetics are against it. And though the principle of appointing the chairman's son to succeed him may ensure continuity, it may also lead to a dilution of that spirit of dash and enterprise which built the company in the first place. And when the tradition extends to finding room on the board not only for the chairman's son but for his brothers, his cousins and his brothers-in-law as well, the damage can be considerable. The company becomes ingrown and inward-looking and professional managers of the kind the company needs most stay away, convinced, often rightly, that no matter how hard they try, the doors

of the board room will remain closed to them. It is a reflection of
this proprietorial instinct that until Lord Marks's death five years
ago only a handful of its hundreds of thousands of shareholders
had the right to vote at the company's meetings: all the voting
shares were held firmly in the hands of the family, who felt that
having built the business they had the right to manage and control
it.

The shareholders have now been enfranchised, but the family,
now in its fourth generation and linked by a whole series of
highly complex interlocking relationships, is still, despite the
presence of a large number of outsiders (of the nineteen members
of the board only five are Sieffs and two are Sachers), the dominant
influence on the board, occupying all the positions of real power.
It may look nepotistic, but so far M. & S. seems to have avoided
most of the snares and pitfalls that lie in wait for the traditional
family company. Its success is partly due to a strong and unusual
streak of ruthlessness and tough-mindedness that runs right
through the company. It is made quite clear to members of the
family, as a number of the younger generation told me, that a seat
on the board is by no means automatic. A Sieff or a Sacher might
get to the board room earlier than others but he has, so David
Sieff, a junior director and son of Marcus, the company's joint
managing director, said, to prove himself first. By no means all
the members of the family have risen in the business: Simon
Marks's own son plays no part in the business, preferring an
unspectacular literary career; Marcus Sieff's nephew, Jonathan, a
former racing driver, now owns a large and successful garage
business and Simon Marks's nephew, Anthony Blond, is a
publisher. But those that do remain are united not only by family
ties but by a common dedication to the business. They have, from
childhood, all been soaked in the ethos of the business, they
understand each others' minds intimately and because they never
stop talking and thinking about the business they are in effect a
board that is in continuous session—even at week-ends. One of
the first things that strikes any visitor to a Sieff house party is that

L

nothing can begin until the day's figures have been reported by telephone from head office.

The indoctrination of a young Sieff, so David Sieff says, starts at a very early age. 'I lived with it as a child. One always heard about it. Indeed I got rather fed up hearing about it. But I suppose the first time I realized that M. & S. was something different, a household word, was when I was about eight or nine when my parents came down to my prep school in Sussex to take me out for the half day. Instead of going out into the country for a picnic as the other boys did, they used to take me round the stores in Brighton and Eastbourne and when I got bored they would give me an ice-cream.' After leaving his prep school young David went to Repton (not a traditional M. & S. school, St Paul's and Manchester Grammar are more usual choices) and for a time toyed with the idea of becoming a film director. 'When I was seventeen I was very much in two minds whether to join M. & S. or go into films. When I told my friends this they said: "You must be mad. If you are actually thinking of working in the family business, do, for heaven's sake. After all, it's an opportunity not many other boys have." ' David Sieff took that advice, joining M. & S. immediately after leaving school. 'I started exactly like all other trainees—in the stockrooms, where I stayed for six weeks. I had exactly the same training as any other boy. The only real advantage I had was this tremendous background. I had in my mind's eye a very vivid picture of a family business growing. And I understood it all the better because when my father talked about the business to me—which he frequently did—he did not talk down to me: he discussed it in exactly the same terms as he would with any of his colleagues and directors. And in those days we were head and shoulders above everybody else.' 'Was it really like this?' I asked. 'Were there no other advantages?'

'I suppose I saw more stores than the average trainee. I was moved about more. But I suppose the other main advantage was the knowledge that I would not be sacked. But at the same time it was made very clear to me that if you didn't work you wouldn't progress very fast and that nobody would give you very much respect.'

What, I wanted to know, did he mean by 'loss of respect'?—and from whom?

'Respect from everybody in the store,' he answered. 'If you are not getting on, people will by-pass you. They will say when your name comes up "He's a jolly nice chap but ... " '

Did he find his first couple of years in the store easy? Did it help to be called Sieff? I asked.

'I suppose', said David Sieff, quite suddenly, 'that in the first six months of my life at M. & S. my father made my life almost intolerable. At that time I was living at home and often when we were having breakfast, my father would leave the table, go to the telephone and ring the store. When he got through he would ask if I was there. He knew perfectly well where I was and chose this method of indicating that I should get to work earlier.

'In the first couple of years I probably did not work as hard as I should have done. I was not involved.' 'Involvement' is a key word at M. & S.; there are people who are 'involved' and there are people who are 'not involved' and everybody knows who is who and which is which. Initially David Sieff was 'not involved'. 'I did it like any other job. It was quite interesting and it occupied my day but then quite suddenly everything changed, and I positively began to enjoy going to work. Being at the store became almost more enjoyable than being at home.'

It was this kind of educative process that Simon Marks doubtless had in mind when he said in 1954, in introducing two new directors, Alec Lerner (who had married his daughter Hannah and has since left the board to go and work in Israel) and Marcus Sieff, to the shareholders, 'I am sure you will agree that the normal method of recruitment to the board should be from within the organization of men bred in its traditions, tested by its problems and educated in its philosophy.' And if this had to be true of members of the family who had grown up in this atmosphere practically from infancy, how much more did it have to apply to outsiders who had only become acquainted with the Marksian philosophy comparatively late in life. The whiz-kid phenomenon, such a feature of other firms who proudly present their thrusting thirty-five-year-olds who have arrived from other firms covered in glory with the scalps of their less successful colleagues dangling at their belts, is one that is entirely foreign to M. & S. They are faintly amazed when the possibility is suggested. 'But what could he offer?' they ask; pointing out that however talented such a mythical creature might be, he would find it quite impossible to make an impact on his own.

And yet if M. & S. is to continue to survive and prosper it will have eventually to reconcile itself, as other family firms like the Wedgwoods or the Montague Burtons have done, to the possibility that the company will one day be run by a professional manager to whom the family means little or nothing. It will change not because the company is in danger of being taken over (it is probably too big for that ever to happen) as Showerings, the cider firm, or Cadburys, the famous chocolate business that is now part of the Schweppes empire, have been; nor because of death duty problems which led to the public flotation of Lord Cowdray's interests; but simply because if the leadership of the company is confined to the members of the family, the chances are that it will run out of talent. It may not happen; Rothschilds have not, Pilkington's have not, the Clarks have not. But it might. It is a possibility that Lord Sieff is wise enough to recognize. But he thinks it will not occur for some time. 'The character of the company will change,' he says, 'but not immediately. I think it will remain a family company for at least another twenty to thirty years yet.'

A visit to Lord Sieff, the president of Marks and Spencer, is, no matter how used one is to interviewing senior businessmen, a somewhat intimidating experience. The visitor to the giant mausoleum at 57 Baker Street where Marks and Spencer has its headquarters is greeted by a clutch of commissionaires who politely inquire as to the nature of your business. From this point a curiously formal procedure is set in motion: one man detaches himself from his desk and takes you upstairs to the directorial suite on the first floor where you are handed over, rather like a baton in some slow-motion relay race, to a second uniformed official who conducts you along wide, *eau-de-nil* corridors fitted with thick and springy carpeting to an antiseptic room bare of all decoration, containing only a metal coat-rack, from which dangle a lonely collection of steel hangers. One's coat is solemnly removed and placed with a reverence that it does not deserve on the rack. From there one is conducted a few yards along the corridor by a third man who ushers one into a waiting-room, which apart from an immaculately arranged bowl of fresh spring flowers, obviously changed each day, is identical to the one before. The third commissionaire departs and after a few minutes a secretary arrives to conduct one on what proves to be the last stage of the journey: through an anteroom in which three secretaries sit gossiping, past a lighted sign which says, in red letters, ENTER, and into the office of the president himself.

It is a large, a very large room; but in no way impersonal. It seemed at first glance to be filled with photographs of children, grandchildren and even great-grandchildren (a feature, I later discovered, of nearly all the offices of senior M. & S. directors) and like the corridors so thickly carpeted as to deaden all sound. It took, or so it seemed, an age to cross this vast expanse and reach the desk at the far end at which an old man was sitting, quite still, his eyes hidden by a pair of green tinted glasses. The effect was altogether most impressive. Even after I had arrived the impression of immobility remained. He listened impassively to what I had to say, but when eventually he spoke the voice was strong and lively with a quite perceptible Manchester accent.

It seemed logical to start any investigation of Marks and Spencer with Lord Sieff, for it was his ideas and personality (together with those of his life-long friend and inseparable companion, Lord Marks) that built and fashioned Marks and Spencer into one of the world's most famous and most admired of retail chains. When Princess Grace of Monaco visited the Marble Arch store in 1968 to buy a pair of nylons, her picture appeared on the front page of practically every national newspaper not because she was a princess and a film star but because her visit illustrated with the kind of dramatic clarity that newspapers love a point that everybody knew but still could not quite believe: that *everybody* shopped at Marks and Spencer: princesses and film stars as well as charladies and bus conductresses. This is what the men at Baker Street mean when they talk, as they often do, of creating a social revolution: a state of affairs in which it is impossible to tell, at first glance anyway, a debutante from a dustman's daughter.

Part of Marks and Spencer's influence stems from its sheer size and ubiquity. Its 250 stores, through which pass some 12 million customers a week, are a central feature of practically every high street of any consequence in the land: there is not a town in England of any size that does not have its Marks and Spencer. Between them these stores are responsible for no less than 10 per cent of all clothes sold each year: the famous St Michael label (named after the firm's founder Michael Marks) is to be found on one out of every five pairs of socks, on one out of every three slips, bras and children's dressing-gowns and on no less than three out of every five pairs of ladies' pants.

But Simon Marks and Israel Sieff have done much more than just build an immensely successful and influential retail chain. In the process they have also created a trading philosophy all of their own—a philosophy which stems from their basic belief that their customers are just as interested in the quality of their goods as they are in their price. And it is this unremitting struggle to combine high quality with mass-market sales that has coloured everything that Marks and Spencer says and does and which gives the firm its peculiar and highly distinctive flavour.*

* It is a reputation that is jealously guarded. In the summer of 1969 Marks and Spencer learnt that some enterprising characters were travelling from door to door offering what they claimed were Marks and Spencer rejects. M. & S. were horrified. A press release was rushed out to explain first that they never had rejects (that

This singularity is apparent even from the outside, for almost nothing about M. & S. is conventional. More than any other retailer it is intimately involved with a large part of the textile industry; its scientists and technologists (themselves an unusual feature) swarm over its suppliers' factories, laying down specifications and giving advice on everything from the quality of the material to the design of the machines, yet it makes nothing itself and invests not a penny in its manufacturers. Unlike other stores it sometimes seems aloof and introspective. It pays little or no attention to what its competitors are up to ('When examining ourselves, which we do constantly, we always judge ourselves by our own standards, not other people's,' says David Sieff); it sets no profit targets either for its managers or the business itself, arguing that if they get the turnover, the profit will naturally follow; and its attitude to its customers occasionally seems to border on the cavalier: if a popular but occasional line runs out, rather than disrupt the whole organization trying to replace it immediately, they simply do not bother, confident in the well-founded belief that the appeal of the stores is such that the customers will keep on coming anyway.

M. & S. is one of the few businesses of its size not to own computers. They did, so the story goes, install an early version once, but Lord Marks was so horrified by the complexities that followed that he ordered it to be taken out again. Nor does the company employ, as others do, hosts of management consultants and other outside experts. 'Experts on tap but not on top,' was one of Lord Marks's favourite slogans and the firm, confident in its own abilities to analyse and solve its problems, has continued to observe this dictum. It does not, again unlike its competitors, do any formal market research. There is, they say, no need. 'Our stores are our best indicator and if something is going to go you

---

was the manufacturers' responsibility) and even if they did they would not carry the St Michael label. The offer therefore, they suggested, was not genuine and should be ignored. The salesmen were subsequently successfully prosecuted under the Trade Descriptions Act.

can usually tell in a couple of hours or so,' a director explains. For M. & S. the process of discovering their customers' likes and dislikes is a much more intuitive and personal process—and one in which everybody at M. & S. from the president and the chairman downwards is involved. Lord Sieff and his younger brother, Edward, the present chairman, may be millionaires several times over but they still have to buy shirts and underpants like everybody else and so it is in the last resort their needs and their preferences which to a very large extent determine what appears in the stores. If the directors do not like it, it will not be sold: it is as simple as that. The first time, so a director recalls, M. & S. tried to market fresh meat (in recent years the food business has been a major diversification, built up by Marcus Sieff and accounting for a quarter of their turnover) the experiment did not come off. 'The blood made the cardboard soggy and as a result, though it was perfectly all right to eat, it did not look right.' M. & S. place great store by appearances—which is why the great smoked haddock experiment also failed. To give the haddock its characteristic yellow colour, M. & S. had used a particularly strong dye. Before it was sent out to the stores it was served for lunch in the directors' dining-room and as it arrived on their plates the dye started to ooze. 'Everybody was horrified. If it stops looking nice, we won't sell it.' This attitude extends far beyond food. A solicitor I know tells the story of another board room lunch at M. & S. In the course of the lunch the conversation turned to the subject of shirts. 'I bet you', said the chairman to the solicitor, who also happens to be a millionaire, 'that your shirt buttons aren't polished on both sides.' The solicitor spent the rest of the meal surreptitiously peering at his buttons to see if this was in fact true. This very personal approach can have disadvantages as well as advantages. Simon Marks was, when it came to matters of dress, a very conservative man who thought that trousers should have turn-ups and that the only colour for shirts was white. Thus it was that M. & S. was one of the last major firms in the country to dispense with turn-ups and to sell pink shirts. But here as elsewhere M. & S. is beginning to change under the influence of its younger directors who reflect the tastes of a younger generation; and though none of them have yet been seen arriving at the office in bell bottomed trousers, they do run to buckled shoes and deep collared shirts.

These practices, which distinguish M. & S. from other businesses, have emerged only gradually, taking all of forty years to crystallize. When Simon Marks became chairman of the company, aged twenty-eight, after a bitter board room row (it is significant that this occurred during the only period in the firm's history when the family was not in control), the company was conventional enough. It was started by Michael Marks as a Penny Bazaar in the market at Leeds (a model of the original stall is still lovingly preserved at Baker Street complete with its famous slogan, 'Don't ask the price; it's a penny.') By the time of Michael Marks's death in 1907, at the early age of forty-four, it had grown into a chain of over fifty stores. And even when it went public some nineteen years later in 1926 with 140 stores making profits of £100,000 a year, it was still a variety chain store, owing much to its street trading origins and competing on exactly the same terms as Woolworths. 'The range of goods now handled by the company', the prospectus describing the public flotation announced, 'has now become very extensive and now comprises Haberdashery, Hosiery and Drapery, Toilet Requisites, Glass, China and Earthenware, Stationery, Confectionery, Toys and Sports Goods, Fancy Goods, Jewellery, Gramophone Records and Music, Cutlery, Household Goods, Hardware, Tin and Enamel Ware, Books and Novels.' It was an image which Simon Marks found difficult to shake off when he began to change the direction of the company. When Israel Sieff went to visit an important textile manufacturer, a firm with which M. & S. subsequently did millions of pounds' worth of business, he was shown the door by the chairman who told him: 'We don't do business with bazaars.'

But by 1926 the company was already beginning to take on an entirely new shape. Two years before, Simon Marks had made what the company's historian Goronwy Rees describes* as a 'decisive' visit to America to look at chain stores there. On his return sweeping changes were made which affected almost every aspect of the company's activities. By far the most important change was the abolition of the old price structure where goods were priced at anything between 1d. and £2, and its replacement with a five-shilling ceiling—a level deliberately set low enough to be within the reach of the working-class families who were M. & S.'s customers. The five-shilling limit imposed a whole new set of disciplines while at the same time opening up an entirely new range of possibilities. Many of the goods that M. & S. had been selling cost far more than five shillings and so these were abandoned. But what to put in their place? The answer was ladies' clothing—a field that Israel Sieff, whose father had run a successful Manchester textile business (he left about half a million pounds when he died), knew a good deal about. And it was largely his knowledge and expertise, plus his determination to eliminate the wholesaler who took a large slice of the profit, that enabled M. & S. to demonstrate to the manufacturers that it was possible to make clothes of the quality they demanded and still sell them within the five shilling limit. It was this decision that marked the beginning of Marks and Spencer's pre-eminence and it is from this decision that all the others have flowed.

Though the turning point can be identified, it came not as a sudden flash of inspiration but as the natural outcome of the almost continuous conversations that Simon Marks and Israel Sieff had been having since they were schoolboys, sitting side by side in the same classroom at Manchester Grammar School. This extraordinary close relationship between the two men, strengthened by the fact that they married each other's sisters, has been one of the mainsprings if not the only one, of the growth of the M. & S. business and the development of the M. & S. philosophy. It is a relationship that Lord Sieff, normally the most articulate of men, finds difficult to describe. 'How can I put it?' he asked. 'It

* *St. Michael, a History of Marks and Spencer.*

would probably sound silly to you as a practical man. I have been asked this many times and I still find it difficult to give a proper description.' There was a long pause. 'I suppose', he said eventually, 'that it was like one body and one soul—David and Jonathan. I would say, particularly with my brother-in-law, that he was always charged with a state of what I can only describe as divine dissatisfaction. That sums up my state of mind too. We used to leave the office and would sit, to the annoyance of our wives, talking for hours about what had happened during the day and what was passing through our minds.'

The subject of their conversations was almost invariably the business: they were constantly worrying about how it could be improved, developed and expanded. Simon Marks was not a man, so those who have worked closely with him say, who leapt to sudden and spectacular conclusions. For him the decision-making process was a painful business involving endless argument and discussion. 'Simon found it extraordinarily difficult to make decisions,' says a man who knew him well. 'It went on and on. It hurt him. He wanted a synthesis of everything. He would sit at his desk and when he wanted an answer to something he would summon somebody, listen to what they had to say and then call in somebody else. This would go on until his room was full of people all giving their opinions. Simon would go on getting people to rephrase and simplify their remarks until what they were saying was both clear to him and them. It was really an exercise in the Socratic method: the constant asking of the question "why?" And then having heard what everybody else had to say he sometimes behaved like an eccentric general who having started the battle would then go and reverse the whole plan.'

But this is not to say that behind all these hesitations and calculated eccentricities Marks did not have a clear and intuitive idea of what the business was all about. Often his decisions seemed irrational. For years M. & S. sold ice-cream. It was one of its most profitable lines. But one day Marks during one of his frequent perambulations about the stores noticed that the customers were dropping the wrappers on the floor. Shortly afterwards orders went out that ice-cream was no longer to be sold. Marks hated dirt as much as he disliked waste and inefficiency and thought that the discarded wrappers were spoiling M. & S.'s immaculate and hygienic image. Cleanliness is something of an obsession at M. & S.; the counters are spotless and the towels in the staff washrooms are changed every day. Pressures to introduce lines whose production and quality they could not control themselves with the same iron-fisted grip that they had over the textile and the food manufacturers are firmly resisted. M. & S. has been built up by offering a rigidly controlled and carefully selected range of goods of a quality that the public appreciated and at a price that they could afford. And Marks sensed that if either side of this equation was altered much of the unique appeal of the stores would be lost. 'He would never say that anybody was wrong,' a director says. 'His most common criticism was: "You don't understand the business." "Why don't you go into gramophone records?" people would sometimes ask him. To which Marks would quite simply reply: "Because it is not our business." ' To Marks 'our business' was shorthand for the whole M. & S. approach: what the men at Baker Street call in their more meta-physical moods *Gestätlichkeit*—the concept of fittingness.

Marks was not an easy man to work for, as his employees often discovered. There was something of an actor in his make-up and he enjoyed putting on a performance to tease and sometimes to frighten his staff. On occasions after giving a subordinate the most dreadful dressing down he would ask kindly: 'Did I upset you?' Anxious to please the junior would answer 'No.' 'In that case', Marks would tartly reply, 'you can't have been listening.' It was not only the head office staff who saw this side of Marks's character. The story is still told in Baker Street of a visit Marks made to the West Country. During a behind-the-scene inspection of the Falmouth store he pretended to become very angry when he noticed that all the shopping bags had been stuffed with paper for the chairman's inspection. The manager was told to unstuff them forthwith. As soon as Marks had left, the unfortunate manager, anxious to avoid another explosion further down the line, telephoned his colleague at Exeter to tell him what had happened. And so by the time Marks had arrived at Exeter all the bags had been emptied and were lying flat and neat on the floor. Marks looked at them. 'Why are they all lying flat like that?' he asked. 'Because I thought that was the way you liked them,' said the manager, not knowing what to think. 'Just because I don't like stuffed bags at Falmouth that doesn't mean I don't want them that way at Exeter,' Marks replied with a twinkle in his eye.

With Israel Sieff, however, Simon's relations were wholly and consistently harmonious. The rapport between the two men was so complete as to be almost telepathic. 'In sixty years I can't recall there ever having been a cross word between us,' Sieff says. There were differences between the two men but they were of temperament and quality of mind rather than of attitude and opinion. Marks was tense and introverted, something of an autocrat, while Sieff, who unlike Marks had a university education, is more relaxed and much more a man of the world. He is a fluent speaker, a skilful writer and in the 1930s he played an important part in the creation of Political and Economic Planning, the research group. Marks was the energizer, Sieff the catalyst. 'Sieff was the iron block off which the sparks flew,' says one man.

The creation and the administration of a great business is a much more intellectual process than many people, including some captains of industry, believe. Certainly this is true of M. & S., which has been successful not only because Simon Marks and Israel Sieff were gifted traders with an instinctive feel for the needs of the mass market, but because, quite simply, they sat and *thought* longer and harder than most of their competitors about what they were doing and why they were there. The object of all those interminable conversations was to reduce any problem to its essentials: first to identify what that problem was and then to work out the simplest way of solving it. It was this fundamental drive for simplicity and clarity of thought, the constant repetition of the question 'why?', that has given birth to many of M. & S.'s most admired innovations. The move into clothing in 1926; the abolition of conventional stock control in 1956 which ultimately led to a 20 per cent saving in head office staff and the disappearance of 26 million pieces of paper each year; the repackaging of their goods in plastic in 1968 which led to an import saving of nearly a million pounds; even the decision to throw out the computer — all these steps flowed from a basic desire to make the business simpler, more manageable and ultimately more profitable.

It is this characteristic that distinguishes M. & S. from all its rivals. And though the ability to think clearly is by no means a Jewish prerogative I think that this intellectual trait, this analytical power, that is so pronounced in M. & S. is ultimately not unconnected with the Jewish values and Jewish traditions which Marks and Sieff patently inherited. When asked about this Sieff, who was brought up in an orthodox family but is not strictly orthodox himself in the way that, say, Sir Isaac Wolfson is, likes to stress the charitable side of the tradition, pointing out that in Hebrew the words for justice and charity are the same, *tsdaka*. 'My father said there are two things I want to tell you that you must remember all your life. God gives to him who gives; and the man who transforms a miserable wretch into a contented mind merits a place on the right hand of God.' It is this injunction, perhaps, the idea that charity involves not just giving money but providing a service for one's fellow man, that is responsible for the atmosphere of moral, almost ideological, fervour, that permeates M. & S. 'It's like no other business I know,' says an M. & S. economist who came from the Transport Commission.

This strand of strong Jewish idealism was further reinforced by Chaim Weizmann, the founder of modern Zionism whom Marks and Sieff met when young and impressionable businessmen in Manchester. The statesman and the businessmen were drawn to one another. The statesman appreciated their energy and enthusiasm. 'They were not hampered by ancient Zionist dissensions, nor were their lives scarred by recollections of persecution,'

Weizmann wrote. 'They were jolly and they loved the good things of life. They helped me in later years to put some kind of organization into my rather disorganized life.' And the businessmen appreciated Weizmann's advice and wisdom. 'He was', says Sieff, 'a man of magnetic personality.' But he was also an extremely distinguished scientist—an organic chemist engaged in fundamental research at Manchester University; work which was to lead ultimately to the discovery of an acetate that was to be an important ingredient in the manufacture of high explosives.

The Jews have produced many famous businessmen but they have also provided outstanding scientists, academics and musicians. It is not easy to analyse why Jews should have made such an outstanding contribution to mathematics, physics, chemistry and biology any more than it is simple to untangle the reasons why many should have succeeded so well in business. But I think part of the answer is to be found in the *shtetl* where the study of the Torah was an inevitable, unavoidable part of a Jewish boy's education. Not all of them, of course, became rabbis, however much their parents might wish it. But it did provide them with an intellectual training of a very special and a very formidable kind. It was a rigorous, scholastic discipline very similar to that which the medieval schoolmen, who were for ever arguing about how many angels could sit on the point of a needle, endured. The points debated by the *yeshiva* (a *yeshiva* is a rabbinical school) were equally obscure and irrelevant. Isaac Deutscher, the biographer of Stalin, who grew up in an orthodox community in Poland at the turn of the century had just such an education. To prove his fitness to become a rabbi he was, so his widow Tamara relates, asked to discuss whether the all-healing saliva of a mythical bird called the Kikiyon, which according to Jewish legend flew over the earth, spitting out its saliva only once every seventy years, was kosher or non-kosher. 'Isaac', his widow writes, 'quoted at length all that had been written on the subject before—all the commentaries, all the learned discussions that had been going on for millenia among the wisest of the wise. He showed command of his sources and a capacity to deal with the most abstruse details. His audience sat enthralled and in complete silence. They nodded their heads admiringly. Then, after a short consultation, they pronounced him, inevitably, fit and worthy to be a rabbi.' Of course one could argue, as Deutscher himself did, that this kind of barren exercise served to stunt rather than stretch the mind, cluttering it up with an agglomeration of useless learning and detail. But on the whole the virtues outweighed the disadvantages: from a very early age young Jewish boys were taught how to argue, to dissect and to analyse.

Some of these traditions had already rubbed off on the young Marks and the young Sieff but they were further strengthened by their meeting with Weizmann, who in the six years that they lived with him not only opened their eyes to the possibilities of science, but helped to clarify their own minds. 'Weizmann', says Sieff, 'had a genius for clarity of thought. He made a definite effort to achieve clarity. In our conversations we always tackled the subject from the very heart of the matter and he made us realize that we must have technical people to do the jobs we could not manage ourselves—after all we were businessmen, not scientists. He educated us in what you might call the scientific, technological and empirical attitude to life: and this very much influenced our business policy.'

Joe Lyons, whose white-and-gold teashops are every bit as much part of the national landscape as M. & S.'s hygienic emporiums, is also a Jewish family business—though the Jewish element is much less noticeable while the family is if anything even more in evidence. It is an amazingly prolific one—at the last count there were over one hundred members—and not all of them by any means have gone into the business. There are distinguished Salmons and equally distinguished Glucksteins in politics, the law, in the universities and in local government. In 1968 the family could boast of two privy councillors, seven knights, six or seven C.B.E.s, three M.P.s, the chairman of the Greater London

Council, a High Court Judge and Sir Keith Joseph, a former Tory Cabinet Minister and a fellow of All Souls who once said that being a Jew made him spark on all four cylinders. But whatever their achievements in the outside world it is the business that has provided the launching pad and which remains the family's focal point. Of the fifteen members of the Lyons board, one of the most highly paid in the country, no less than nine are Salmons, Glucksteins and Josephs; while the chairman, Geoffrey Salmon, has the distinction of being both a Salmon and a Gluckstein: his grandfather on his father's side was the original Barnett Salmon while his maternal grandfather, Isidore, was one of the four founding Glucksteins. He is a pleasant, approachable man with a rather woofly manner and a jerky way of speaking, much given to explosive bursts of laughter and fond of quoting Hilaire Belloc. In the ninety-odd years that Lyons has been in the catering business it has had ten chairmen but only one—Joe Lyons himself—has not been a Salmon or a Gluckstein.

There are similarities between M. & S. and Lyons: both are family businesses and both have grown and prospered initially by providing for the needs of the working classes. But there are also important differences. While M. & S. represents the positive virtues of the family business, so Joe Lyons has, until very recently, demonstrated the negative ones. It is a huge business: in 1969 it had a turnover of £129 million, sold 38 per cent of all ice-cream eaten in Britain, had very nearly a quarter of the frozen food market, operates a nationwide chain of teashops (currently being reduced), a string of restaurants and hotels, including such famous landmarks of Edwardian London as the now vanished Trocadero, and has interests in France, Ireland, Kenya, Luxemburg, Malawi, the Netherlands, Rhodesia, South Africa and Zambia. In its heyday its Nippies (as the public affectionately called its red-dressed waitresses) were to be found at nearly every great occasion, from Wimbledon to Buckingham Palace garden parties, handing out the strawberries and cream. In 1924 and 1925, when more than 27 million people trooped up Wembley Hill to

M

view the marvels of an already vanishing empire laid out in the turreted pavilions of the British Empire Exhibition, it was Lyons who provided both the buns and the cups of tea in the general enclosures and the cold salmon salads in the private dining-rooms; and when the Masonic Banquet was held at Olympia the following year 1,300 Nippies were on hand to serve the 8,000 guests. But in recent years much of this glory and profit has faded. Although it operates in a growth area it has not been, for all its size, a growth business. For many years, its profits rose only slowly while its return on capital, largely due to the soaring values of its properties, actually fell.

For this comparative decline the family was largely to blame, for so obsessed had they become with family mystique and family mythology that what was originally a dynamic and creative force had become hardened and fossilized into a set of unworkable and seemingly ineluctable rules and regulations. It is changing now, but until a couple of years ago it was an unwavering tradition that the oldest member of the family should automatically become chairman as of right, irrespective of his abilities; that no outside member, no matter how able, could be a full member of the board (they were called, revealingly, employee directors), and that no decision involving an expenditure of over £2,000 should be taken without the sanction of the board. All the power was concentrated in the hands of the board. Practically every operating division was supervised on a day-to-day basis by a member of the family: Mr Neil looked after the ice-cream, Mr John the tea, Mr Robin the bread and Mr Brian the catering. As they were often members of the board as well, the lines of demarcation that should exist between the board and its managers were blurred and indistinct and the whole thing became hopelessly entangled. This situation developed not because the Salmons and the Glucksteins were greedy or power-hungry but as a result of an attitude of mind. 'I have always regarded the business as a kind of extension of the family,' says Geoffrey Salmon. 'It is the family in business, as it were. In a family business the board and the family are inextricably mixed up. The managers are the directors and the directors are the managers. It's how a family business works.'

Such difficulties are common to many family businesses, but at Lyons there is another complicating factor, making the solution all the more intractable: the special traditions of the family itself, which have percolated not only the management of the family's own affairs, but that of the business as well. The Salmons and the Glucksteins arrange their affairs in a truly remarkable manner. The principle of share and share alike is common to many families (indeed it is written into the Church of England's marriage service) but the Salmons and the Glucksteins have carried it to an extreme. The family has a vast fortune (the value of the family directors' shares in the company alone totalled at least £4 million in 1969) but no member is rich in his own right. It is the family who decides how it shall be apportioned and how much each member shall have. It is no accident that those Salmons, Glucksteins and Josephs who are Lyons directors all have exactly the same number of shares: in 1969, £8,549 of ordinary voting stock. There are, it is true, minor variations in the holdings of the ordinary non-voting stock, Sir Julian Salmon having as much as £533,036 while Ivor Salmon and some others of the younger generation have only £522,176, but the general principle still seems to hold good. It is a principle that extends far beyond the mere sharing out of the money: houses, cars (the Humber Super Snipe seemed, until it was discontinued, to be the family choice) and even jewellery are distributed on much the same lines. All this has been described in a novel, called, inevitably, *The Family*, written by the novelist and actress, Yvonne Mitchell, who was, before she married, a Joseph, a cousin of Sir Keith's. And although the names have been disguised—in the novel the firm is called Appelby's and the three families, Gregory (the Glucksteins), Dance (the Salmons) and Coleman (the Josephs)—the sources of her inspiration are fairly plain. The book has not been exactly well received in the family, which naturally dislikes having the thinly disguised skeletons in the family cupboard paraded for public view. 'I don't think it was a very good book,' said Sir Louis Gluckstein who, besides being chairman of the G.L.C., administers the family's business at their weekly Wednesday meetings at his office at 166 Piccadilly, 'It is not very well written.' Outside the family the book got rather good reviews.

To check Miss Mitchell's reliability as a guide (for she had warned in her preface that a writer's world is made up of 'fact, half-truth and imagination') I went to see Mr Isidore Gluckstein, the last surviving member of the second generation, who retired in 1960 aged seventy, after five years as chairman. He now lives in a charming Tudor cottage in pastoral Hampshire, just off the Hog's Back. A huge jigsaw was lying half finished on the table by the window and after our talk I was taken to admire the roses in the garden. 'Was there', I asked, 'any truth in the story that all the family's possessions were equally shared?' 'Yes,' he said. 'Whatever comes into the directors' pockets belongs to the family; whatever you draw wherever you make it. I don't think that if I backed a horse and it came home they would ask me for the winnings—though if I was not so lucky they might repay my losses. But any money I make—if you were paying me for this interview, which you are not—would go to the family.'

Joe Lyons may be a capitalist business run by arch-exponents of the capitalist system, but the family to which they belong is the nearest approximation I can find to a soviet: all goods and chattels are shared and all decisions made communally after lengthy family discussions which only come to an end after everybody has been consulted and everybody has agreed. Sir Louis, the family historian and guardian of its records (which are kept in an imposing red leather-bound book), may preside over the family meetings, but he does so because he has proved in years of local government service to be an exceptionally able administrator; not because he is head of the family. Strictly speaking there is not one for everybody has, so I understand it, an equal voice and an equal share.

It may be a splendid and admirable way to run a family, but

when the same principles are applied to the business the disadvantages are obvious. Did they ever have rows and disagreements? I wondered. 'Oh no, listen,' said Geoffrey Salmon emphatically, 'this was a family responsibility, a family team. All major decisions were taken by members of the family. It was the accepted order of things. We were trained to take command.' Another director makes the same point, though not being a member of the family he puts it rather more sharply. 'For anything significant to happen', he says, 'it needed the approval of the whole family. And if one or two could not reach agreement, as sometimes occurred, nothing happened.' It sounds absurd and it is easy for outsiders to criticize but the weight of nearly a hundred years of tradition is not easily or lightly sloughed off. 'It has been a most traumatic experience,' says Geoffrey, pondering the changes that have overtaken the company in the last three years and which have included the introduction of a Freudian psychologist from the Tavistock Institute, the home of Freudian orthodoxy, to psychoanalyse in effect the whole company.

Traumas have, so the psychologists say, their origins in the experiences of childhood—and this is just as true of Lyons as it is of an individual. The idea that the company was a family responsibility and that everything should be pooled was born very early in Lyons's history, even before the decision was taken to go into catering. The company was created not by one man but by five: Barnett Salmon and the four Gluckstein brothers, Monty, Isidore, Joseph and Henry, the sons of a poor Jewish immigrant, born in 1821 in Rheinburg, a small town in Germany, who started as enterprising tobacco merchants in the East End, selling cut-price cigars ('The more you smoke, the more you save,' was one of their favourite slogans). They were an exceptionally united family, helped perhaps by the fact that when their father Samuel Gluckstein died in 1873, aged fifty-two, they were all still very young, the eldest, Isidore, being only twenty-two. Even before Samuel died the pooling instinct was very strong. As a boy in the East End he was extremely poor and he decided when still very young that the only way for him to prosper was, so family legend has it, for him to share all he had with his best friend. The proposition was put to the friend and it was agreed that Samuel should be the treasurer of their joint fortunes. For a few days all went splendidly, but then the friend returned and asked Samuel for his money back. 'Why?' asked Samuel, 'I thought that it was agreed that we should share it.' 'I know,' said the friend, 'but I have been thinking. If I can't trust myself, I can't trust you either.' No such doubts troubled the four Gluckstein brothers and their brother in-law, Barnett Salmon, who had married their eldest sister, Helena. Shortly after they had taken over their father's tobacco business they held a meeting at their house in the East End, where after much discussion it was agreed that the proceeds of the business should be equally divided amongst them, no one getting either more or less than any other. In short, the family would be responsible for the family whose motto was, they reminded themselves, 'Union fait la force'. It is a precept that is still religiously observed.

The story of their rise is a mixture of foresight and good fortune. The foresight was provided by Monty, the salesman of the family and a teetotaller who, travelling around the country selling his cigars, known endearingly as You-needas, came to realize that what the respectable Victorian family needed even more than his cigars was a place where they could buy a good cup of tea. In those days almost the only places of refreshment were pubs, and no Victorian father was willing to expose his wife and family to the scenes of drunkenness and depravity that were, he supposed, the features of such institutions. There were, it is true, cafés where it was possible to buy a cup of tea, but they were usually dirty and the service was indifferent: not for nothing were they known as 'slap-bangs'. And so it was that Monty, with the approval of his brothers and his brother-in-law, Barnett Salmon, went into catering with the object of providing cheap, and above all, clean establishments where non-alcoholic beverages and refreshments were sold. The first step in this direction was taken in 1888 when the Gluckstein boys took on the catering for a pavilion at the Newcastle Exhibition. It was such a success that further commissions of a similar kind followed, first in Newcastle and then in Paris, where the arrival of a whole bevy of waitresses caused a certain amount of embarrassing misunderstanding. The worldly French, though used to the idea of waitresses in hotels, found it difficult to believe that the mission of the Salmon and Gluckstein girls was as innocent as it appeared. When Mrs Isadore Gluckstein, who was in charge of the expedition, discovered what the French were thinking she was profoundly shocked and the party packed their bags and returned to England the very next day. This setback, however, was only temporary and the family went on in the next few years to open a whole chain of teashops: the first in Piccadilly, then the Trocadero, just up the road, fronting the Circus itself, and then eastwards into the City where a shop was opened in Throgmorton Street, just opposite the Stock Exchange—presumably to quench the thirst of the brokers and the jobbers.*

The good fortune came in the shape of 'Buck' Duke, the American tobacco magnate and the first of what was to prove a whole series of American invaders, intent upon taking over the fragmented and family-dominated British tobacco industry. Unlike many of his successors Duke was not successful. The Wills of Bristol and the Players of Nottingham were so alarmed by Duke's presence that they sank their differences and banded together to form what is now known as Imperial Tobacco. Salmon and Gluckstein were beneficiaries of this struggle. To fight off the Americans, the Wills and the Players needed a strong retail chain. S. & G., with its hundred or so shops up and down the country, fitted the bill perfectly and in 1901 the brothers, who by this time were becoming increasingly involved in catering, sold out to Imperial for over £100,000—a price which reflected the ardour

---

* It is a function that it is still performing. Unlike the other teashops, Throgmorton Street has never had a facelift. Its elaborate wrought-iron decoration and Art Nouveau lettering remains just as it was at the turn of the century, reflecting, as so much else in the City, a yearning for things past.

with which they were being courted by both sides. But though the price was highly attractive and the money sufficient to enable them to establish their white-and-gold shops nationwide, they did not abandon the tobacco business without much regret and foreboding. Tobacco was a respectable business while 'slap-bang' catering very definitely was not. And if there was anything that the Gluckstein boys valued above their business, it was their name—which is why the business is called J. Lyons, after one of their friends, a cheerful Irish Jew with a gift for funny stories, rather than Salmon and Gluckstein. As it turned out, however, they have had no reason to regret their decision.

All this makes it easier to understand why the process of change sweeping through Cadby Hall, the former piano factory at Olympia that is now the headquarters of the Lyons's business, is so painful. To the outsider it may not seem all that radical. The chairman and the managing director are still members of the family, as are the majority of the directors of the board; nor, apart from the lone psychologist who is there, he says, only as a catalyst to help the company understand its own workings, is there any evidence of management consultants, those visiting firemen who are apt these days to descend in extremely expensive droves at the slightest hint of trouble. The company is determined to discover its own route to salvation. The first visible signs of change occurred three years ago when, in a fit of introspection, the directors circulated to all senior members of the staff a document, marked Private and Confidential, which has since become known as 'The Fateful Green Report'. 'We are', it said, 'very ashamed of our performance: we must do something to improve it.' In companies such as Lyons disentangling cause and effect is a difficult and hazardous business, but in any event it was shortly after the circulation of The Fateful Green Report that Geoffrey Salmon was appointed chairman. 'I was', he says modestly, 'thought not to be unsuitable for the job.' At the same time a number of members of the family were quietly informed that their future in the business was not quite as rosy as they had perhaps been led to expect. In one respect Geoffrey's appointment followed the traditional pattern: he had started, like all other young Salmons and Glucksteins, first in the Trocadero ('It had the best standard of cooking and it was thought we should start off at the best place') and later in the kitchens of Cadby Hall. By the time he was twenty-four he was on his own, managing one of the company's bakeries. It was the beginning of a steady and predictable climb through the business. But in another respect Geoffrey's elevation was an important break with tradition: he is the first chairman in Lyons's history to be appointed on grounds of merit, rather than age. Since then the business has been extensively reorganized; sharp distinctions have been drawn between the functions of the board and those of management and the business consolidated into three main divisions, one for food, one for property and administration and one for catering. And three non-family men now occupy key positions; with one as food overlord, one in charge of the company's finances and one as head of personnel. Already the benefits are beginning to show in the profit and loss account. It may all sound pretty undramatic but it is what the creation of a modern corporation is all about. It would be silly to pretend that after nearly a hundred years of family rule Lyons is going to turn itself into an I.C.I. overnight, but the process has undoubtedly begun. The family has started to draw back.

Chapter Nine

The Property Game

In most of the industries in which they have become involved the Jews, as in the country at large, are in a minority; not always an inconspicuous one, but still a minority. Of property this cannot be said, however much some Jews, sensitive to the criticisms that have been heaped on the property developer's head, would like to deny it. In this field and this field alone, the Jews throughout the extraordinary boom of the last couple of decades have reigned supreme. They have, of course, not enjoyed a monopoly; some of the most successful post-war developers have been non-Jews — insurance clerks like Nigel Broakes of Trafalgar House and retailers like the late Sir Henry Price of Fifty Shilling Tailors have been particularly successful. But it remains true that the techniques and stratagems necessary to set the boom rolling were, if not invented, then carried to their logical conclusion by a small band of second-generation Jewish entrepreneurs of mainly East European origin who were fortunate enough to inherit the commercial instincts of their fathers and grandfathers. In his brilliant analysis, *The Property Boom*, Oliver Marriott calculates that between 1945 and 1965 at least 108 people made a personal fortune out of property in excess of £1 million; of that number just on 70 per cent are, by my reckoning, of Jewish origin. Through their spectacular success as property developers the names of Jack Cotton, Charles Clore and Harry Hyams have become household words

—synonymous with great wealth and entrepreneurial dash. The use of their talents has led in the last twenty years to a dramatic change in the face of Britain. In almost every town centre, and especially in London, old Victorian and, often more controversially, Georgian buildings have come tumbling down, to be replaced by shiny, anonymous, steel-and-glass office blocks of a size and height unimaginable even ten years ago. In London the changes have been particularly evident: in 1960 there were no buildings higher than St Paul's in the City of London, now in 1970 there are five and at least one more is planned. But the activity of the property developers has had more than a physical effect: mental attitudes have been altered as well. In the early years of the boom the profits made by the developers were so spectacular that staid and respectable institutions like the Church Commissioners, the pension funds and the life assurance companies, all of them large property owners, who had hitherto regarded their properties as a source not of profit but of investment income, began to realize the true size of the gold-mine on which they had so passively been sitting. Gradually, often guided by the developers, they began to develop on their own account, thus changing the face of London still further—until George Brown's office ban in 1964 brought the whole giddy process to an abrupt but, as it transpired, temporary halt.

Some of these men, like Clore and Sir Max Rayne whose career I shall discuss later, have branched out, away from property, using the cash which they acquired from their property dealing to build industrial empires whose assets are worth millions of pounds. Others like Sir Harold Samuel, who in 1969 became, with the acquisition of the huge but ailing 105-year-old City of London Real Property Company, the largest property owner in the world, and Harry Hyams have remained property men pure and simple. But in the beginning they were all entrepreneurs. 'Entrepreneur' is now a fashionable word, especially in Tory circles, used quite indiscriminately to describe anybody who displays the faintest glimmerings of business acumen, from the part-time launderette owner to the multi-millionaire tycoon. But the word has a quite precise and specific meaning. The Shorter Oxford Dictionary lists three definitions: 'the director or manager of a public musical institution'; 'one who gets up entertainments'; 'a contractor acting as an intermediary between capital and labour'. It is this third and last category, which only acquired general circulation in 1885, which perfectly describes the property developer. However entertaining the activities of these men have been, in essence the property developer is nothing more than an intermediary. Very often he has had no assets, not even owning the bricks and mortar that he created. All the property developer provides is flair, imagination and vision, leaving it to others to supply the cash, the land and the raw materials of the trade.

But why the Jews? The explanation is complicated and not immediately obvious. It is possible to argue that they prospered in retailing and tailoring because these were, for reasons that I have already explained, the main trades of the ghetto. And the subsequent success of people like Sir John Cohen, or even Sir Isaac Wolfson, can be seen as the result of the diligent application of lessons learnt in the slums of London's East End or Glasgow's Gorbals. The same argument, however, cannot be used to explain the Jews' undoubted success as property dealers. This is an activity that was, except on a very modest scale, unknown in the ghetto. In Russia and Poland the Jews were forbidden to hold land or property and even though no such barriers existed in England the immigrants were for the most part too poor, too low on the economic ladder, to consider dealing in property. It was only after a number of these rungs had been scaled that they began to look about and perceive just how wide the economic horizon really was. Nearly all the Jewish property developers are second-generation immigrants who though they may have started, like Max Rayne, in their father's workshops, could see much more clearly than their fathers the restrictions and limitations of life as a cut, make and trim tailor in the East End. To a highly intelligent and ambitious boy like Rayne, totally uninterested, he says, in his father's moderately prosperous business, the escape route was obvious. Like hundreds of others he worked during the day in the workshop but in the evenings he laid down the scissors and took up the books, attending evening classes in the hope of becoming a lawyer. 'I think one had a desire for professional qualifications,' he says. 'One has always felt that one wanted training.' Rayne was the family's eldest son and it was an ambition that his parents did much to encourage: a respect for learning has always been a feature of the traditional Jewish household—a mixture of the cultural traditions of the *shtetl* and a very strong desire for the status that goes with professional qualifications. Rayne though he studied hard never did achieve his ambition to become a lawyer, for the effort of working during the day and studying during the night proved too much for him. 'I worked during the day, went to lectures in the evening and then had to come back and do some more work, packing parcels and delivering them to the railway stations at night. Only then would I come back and write up my notes. It simply wasn't on.' Other boys in much the same situation as Rayne faced similar pressures and it is for this reason that so many of them, though they would perhaps have liked to be doctors, lawyers or architects, turned to a slightly less rigorous profession, estate agency. It was a convenient half-way house, a compromise between a fully fledged commercial career and a full-blooded professional one; an ideal profession for a boy anxious to acquire middle-class status but deprived of the opportunity, and sometimes lacking the ability, to become a paid-up professional.

A remarkable number of the 108 property millionaires started in this way; over 50 per cent according to Marriott's calculation. Jack Cotton, whose father had founded a flourishing import/export business in Birmingham and who was educated in the Jewish house of Cheltenham College, trained as an auctioneer but began with a small estate agency of his own, Cotton, Ballard and Blow, which dealt mainly in residential property and factories in and around Birmingham; Alec Colman, another Midlander and an early associate of Cotton, began with the support of the local building society manager as a seventeen-year-old estate agent in his native Tipton—an area inhabited largely by blast-furnace men and so devoid of Jews that, so Colman says, people didn't ask for the Colmans; they merely said: 'Where do the Jews live?' It was this feeling of isolation plus the opportunities of the big city that led the family, two years after Alec had opened shop, to move to Birmingham where there was an established Jewish community. But for all the activity in the provinces the real centre remained in London—and more particularly at the College of Estate Management in Lincoln's Inn Fields, whose evening classes were in the 1930s attended by an extraordinarily large proportion of today's property developers. Sir Harold Samuel, of Land Securities, Marcus Leaver of Allied Land, Felix Fenston of Metropolitan and Provincial Properties and Jack and Philip Rose of Land Investors all acquired at least some of the rudiments of their trade at the College.

As young estate agents the Samuels and the Roses had a ring-side seat. From their vantage point as young clerks in West End and suburban offices they could watch and sometimes, as far as the ethics of the profession allowed, even participate in the great property game. They saw the dramatic effect of the twin forces of inflation and demand on the price of land and property and, as they were often responsible for the mechanical side of these deals, they could hardly fail to notice just how large the profits generated were. For the ambitious lad the rewards could be high, even if he stuck to estate agency and resisted the temptation to start developing on his own. 'In 1938 as the result of deals that I negotiated', a man who has since been responsible for more new shopping centres than any other developer in Britain told me, 'I earned £2,000 for myself on commission.' Nearly every property man who went through this particular mill has similar stories to tell. 'When I was eighteen', says Jack Rose, who started as a clerk in a Baker Street estate agency, 'a man came to me, wanting to sell a shop at Rainham in Essex for £800, on which he was getting a rent of fifty pounds a year. Before I bought it I went down to

Rainham to have a look and after I had seen the shop, which had been a launderette, I went to the place next door which happened to be a hairdresser's. It was a much smarter place and while I was having my hair cut I managed to find out everything I needed to know: how prosperous the place was, how many customers he had and what rent he was paying. It turned out to be seventy-five pounds a year. That decided me. I knew that if I bought the property, spent a few pounds on fitting it out as a hairdresser's, I would have no difficulty in persuading him to move to my shop next door. I managed to buy the property and then I got a firm to fit it out as a hairdresser's shop and when it was finished I rang him up and offered him the place at slightly less than he was paying. He was delighted. So was I. The higher rent had increased the value of my shop enormously and by the time I had completed the deal I had doubled my money.' It was a small, insignificant deal but Rose had grasped early just what a potent effect demand and inflation can have on the value of a property. It was their consummate understanding of these fundamentally simple principles that was to make his and many other people's fortunes. He and his brother Philip are now between them worth some £10 million.

The choice of profession then is part of the answer; but only part. In the first place not all the Jewish developers were estate agents. Lawyers, furriers, shopkeepers and garment manufacturers also turned their hand to property dealing. For some, like solicitors who spent much of their time conveyancing, and shopkeepers, it was a natural extension of their business; for others, like Max Rayne who left the Air Force with no qualifications at all, property seemed a natural home for what little capital they had. When Rayne left the Air Force as a corporal the great office boom was still nine years away. 'I wasn't thinking so much of the profits that could be made,' he says. 'I didn't know that they existed. I think one was simply thinking of a secure investment that kept pace with the effects of inflation and really required minimal management. Investment in property did deal with the constant erosion in the value of money and property let produced a fairly safe income with minimal management.' Even before he was demobbed Rayne was taking an interest in property. Every time he got a thirty-six- or a forty-eight-hour pass, instead of going home, he would travel round the Home Counties looking for bargains. He was particularly interested in housing estates which had fallen into disrepair because of the war; though he did buy a row of such houses in Croydon his early efforts were none too successful and it was not until he almost accidentally stumbled into office development, erecting what proved to be a highly profitable deal around the new headquarters of the family business in Wigmore Street, that his career as a developer really began to blossom.

But while not all Jewish developers were estate agents, not all estate agents were Jews. Theoretically if the young Jewish clerks could spot the opportunities presented by the burgeoning housing estates of the 1930s, so too could their Gentile colleagues. But the fact remains that though many of the large West End estate agencies like Jones, Lang and Wootton, Hillier Parker May and Rowdon, and Healey and Baker were built up by enterprising Gentiles who profited in the 1930s from the insatiable hunger for property of such multiples as Marks and Spencer and Woolworths, very few of these men turned developers themselves. How can this be explained?

It is here that we enter somewhat dangerous and boggy ground. Loose generalizations about the economic activities and characteristics of the Jews have in the past been made with such disastrous consequences that a certain amount of caution is required. Nevertheless the predominance of the Jews in property is sufficiently striking to call for some comment. The Jews themselves, always an introspective people, offer a vast range of explanations, some plausible, some highly fanciful. 'Throughout our history', says Jack Rose, 'the Jews have always loved the land. It is evinced by the fact that they pushed off to Egypt 4,000 years ago. It's a pity they turned left instead of right, but then you can't think of everything.' It is an interesting theory, but I think Max Rayne's

answer is probably nearer the mark. 'Like all immigrants', he said,
'we came with very little money and our problem has always been
to create capital. Income one could, with a little luck, always earn
... but the accumulation of capital has always been a very difficult
business—certainly it was for us for we started with very little.'

Many of the developers I met have interests which are very
often depressingly one-track. Many of them, it is true, collect
pictures and raise pedigree cattle at the week-ends (Sir Harold
Samuel has a particularly fine collection of Impressionists at his
week-end farm in Sussex, and Harry Hyams has spent part of his
£30 million in acquiring Ramsbury Manor, previously the home
of Lord Rootes and one of the finest examples of Queen Anne
architecture in the country), but these interests are not reflected
during office hours. Rayne, who also collects pictures (mostly
modern) and who was knighted in 1969 for philanthropic services
(a large part of his fortune has been given away to charity), is
something of an exception. Not only has he married outside the
Jewish community and into the British aristocracy—his second
wife is Lady Jane Vane Tempest Stewart who assumed the Jewish
faith after her marriage—but his style is altogether cooler and
more analytical than many of his rivals. Nonetheless his early
steps were typical of many and it is for this reason that his name
appears so frequently in the following pages.

In a capitalist society there are many ways of accumulating
capital: the conventional route, followed by many of the immigrants, was to build up their trading businesses, ploughing back
the profits, to a point where the business was sufficiently secure
and sufficiently sound for the shares to be floated off to the public,
thus establishing an external value for the business and at the
same time giving the proprietor, always providing of course that
he retained his shares, a sizeable capital sum. But even for the
most successful the road to public status was frequently hazardous
and nearly always long. Sir John Cohen, for example, had been a
market man for thirty years before he reached this stage and Marks
and Spencer had to wait even longer—it was not until 1926, forty

N

years after Michael Marks had first set up his stall in the market place at Leeds, that the firm finally took the plunge and went public.

The young potential property developers could not or would not wait that long. They were more self-confident and better educated than their fathers and they looked around for alternatives. They did not have to look far for in a sense the answer was right under their noses—in the shape of hundreds of office blocks that were, immediately after the war, lying empty and under-used. The bombing had flattened a large number, but many of those that remained were legacies of the Victorian era, with large lobbies and high ceilings which were designed for more spacious days. At first sight, one might think, offices were the very last commodity that would appeal to a young capital-hungry entrepreneur with scarcely a penny to his name: they were often extremely expensive to run and could be even more expensive to develop. This was true enough. But what the young property men gradually began to realize (and what correspondingly the owners of the buildings, the pension funds, the life insurance companies and the trustee solicitors often failed to appreciate) was just how drastically the arithmetic of the property business, though still hedged around with the restrictions imposed by the Labour Government, had been altered by the war. In the pre-war years the price of office property had remained static for years at a time, barely fluctuating year in year out. And when war came prices dropped like a stone. Regent Street was practically deserted. 'If you had seen Regent Street before the war and then seen it during the war you would never have believed that the shops there would recover even their former value,' says a solicitor who for many years was Jack Cotton's right-hand man, negotiating many of his most important deals. 'It was a desolate sight. I let a shop for a client in Bond Street for five pounds a week during the war. When he came back in 1947 and discovered what had happened and what I had done, he issued a writ for negligence. He thought I was some sort of crook.' But immediately after the war the picture changed suddenly and dramatically. Under the impetus of the shortages created by the bombing and the release of the pent-up demand as firms and shopkeepers began to return to the capital, prices began to rise astronomically. Suddenly everybody wanted property and the rents began to reflect the demand. And as rents rose, so naturally did the value of the property. It was a phenomenon that was not confined to offices: houses benefited too, as Alec Colman discovered. At the outbreak of war the houses that he was building on the estates round Birmingham were worth perhaps £300 a piece; throughout the war they stood empty, and Colman was only saved from bankruptcy by the help of a friendly building society manager. But when eventually peace came Colman discovered to his delight that the houses he had nursed through the war had more than tripled in value.

The effect of rising prices on offices was more complicated — but more dramatic. Of the hundreds of similar deals that were being done at that time, let us take just one example which illustrates the general principle. The development boom did not really take off until 1954 when building restrictions were removed, but the basic arithmetic remained the same throughout the post-war period. It was in 1947, after the abortive experiment with the housing estate in Croydon, that the beauties of office development first began to dawn on Max Rayne. His father had taken a twenty-one-year lease on a small building in Wigmore Street as a new home for the tailoring business. At first they thought that it was just what they needed, but they later discovered that the rooms were so small that only the ground floor and the basement were suitable for the operations they had in mind; the remaining four floors were, as far as they were concerned, quite useless. At the time it looked like a setback but as it turned out it was very fortunate, for it set Max Rayne thinking hard about how to put the building to best use. Some of the floors were occupied by tenants and, as their leases expired, Rayne came to realize just how high rents in the area had risen. It put an entirely new complexion on the deal. Rayne now realized that in fact he had a bargain, for the new rents that were coming in more than covered his father's outgoings: they were in effect occupying the building for nothing. This was a happy position to be in and many men would at this point have simply sat back and enjoyed it. But it still did not solve Rayne's need for capital. 'I had developed', he explains, 'an investment which was showing a very substantial revenue surplus but still did not give us any money.' And because his father's lease was so short, there was not much hope of getting any either. Rayne and his father counted up their savings and tried to cut this knot by making an offer for the freehold but the trustees, conscious that they were the appointed guardians of their client's investment and anxious not to lose the income that the property was producing, refused. Rayne was not to be put off, however. 'I used to lie awake at nights thinking how I could overcome this obstacle,' he says. 'And it suddenly occurred to me that if they wanted income and we certainly did not want to part with the capital, the answer might be to offer them a higher rent and see if one could get a long lease.' This is exactly what Rayne did. It did not really matter very much to him whether he got the freehold or a long lease: provided it was long enough it was just as easy to raise money on a leasehold as it was on a freehold. The upshot was that Rayne got a fifty-year lease ('The lawyer was very excited, he thought it was a marvellous deal for his clients') which he immediately took round to the bank, who were delighted to lend him £14,000 on its security. As a result of this essentially very simple manœuvre Rayne now had, thanks to his own acumen and the beneficial workings of inflation (which is often not quite the monster that economists make out), a fifty-year lease, a substantial income from the surplus floors which was more than enough to repay the loan, and the capital which he had been trying so hard to acquire. Admittedly £14,000 was not the £12 million Rayne subsequently made out of property, but it is fair to say that without it he would never have got there.

Raising money on a long lease was one way of generating capital but it was only the first, comparatively crude step. Strictly speaking, as it involved no physical change to the building, it was not even development. It was only when the developer succeeded in changing the nature of the asset from something which seemed worthless into something that was evidently desirable that the money really began to gush. Often the whole building had to be pulled down and rebuilt—always a costly exercise. But sometimes the necessary transformation could be accomplished with an astonishingly small outlay—as Sir Harold Samuel discovered. In 1946 he acquired the Regent Street Arcade, which ran from just by Oxford Circus to Argyll Street, next to the Palladium. It was not a very prepossessing purchase: the shops were shabby and the offices above were under-used and partially empty. Samuel was not content to leave the arcade as he found it. By closing off the ends and by installing a grand entrance giving out into Oxford Street he entirely altered the character of the site. The stratagem proved successful. Within a week he had rented the refitted offices for £100,000 to the Bank of England, who needed more space for an army of clerks, recruited to hand out Government bonds to the owners of the shares of the steel companies which the Labour Government was in the process of nationalizing. As he had only paid £250,000 for the Crown lease, the couple of thousand he had laid out to modernize the buildings was obviously money well spent.

But a need for capital, which is after all common to all immigrants of whatever race and nationality, was not the sole motive force behind the activity of the Jews in the property market throughout the 'fifties and early 'sixties. Combined with this hunger for capital there is, I would suggest, another trait which has emerged as the result of their centuries-long sojourn in the market place: an almost instinctive feeling, most noticeable in the East European generation of immigrants, for the market value of any article whether it be a pair of bootlaces or a multi-million pound office block. 'We have been forced to work on tiny margins,' said Jack Rose, 'and this has sharpened our skills as valuers. We have had to work to the last penny; to calculate how much an article is worth and how much it can be sold for. We are the best valuers. We are not so interested in how it is made but we are very interested in how much it is worth; how much it can be sold for.' At the risk of being accused of perpetuating the stereotype I think there is a lot in this; at least as far as the property developers, in whose minds the memories of the East End are still very fresh, are concerned.

It is not so easy as it sounds to see the profit in property. It often involves a good deal of imagination, foresight and simple guesswork, for the real value of an office block is usually gauged not by its worth at the time it is purchased but what it will fetch in five or even ten years' time. Crystal ball gazing is always a dangerous exercise, but in this case it is made even more difficult (and risky) by the multiplicity of factors involved. Rents which ultimately determine the value of a commercial building are a notoriously sensitive economic indicator which respond quickly and often violently to the general economic climate; to the level of demand; to the Government's and, often more importantly, to the local authorities' own plans. A new motorway or the decision to build, or not to build, a new town can have drastic effects, for good or ill, on the area concerned. But for those who were prepared to take the risks, to gamble on their judgment, the rewards in this post-war period were frequently considerable.

That they were not reaped by the existing post-war owners was, I think, largely the result of an attitude of mind. The insurance fund managers and the trustee solicitors were, like the chartered surveyors who advised them, for the most part conservative folk who looked at property through spectacles that were coloured by pre-war experience. The solicitors who sold Max Rayne his fifty-year lease did not regard the Wigmore Street block as a commodity that was to be bought and sold but as an investment that would produce a safe and steady return for their clients. And consequently they failed to appreciate just how valuable their property had suddenly become. The City of London Real Property Company, which in 1969 became the focus of a strenuously

contested takeover battle, in which Sir Harold Samuel's Land
Securities eventually emerged victorious, is just such an example
of commercial short-sightedness. Its origins were opportunistic
enough. It was the creation in 1864 of two brothers, James and
John Innes, who were shrewd enough to invest the fortune that
they had made out of the West Indian sugar trade (an activity in
which incidentally the Jews were heavily involved in the eighteenth century—it was sugar that was the foundation of the
Henriques family fortune) in property in the City of London.
By 1914 they had built up a portfolio worth £2½ million, consisting
almost entirely of tall Victorian offices that were crammed into
the few hundred yards that separates the Tower of London from
the Bank of England. They owned a sizeable chunk of the most
valuable tract of commercial property in the country and were
landlords to more stockbrokers, shipbrokers and insurance men
than any other group in Britain.

By rights they should have been sitting on a gold-mine, whose
value was enormously enhanced by the war. The Blitz was in a
sense the best thing that could have happened to C.L.R.P.; their
buildings were so densely packed that one-third of their portfolio
was destroyed in a single night. But the opportunity was largely
missed. The property was redeveloped all right. But instead of
letting them out on short leases, studded with break clauses which
would have enabled them to raise the rents at frequent intervals,
thus keeping pace with inflation, C.L.R.P., which was administered largely by practitioners of the old school, retained its pre-
war policy—initially letting out its buildings on longish leases
with no break clauses. In 1969 C.L.R.P. paid the price for this
mistake. The shortage of office space in central London had been
aggravated by George Brown's clampdown in 1964, driving the
price of existing offices sky high. The value of C.L.R.P.'s portfolio
reflected this trend. In three years their assets rose by 120 per cent
to a truly impressive £220 million. On paper C.L.R.P. was worth
a good £18 million more than that of its attacking rival, Land
Securities. But it was nothing like as productive. Because the rents

had been fixed when the long leases were first assigned ten or twenty years before, earnings had failed to keep pace and the shareholders began to get restive. At the same time Corporation Tax, introduced in 1965, and rising interest rates, had dealt property developers, who all rely on high capital profits and a rising rent roll to offset their interest charges, a number of body blows. And as the C.L.R.P. share price fell, the company became vulnerable—attracting first the attention of Nigel Broakes and then Sir Harold Samuel.

C.L.R.P. is not an isolated exception. Other institutions like British Rail, whose central London terminals are ideal locations for office development, and many of the charities, have through a mixture of bureaucratic caution and muddle also missed the property boat. The new Euston Station may be a very fine example of twentieth-century railway architecture, but commercially it would have been a good deal more impressive had a twenty-storey office block been sited, as was originally intended, on top of its flat roof. The towering skyscrapers of Joe Levy's Euston Centre which dominate the station provide an illustration, modelled in steel and concrete, of just how badly British Rail has been left behind.

Not all the institutions have been so laggardly. Some, like the Church Commissioners, have been taken in hand by the developers and taught to taste the joys of property development for themselves—to the mutual advantage and profit of both parties. No developer has done more to educate the institutions than Max Rayne, whose alliance with the Church Commissioners has proved to be one of the foundation stones of his career. The Church Commissioners are probably Britain's largest landlord: in 1967, when they were last revalued, their property assets amounted to £45 million. In 1955 the Church Commissioners announced that Eastbourne Terrace, a vast cliff of Victorian flats and small one-night hotels which they had owned for many years and which had fallen into disrepair, was for sale. Tenders were invited. Rayne heard of the proposed sale through a contact in the Norwich

Union and as soon as he got the details he began to work out his own sums. 'I looked at the spot and I thought "Here's Paddington Station and here's Mayfair, not a stone's throw away"—it should be very valuable. Bearing all this in mind I produced what I thought was a proper valuation for the redeveloped site at a rather conservative predicted rental of ten shillings a square foot. And when I had done the sums I looked at them and said "Well, that's very interesting. What I can't understand is why the Commissioners should want to sell it. They must be absolutely mad." ' To cut a long story short, Rayne eventually persuaded the Commissioners to keep the site and, with his help, to redevelop it. The subsequent rebuilding of the site, at a cost of £1¾ million, so enhanced the value of the buildings that by 1966 the joint company which Rayne had formed with the Commissioners to finance and supervise the work had made a profit of £5·8 million—half going to the Commissioners who had put up all but a £1,000 of the money and half to Rayne whose idea it was in the first place.

In retrospect it all sounds absurdly easy. If it was so obvious to the developers, why was everybody not doing it? As I said earlier it all comes back, in my view, to an attitude of mind, conditioned by historical experience. Most of the developers grew up in an entirely different atmosphere, subject to much fiercer pressures. They were ambitious men, eager for capital gain, and unencumbered by a stifling weight of tradition. They felt none of the mystique which the middle classes had invested in bricks and mortar. For the Jews it was simply another commodity whose profit potential had hitherto lain largely unrecognized. And it just so happened that because of a chain of historical and social accidents they emerged on the scene at the very moment when the property market was undergoing one of the most violent transformations in its history. This was not, however, the only factor: like all entrepreneurs they were willing to take risks.

The Jews have, as innumerable studies have demonstrated, probably fewer of the conventional vices than most people. The social workers combing the East End in 1890s invariably reported that cases of drunkenness, illegitimacy, adultery, divorce, prostitution and thieving were rarely found among the Jewish immigrants, whose family life was for the most part exemplary. But they were, so the same social workers said, extremely fond of gambling. And it is this gambling instinct that partially explains the developers' success. The property business now has a very solid, institutional look about it; many of the original entrepreneurs have, as they became older and profit more hard to come by, sold up and departed. Much of the business is now in the hands of anonymous insurance companies or in massive agglomerations like Land Securities. But in the beginning property was a highly speculative commodity, fraught with uncertainty and risk. The early property developers were in effect gambling; an activity made all the more exciting by the fact that they were using other people's money. Any number of things could go wrong: the expected demand could fail to materialize; the carefully nurtured tenant on whose income the developer depended could at the last minute change his mind or the equally carefully nurtured local authority could, if the borough's planning officer was feeling liverish that day, refuse the essential planning permission. And any one of these eventualities could spell disaster, threatening the whole elaborately constructed edifice with collapse. This is what very nearly happened to Max Rayne. In 1951 he had already embarked on the most ambitious project he had so far undertaken: the redevelopment of a large block which belonged to Selfridges and which stood at the back of the store in Baker Street. All the bricks had been assembled. He had backing—£1 million from the Norwich Union—a tenant in the shape of Marks and Spencer, which had outgrown its original Baker Street headquarters, and a building licence—an essential prerequisite in those restrictive days and only granted to a developer when he could prove that he had a tenant lined up. But at the eleventh hour disaster struck: Marks and Spencer had decided that they wanted something bigger and immediately the bricks began to crumble. No tenant, no building licence; no building licence, no £1 million. But Rayne had already agreed to buy the site and was committed. 'I had a commitment to put up a large and expensive building. I had no tenant and no building finance; I didn't even have the money to pay the ground rent,' he said. Rayne was rescued from this uncomfortable hole by another property company which was sufficiently convinced by his figuring to agree to take a 37½ per cent stake in the project—and with this support it proved not too difficult to persuade the Midland Bank to advance the necessary cash, even though they still had to find a tenant. In the event the deal went through and Rayne made a profit of £850,000.

Rayne denies either that he was taking a risk or that he was lucky to emerge unscathed. 'There was nothing speculative about it,' he maintains. 'The calculations on which I had gone into the thing were such that they convinced not only me but several other people as well that it was worth going ahead with. The deal was inherently sound and my view was that it couldn't come to any great harm.' Maybe not. Rayne is not the kind of man who gives the impression that he skimps his homework. But even though the odds were, as it proved, stacked in his favour, he was still gambling—gambling on his judgment that prices would rise sufficiently in the near future to show him a handsome profit.

The property developers may have been gamblers but the best of them were by no means wild or indiscriminate ones. Like all good punters they tried hard to minimize the risks by paying close and expert attention to the form. It is noticeable that the most successful developers, in their early years at least, specialized; sticking to those areas and types of property they knew well and ignoring those they did not. That there was no magic formula is indicated by the fact that whenever they strayed off the beaten path their efforts were not usually crowned with success. Jack Cotton is a case in point. His first venture in America was the giant Pan Am building which towers above Grand Central Station in New York, dominating Park Avenue. The difficulty this development encountered was one of the many reasons for the sad decline of his joint company with Charles Clore, City Centre Properties (it has now been swallowed up by the ubiquitous Sir Harold Samuel). Many companies, including Land Securities, have reason to regret the headlong dash that they made into Canadian property in the late 'fifties. Nor have similar adventures in America and Australia yielded quite the dividends that their promoters were hoping for. The pioneers, like Samuel and Rayne, prospered initially because they made it their business to find out more about the property in their chosen field than anybody else. For many years the majority of Rayne's deals involved buildings which were not more than two miles at the most from his Wigmore Street office, most of them north of Oxford Street, at that time a most unfashionable district as far as offices were concerned. For a business with such a reputation for hard-headedness, property contains a surprising element of fashion. To a certain extent they all play follow-my-leader and it is not until one big firm has made the move that the others summon up enough courage to follow. Sir Harold Samuel in the days immediately after the war operated on a larger canvas than Rayne, but the principle was the same. The Samuel strategy was simplicity itself. 'He drew a line from Marble Arch to the Aldgate Pump, reckoning that was the main trading route and that anything he bought along that line would be all right. He walked along Oxford Street looking at the names of the companies that owned the properties; it was all quite simple: they were all written up on plaques. Mostly they were old City companies whose shares were standing way below their asset value because nobody, including them, realized what they were sitting on,' says a man who has followed Samuel's career closely.

Because property was in those days such a personal business, an intimate knowledge of individual properties was one of the developers' greatest assets. Some of the best developers have, after twenty years in the game, become walking encyclopaedias — mines of information about almost any property in London you

care to name. When I went to see Jack Rose in the summer of
1969 I was treated, quite by accident, to just such a display of
virtuosity. When I was shown into his office he was in the middle
of a telephone conversation with a man from the Irish Pig and
Fatstock Marketing Board who thinking, quite mistakenly, that
Rose owned his building had rung up to complain about the
window sashes—which, he said, were sticking. 'Hang on a
moment,' said Jack Rose, 'where did you say you were—3 to 4
Great Marlborough Street? I know where that is. If my memory
serves me correctly you are right on the corner where Poland
Street goes across.' The voice at the other end of the telephone
confirmed that that was indeed where he was speaking from. 'Ah,'
said Jack Rose, a broad grin spreading across his face. 'I don't
think that's one of mine you know. I'll think you will find that the
building is owned by Land Securities. But I'll tell you what I'll do.
You send me the deeds and I'll mend your window sashes— all
right?' There was a polite public school burble at the other end
and the conversation ended in chuckles.

Jack Rose's knowledge is probably more extensive than most,
but many of the professional developers could put on a similar
performance if necessary. Some, like Louis Freedman of Raven-
seft, the shop group which is now part of Harold Samuel's
empire, acquired their knowledge during the war, using forty-
eight-hour passes from the R.A.F. to inspect cities like Plymouth
which had been flattened by the German bombers. He was
appalled at the disaster but not so stunned that he failed to
notice hardly any of the shops remained standing. Others,
like Max Rayne, began quite simply by investigating their own
patch.

It was these skills, deployed over the last twenty years, that have
enabled the developers to establish their supremacy in such spectacular fashion. They were not geniuses, they were not, once
removed from the arena which they had come to know so well,
even particularly infallible businessmen, as the variegated fortunes
of Charles Clore's Sears Holdings and Max Rayne's London

Merchant Securities would seem to indicate. Their particular aptitudes happened quite by accident to coincide with a situation in which they were allowed to exercise those aptitudes to a quite remarkable degree.

Chapter Ten

The Business of Charity

> 'It's like a platoon of Lewis guns that do not fire straight
> ahead but at an angle, so that nothing in the field of fire
> should be missed. If you are a Jew in Leeds it's very hard
> to escape giving.'
>
> a leader of the Leeds Jewish community
on fund raising.

> 'Charity saves from death.'
>
> an old Jewish proverb.

If gambling is the most conspicuous of the Jewish vices, then
philanthropy is the most noticeable of their virtues. The Jews are
by any standards an extraordinarily generous people. And much
of this generosity is, as one would expect, devoted to looking
after their own. For the most part, the Jewish poor, young and
old, are exceptionally well catered for. In every town in Britain
where Jews are to be found in any numbers they have gone to
great lengths to plug the gaps left by the Welfare State and to erect
an impressive superstructure of voluntary services: in the East
End and elsewhere Jewish youth clubs, old people's homes, meals
on wheels and hospitals have proliferated. In London, the home
of 60 per cent of Britain's 400,000 Jews, there are at a rough count
34 such institutions and in Leeds, that stronghold of provincial
Jewry, there are no less than 120 separate organizations all

devoted in one form or another to the promotion of Jewish welfare. In many fields the Jews have led the way: the Jewish Board of Guardians (now the Jewish Welfare Board), founded by a group of altruistic businessmen, was one of the first voluntary bodies to ease the rigours of the Victorian Poor Law, and it was these same Jewish businessmen who saw very early the need for youth clubs and recreational centres in the East End to brighten and widen the drab lives of the immigrants. In 1896 the Henriques family founded the Brady Club where the widow of Sir Basil Henriques, himself a famous East End magistrate, still lives and works; Bernhard Baron, the tobacco millionaire and founder of the Baron Cigarette Machine Company (which later became Carreras) had already given away over £1 million—part of which went to establish the Bernhard Baron Settlement; and in 1901 a group of philanthropists led by Sir Bernard Waley-Cohen followed suit, setting up in the Commercial Victoria Club on the site of a working man's café known as the 'Tee Too Tum'.

The need is no longer so pressing but the institutions still remain: the soup kitchens of the 1890s have become the suppliers of kosher meals on wheels for those who have been left behind. Not all the immigrants by any means have succeeded in clambering out of the ghetto. Behind the aggressively commercial façade of the Whitechapel High Street there are still crumbling Victorian blocks and mean, jerry-built two-storey houses which are the homes of the Jewish poor. Their children may live in smart semi-detacheds in Ilford, Wembley or Edgware but their parents, the garment workers and the furriers of the ghetto, still remain. In some ways their plight is worse than it was fifty years ago, for they have lost that mutual support that was such a feature of ghetto life. 'As far as Jewry is concerned', says Phyllis Gerson of the Stepney Jewish Girls' Club, which provides a meals on wheels service for the entire East End, 'we are inundated with problem families.' Some of the old people serviced by the club are isolated because they are sick; their lungs affected by fine particles of fur which have penetrated their lungs in the course of a lifetime of fur cutting and dressing in the workshops along Upper Thames Street. Others are isolated because in their old age they have forgotten all their English and reverted to Yiddish—and there are few enough Jews in Britain, let alone the East End, who can speak that language now.

The Jewish middle classes have always recognized and responded to the plight of their poor. And this remains as true today as it was in the days of Lady Rothschild's Four Per Cent Industrial Dwelling Company or the Lord Mayor's Mansion House Fund of 1882. Most of Phyllis Gerson's helpers seemed to be either student teachers on holiday or retired businessmen from well-to-do middle-class suburbs like Wembley, Finchley and the Hampstead Garden Suburb. One morning in the early spring of 1969 I did the rounds in Stepney with Sol Rubin, a small neat man of sixty-eight who wore a carnation in his buttonhole and who turned out to be a retired shoe manufacturer with a factory employing 300 people in Bethnal Green. 'I'm still called the managing director but it is my twenty-nine-year-old son who does all the work.' Watched by two girls from the hairdresser's shop opposite the club, we packed the metal boxes containing some dozen lunches and some hydrangeas from the garden of Rubin's house in the Hampstead Garden Suburb into the boot of his Rover 2000 and set off down Whitechapel Road. For Rubin this was a regular routine, for he made the twenty-minute journey from the Suburb to the East End most mornings. His handing out of the lunches was decidedly brisk—idle chat was not encouraged. We started out at eleven o'clock and were back again at eleven forty-five. In that three-quarters of an hour we had visited a good cross-section of East End housing—and East End Jews: everything from dark, damp, two-room apartments in The Buildings to bright, modern council flats, and everybody from lonely, broken-down furriers to cheerful, tea-making Mums. Half-way through, Rubin lit a large cigar. Together with the carnation and the Rover, it lent a bizarre touch to the morning's excursion, but if Rubin was aware of the oddity he made no mention of it.

o

Providing help and comfort for the Jewish poor is a continuing preoccupation stretching back through the voluntary organizations, the Welfare Board and the synagogues for a couple of hundred years or possibly longer. The concern is genuine, the help considerable, but like all voluntary efforts and despite the co-ordinating influence of the Welfare Board it tends to be a little patchy and haphazard. But while it still goes on some of the enthusiasm — and some of the money — has been diverted into an entirely new channel which was opened up by the creation of the State of Israel in 1948, which in turn has led to the establishment of what its critics call the Zionist machine. There is nothing haphazard or amateur about the Joint Palestine Appeal which is the main instrument of British Jewry's fund raising efforts for Israel. It is, as one would expect from an organization dominated by Marks and Spencer, a most professional concern. 'They run it like an extension of their own business, never using two men when one will do,' says one insider. The J.P.A., as it is universally called, is housed in an office block in Lower Regent Street and the exterior is not impressive. Like practically every other official Jewish institution I visited, Rex House is remarkable for its shabbiness and air of general improvisation. At ten o'clock one morning I passed a man solemnly sitting at his desk in the lobby conducting what sounded like a rather confidential interview with a visitor. The desk was just opposite the commissionaire and not six feet from the main door into Lower Regent Street through which people were constantly coming and going.

But appearances are deceptive. The J.P.A., originally the United Palestine Appeal, was founded in 1942 with the amalgamation of the Palestine Appeal and the Jewish National Fund which now exists in another form. At first sight it would seem to be a rather top-heavy organization. It has four honorary presidents, one president, one chairman, one deputy chairman, two vice-chairmen and ninety-three vice-presidents. Together they are a roll-call of the middle-class Jewish Establishment which has now taken over the leadership of the community from the older, more patriarchal aristocratic families, who though they often support the Zionist cause play little if any part in the affairs of the J.P.A. In fact the J.P.A. is not quite as top-heavy as it looks, for not all its members are active and a place on the notepaper is more an identity badge than anything else. The real administrative work of the J.P.A. is done by a handful of businessmen, led by the Sieffs of Marks and Spencer; its director Lavy Bakstansky was the first Jewish president of the London School of Economics debating society and is married to a professional ballroom dancer who in the week after the Six Day War ran dancing lessons for Israel. The real, grassroots fund raising work, however, is done not at Rex House but in the field. Supervised by head office in London and by branch offices in Glasgow, Birmingham and Leeds is a veritable army of some 3,000 to 4,000 voluntary workers all organized into some 250 committees which are centred either round their trade or the area in which they live. Any trade in which there is a significant number of Jews has been organized into a committee: there are committees for bankers, chemists, costume jewellers, diamond workers and jewellers, doctors and dentists, the food trade, the fruit and vegetable business, the fur trade, furniture and timber, hotel and catering, metal, millinery, property, sportsmen (this is a J.P.A. euphemism for bookmakers), shoes, textiles and 'the knights of the toy and gift trades'. And for anybody left over there is the president's committee and the central list, which contains, so Bakstansky explained, a large number of the friends of Marks and Spencer. Each committee has its own hierarchy of presidents, vice-presidents, chairmen, etc., who report either direct to Bakstansky or to one of his dozen helpers who keep a watchful eye over their allotted committees. Not all the committees are equally effective, though the differences in the sums raised also reflect the economic and occupational distribution of the Jewish population. It is perhaps to be expected that the rag trade would provide a large part of the money: in 1967, if one includes the president's list, they contributed over £600,000—between one-quarter and one-third of the total. The bankers and the doctors are perhaps less generous though nothing like as numerous: between them they produced just over £17,000. The disparity is, I think, revealing for it indicates that the main weight of Zionist support comes not from the old-established assimilated families, or from the young professionals, but from the second generation of self-made businessmen for whom Israel has, for reasons that I shall try to explain later, a particularly powerful appeal.

All this goes on as a matter of routine, year in, year out. The J.P.A. fund raising dinners have for many Jews become just as much part of the Jewish calender as *Yom Kippur* (The Day of Atonement) or *Rosh Hashanhah* (The Jewish New Year). But at the beginning of June 1967 this routine was sharply and dramatically interrupted by the outbreak of the Six Day War. The response of British Jewry to the crisis which they saw as threatening not only the lives of the Israelis but also, in a more complicated way, their own existence, was immediate and dramatic. Stories are still told of the extravagant and selfless gestures that were made by Jews (and some non-Jews too) at that time. How a weeping girl, in tears because she had nothing to give, arrived at a synagogue in Kenton and handed in her engagement ring; how many families raised money by mortgaging their houses; and how businessmen left their businesses for weeks at a time to help with the fund raising. In a little over two months the 400,000 odd members of British Jewry raised a total of some £16 million. It was an astonishing achievement, especially when one remembers that the American Jewry, some 5½ million strong, contributed only £40 to £50 million—proportionally a much smaller amount. That the British response was so overwhelming was of course largely the result of the spontaneous reaction of a large section of British Jewry; it is estimated that one out of every two families contributed. But some of the credit must go to the J.P.A., for without its efficient organization some of the impact would undoubtedly have been lost. The emergency campaign of 1967 saw the J.P.A. machine at its most effective.

The wheels began to turn before the war had broken out. On May 24th many of the leaders of the J.P.A. met at Lady Marks's house in Grosvenor Square for what was, as they thought, a normal campaign meeting. The guest speaker was Sir Alec Douglas-Home. He had been to Israel recently and they were anxious to hear what he thought of a situation that was, with the closing of the Straits of Tiran by President Nasser only days before, beginning to look increasingly menacing. It was at this meeting that they decided that things looked so black that an emergency campaign for Israel should be started immediately. The meeting was on a Friday and that week-end the J.P.A. officials at Rex House worked overtime, combing their registers for the names and addresses of the 'big givers' to whom they then sent telegrams summoning them to a meeting the following Tuesday in the big room on the top floor of Marks and Spencer's headquarters in Baker Street. There were two meetings at St Michael House that day: the first, held at three o'clock in the afternoon was for a carefully selected group of people—the big guns of British Jewry, the older families as well as the middle-class millionaires. Among those who came were Lord Rothschild, the Goldsmids, the Djanoglys of Nottingham Manufacturing, the textile group which is one of M. & S.'s biggest suppliers, Sir Isaac Wolfson and, of course, Lord Sieff. The atmosphere, according to those who were there, was already electric, but a further charge was added when Lord Rothschild or his representative (accounts vary) stood up at the beginning of the meeting and said, quite simply: 'You can count me in for £1 million, payable in cash within seven days.' Everybody was taken aback—not least the organizers who up until that moment had been thinking in terms of a *total* of £2 million. 'It was this meeting', one of the organizers told me, 'that set the tone and the level of the campaign.' The second meeting at St Michael House which was held at five-thirty was less exciting but much larger—about 400 to 500 people came. 'A lot of people went to the meeting not knowing what it was all about and thinking that it was just another appeal.

But when they heard what had happened at the earlier meeting, the atmosphere changed abruptly.'

While all this was going on, telegrams continued to pour out of Rex House summoning as many J.P.A. supporters as they could trace to meetings in synagogues up and down the country. This was a departure from normal practice; the synagogues are not usually used for fund raising meetings. 'We wanted to impress people with the urgency of the situation,' says Cyril Stein, the young managing director of Ladbrokes, the famous bookmakers, who played a leading part in organizing the emergency campaign. Apparently people were impressed, for on that Wednesday evening some 2,500 people turned up to hear what the J.P.A. speakers had to say. 'We ran fund raising like it had never been run before,' says Stein. 'We told them that we were raising money not to support arms but to take responsibility for essential services like hospitals and schools. We told them that the people in Tel Aviv were within ten minutes' flying time from the air raids. "If you have thousands, give thousands, if you have only pennies, give pennies," we said.' Not all the fund raisers were professionals, they were not even all committed businessmen. Everybody was involved, even the schoolchildren. According to the *Jewish Chronicle*, which until the total became embarrassingly large published detailed progress reports of the campaign, the girls of the Henrietta Barnett School in the Hampstead Garden Suburb raised money by organizing a class-by-class canvass and one girl even visited the Wentworth Golf Club where she found Bob Hope and Bing Crosby playing a friendly round. She told them of the school's drive for Israel and returned triumphant, clutching a handful of notes. Support from the world of show biz was particularly strong. At a meeting at the Café Royal attended by 450 performers, managers, agents and executives £300,000 was raised within an hour; the Grades of the Grade Organization and Associated Television gave £40,000; the Bernsteins of Granada Television gave £35,000.

'It was', says Maurice Edelman who was there, 'a miracle of

almost Biblical proportions.' Almost the only body in the community that did not contribute was the United Synagogue—not
only was it prevented by its constitution from doing so but at the
time it had an overdraft of £800,000. By June 9th, one day before
the war ended, the J.P.A.'s emergency fund stood at £6 million;
to which Manchester had contributed £350,000 the Hampstead
Garden Suburb £200,000, Edgware £60,000, Edinburgh nearly
£30,000—a sum sixty-seven times greater than its usual total—
and the Coombe Hill Golf Club £70,000. But even after the guns
had stopped firing the enthusiasm did not die away. Money continued to roll in and a public relations firm, Voice and Vision,
one of whose directors, Moss Murray, is an ardent Zionist, was
retained with a brief to keep things on the boil. Apart from producing some 10,000 car stickers which read 'STOP NASSER NOW'—a
slogan designed to appeal to Jews and non-Jews alike—Voice and
Vision's main contribution was the production of a large, 320-page
book called *Six Days in June* and designed to commemorate the
war. It contained one or two specially written feature articles, but
for the most part it was made up of nothing but advertisements—
thus giving Jewish businessmen a further opportunity to demonstrate their loyalty. This too was a classic fund-raising device. One
of the most noticeable features of the J.P.A. Year Book is the
large number of advertisements that it contains, all grouped under
the relevant trades. As each page in *Six Days in June* cost £500 it
was potentially a most effective fund raising instrument. Originally it was intended to include a number of pages printed on
golden paper; these Golden Pages, as they were called, cost
£1,000. Because of technical difficulties the Golden Pages never
materialized and the advertisers had to be content with a thin gold
line around the border of the page. The price, however, remained fixed at £1,000. By the following January when the book
finally appeared, ready for distribution to the 70,000 people who
had contributed to the war campaign, another £200,000 had been
gathered in.

*

However fascinating the mechanics of Jewish philanthropy may be, the really interesting and fundamental question remains. Why is it so widespread and so successful? What is it that drives the Jews to give out of all proportion to their numbers and in some cases out of all proportion to their wealth? As many of them are businessmen the community's average income is probably a little higher, but not very much, than the norm. But it does not explain their generosity, which in the case of Sir Isaac Wolfson and Sir Max Rayne, both of whom have set up charitable foundations, has been on a scale matching that of their businesses. The Wolfson Foundation, run by a genial ex-major general called Ray Leakey, has assets of roughly £40 million (any estimate must be approximate as the main assets are in the form of Great Universal Stores shares and the value of these naturally fluctuates) and an annual income of £1·5 million, making it the second richest foundation in the country. Only the Wellcome Trust is larger, with an income in 1969 of £1·75 million. Since its establishment in 1955, the Wolfson Foundation has given away over £15 million, with another £2 million in the pipeline but not yet allocated. Only a relatively small proportion of the money goes to Jewish causes; the bulk of it is reserved for education, health, social welfare and the arts—in roughly that order. In the last nineteen years the Wolfson Foundation has set up one entirely new Oxford College, named after its benefactor, has supported another fifteen university colleges and institutions in this country (where the bias has been towards the older universities), in Africa and the West Indies; has helped nineteen hospitals and has supported a whole host of other activities from the Leaf Protein project at the Rothhampstead Agricultural Experimental Station to setting up a baby clinic in Dar es Salaam. The Rayne Foundation is smaller but run on very similar lines. And though only about 8 per cent of its income goes to the arts it is best known for its much publicized purchase for the National Gallery of Cézanne's 'Les Grandes Baigneuses'; a patriotic act which cost the foundation £750,000 and which, so its secretary Air Commodore

Milligan says, 'brought in a shoal of rude letters from all over the world'.

There are of course important tax advantages in transferring the ownership of a business to such a foundation. The owner loses much of his capital but by means of ingenious juggling, using preference shares, it is still quite possible, as Max Rayne explained to me, to retain both control of the business and much of its income. To suggest that this is the main reason why Sir Isaac and Sir Max have set up foundations would be both inaccurate and uncharitable. But when these and other businessmen are asked why they give so much, so frequently their answers are not very revealing. They provide the answers that one would expect from any rich man with a vestige of a social conscience who realizes that he has been clever enough, or lucky enough, to create more wealth than even the most profligate can hope to consume. 'Let's face it,' said Arnold Ziff, a Leeds businessman who besides building up the Stylo shoe business has made a fortune out of property on the side, 'I have a nice house, a wife and children ... I don't have a house in the country or a house in the Bahamas. I may take the wife to the South of France for a week but when the family go on holiday we go to Bournemouth or Blackpool. I really haven't anything else to spend my money on. I only need three meals a day ... In fact if I eat more than two my figure suffers so ... ' Another property man put it this way: 'One day I woke up and found that I was living at a certain rate that my present income after tax and investments would keep me very much the way I am living now until I was ninety-five and I began to worry: am I really making a contribution to the economic life of this country? Am I a social parasite? I have already provided enough for my children. I feel I am at the top of my social ladder in my own profession and you only get these feelings when you don't have to make any more money. What next, I asked myself? And the answer I came up with was: charity.'

Max Rayne offers a more sophisticated variation on this theme. 'A large percentage of Jewish people are recent immigrants who have needed to create security for themselves ... Having generated the impetus they have, if you like, overrun and created a surplus and many of them have had the sense to realize this and done something about it by giving that surplus away. If a man has a great fortune he knows jolly well that he is not going to spend it all in his lifetime. Unless you are looking for an empire and eternal power—the foundation of a dynasty—there is no point in hanging on to too much of it. I probably overdid it and gave a little too much away but that's neither here nor there.'

This is undoubtedly true as far as it goes, but the root causes of Jewish philanthropy are more tangled and complicated than this. Giving money away has always been as much part of the traditional Jewish ethos as making it; if anything the charitable instincts are the stronger, for as we have seen, these remain long after the money-making ones have faded. 'Distance does not dilute this faith,' Lord Sieff has said. 'It has strengthened it. If a Jew faithful to his creed hears a real call for charity he will never refuse. This is the very warp and woof of being a Jew.'* The charitable habit is instilled into the ghetto-born Jew almost from the moment of birth, for an obligation to provide for the needy is one of the strictest of the 613 Talmudic injunctions that an orthodox Jew must obey. Lord Sieff, who was brought up in an orthodox home, still remembers walking the streets of Manchester with his father, handing out golden sovereigns to the beggars they happened to meet. As Mark Zborowski and Elizabeth Herzog point out in their penetrating study of ghetto society *Life is With People*:

Life in the shtetl begins and ends with tsdaka (a concept that embraces social justice as well as mere alms giving). When a child is born, the father pledges a certain amount of money for distribution to the poor. At a funeral the mourners distribute money to the beggars who swarm the ceremony, chanting 'Tsdaka will save from death.' At every turn during

* Quoted by Kenneth Harris in the *Observer*, June 30th, 1968.

one's life, the reminder to give is present. At the circumcision ceremony, the boy consecrated to the Covenant is specifically dedicated to good deeds. Every celebration, every holiday, is accompanied by gifts to the needy. Each house has its round tin box into which coins are dropped for the support of various good works. A home that is not very poor will have a series of such boxes, one for the synagogue, one for the yeshiva (the rabbinical school) in some distant city, one for 'clothing the naked', one for 'tending the sick', and so on. When something good or something bad happens, one puts a coin in the box. Before lighting the Sabbath candles, the housewife drops a coin into one of these boxes.

This religious tradition which goes back thousands of years and which has its origins in the Old Testament ('In the hour of man's departure, neither silver nor gold nor precious stones nor pearls accompany him, but only Torah and good deeds') has been reinforced by historical circumstances. For centuries the Jews were a poor people, living apart from the mainstream of Western European life. And this poverty and isolation fostered a very strong sense of communal identity. As the Bible says: 'Abraham taught the children of Israel that they are dependent on each other for survival ... that each man must live for the other.' Both their salvation (in the religious sense) and their survival depended on their ability to cling together and on their willingness to help one another. 'To be isolated', say Zborowski and Herzog, 'is hideous, pathetic and dangerous. Only when man has a functioning place in a group can a man be happy, "beautiful" and safe.' It was this principle, enunciated by the rabbis, that led to the creation of the ghetto's numerous welfare institutions: the charitable funds, the public kitchens, the provision of clothing, the hospitals, the homes for the aged and the burial funds. To put it at its crudest, these institutions were the ghetto's mutual insurance policy, reassuring the richest that if, as could easily happen, Fortune's wheel should turn, they too would be looked after.

Charity, then, is one element in the Jews' constant struggle for survival: throughout their history a concern for security has been an ever present theme. And though as far as the British Jews are concerned the ghetto and all its uncertainties are now far behind them, this sense of insecurity still remains. 'How on earth can you feel secure when you know that there are golf clubs that won't let you in because you are a Jew, or certain businesses which you can't reach the top for the same reason, no matter how hard you try?' a property millionaire asked. 'Being Jewish', says Louis Mintz, the clothing magnate, 'you are penalized a little bit and realizing this you try and do a little better. When I hear an anti-semitic remark—like when I'm driving and I make a mistake and the driver winds down the window and shouts "You little Jew Boy"—I get palpitations you can't express.'

For these men, both second-generation immigrants, and others like them the existence of Israel is profoundly comforting. It is not only the fulfilment of a Biblical prophecy; it is what its original name suggests—a home for the Jews; a place of refuge and of shelter. 'Deep down', says John Cohen of Tesco, 'I have always had the feeling that something could be stirred up again: that somebody may start screaming and shouting and that we may have to take our bundle and run. I support Israel because I feel it is a sort of duty. I feel about Israel like the Roman Catholics feel about Rome or the Greeks about Athens. But I also feel that our security in this country is centred around Israel. If Israel goes it will make it a lot worse for us . . . It's an insurance policy as far as we are concerned.'

Not all Jews by any manner of means feel this way either about themselves or about Israel. Feelings of insecurity are always relative and many Jews are too well established and have been in England far too long for such feelings to be anything more than a folk memory. Even to the sons of the Russo–Polish immigrants the pain of the recent past has faded. 'I really haven't got a perse-cution complex, you know,' says Arnold Weinstock, who in the last five years has built up the largest electrical combine in Britain in such a spectacular fashion that his name has become a synonym for industrial efficiency. Weinstock is a good twenty years younger than the men I have quoted above; he was only a schoolboy during the Fascist riots of the 'thirties; he never had a Jewish education ('There used to be a rabbi who came to teach me Hebrew but I used to stand at the top of the road with my bicycle and when I saw him coming I used to ride in the opposite direction') and has never mixed very much in traditional Jewish circles. 'It is not my style,' he says. But even for a man who is as seemingly detached from the Jewish world as Weinstock, Israel, which he visited in 1949, still has considerable appeal. 'They are a beleaguered people with enemies on all sides and one always has some sympathy with the underdog. Besides they are Jews and I am a Jew ... '

Normally these feelings lie some way below the surface. Like many Jews, Weinstock does not feel the need to be constantly expressing his Jewish identity by supporting Israel and working for Jewish causes. And it is only when Jewry appears to be threatened, as it manifestly was during those six days in June, that these feelings re-emerge. 'Once again', says Cyril Stein, 'the whole spectre of Jews being exterminated was being raised.' The danger was obvious and dramatic. It was a situation to which no Jew, no matter how secure and how assimilated, could fail to respond. By all accounts it was not just the 30 per cent of the community who are the J.P.A.'s regular supporters who reacted to Israel's plight. Jews who had never given Israel a second thought and who regarded the J.P.A.'s fund raising efforts as vulgar and offensive suddenly became ardent Zionists. The Israeli embassy in London was besieged with offers of help from young professional people anxious to join the fighting and had to install extra telephone lines to handle all the inquiries. It was the Spanish Civil War all over again, though this time it was not the Communists but the Jews who were fighting for their lives. 'Two very unusual things happened,' says Cyril Stein. 'People who didn't even regard themselves as Jewish, suddenly became involved.

People for whom Israel had had no special significance, who had regarded it as just another country—like Ireland—were rushing off to join the fighting.'

In responding as they did to the Israeli crisis the Jews of Britain were in a sense obeying an old instinct. 'Throughout the ages', says Lavy Bakstansky, the director of the J.P.A., 'our secret weapon has been the readiness of our men and women to give up time and money. The main driving force behind giving is the old feeling that their only hope resides in their readiness to help one another in any emergency.' But the Jews' desire for security and their readiness to defend themselves when threatened is not the fund raisers' only secret weapon. They have others, equally powerful, in their armoury. Religion is no longer the cohesive force that it once was. Dr Ernest Krausz has done a detailed survey of the Jewish community in Edgware in the course of which he discovered that though 100 per cent still circumcise their children and over 70 per cent still observe the major Jewish festivals only 13 per cent go to the synagogue once a week or more. But though this is a trend that worries the rabbis it does not indicate, I think, that Jewish society has lost all of its cohesiveness. Many, like Max Rayne, still feel a continuing need to identify themselves as Jews—and not just when Jewry is threatened. 'I knew I was a Jew but the first time I realized that this was anything different was after Hitler came to power. I was then at school and for the first time people spoke of Jews—I had never thought of myself as a Jew in being any way different from anybody else. I knew that I was Jewish by religion, but there seemed no difference between going to a synagogue or going to a church or a chapel. But then it gradually began to dawn on me that even if I didn't feel any different, others did. And I remember how impressed I was when the late Lord Melchett, the father of the present head of the British Steel Corporation, resumed his Jewish faith. And I remember what a tremendous thrill and a tremendous source of encouragement this was to those humble members of the Jewish community which I knew. I've never forgotten this. To do the opposite would, I think, be a dreadful thing to do. One has to identify oneself.'

Giving money to Jewish causes and taking part in charitable activities is a traditional and convenient way of doing this and one, so the sociologists say, that is widely practised. In his travels round Edgware, Dr Krausz discovered that while only 13 per cent went regularly to synagogues, no less than 35 per cent were active supporters of Jewish clubs and charities and another 40 per cent had participated at some time in the past. Charitable work plays an important part in the social life of any Jewish suburb. For many middle-class housewives having the ladies in to tea to raise money for the old people's home is part of their regular weekly routine; similarly the J.P.A. dinners perform a dual function where the practical business of money raising often seems to take second place to social chat and gossip about the business.

Religious traditions, compassion for the poor, a desire for security, a need for identity are some of the driving forces of Jewish philanthropy. But prestige and status are just as important. Anybody who gives to charity can expect the approval of his fellow men, but in Jewish society the rewards for those who support good works are perhaps greater than elsewhere. Not only is the Jewish donor assured of 'the recording angel's credit mark' when he dies, but he is also assured of earthly prestige while he lives. In ghetto society the greatest respect was reserved for only two classes of men: those who were learned in the law and those who had served the community. To these men were accorded the places of honour on the Western Wall of the synagogue. It's a tradition that still lives on today: to give to charity is one way of demonstrating your goodness both as a man and as a Jew. Preferably people should only hear of your charity by accident, for the tradition is that giving is best when done anonymously. But people are only human and while many give, most donations have names attached. Indeed one of the most conspicuous features of many Jewish institutions is the large number of plaques

announcing that this clock, or that bookcase, was given by Mr
and Mrs Blank. I have even seen a van in Israel on which the
names of the donors were painted on the side in large letters. This
tug of war that goes on in many Jewish hearts between a desire
to obey the Law to the letter and a natural desire to advertise
their generosity is the source of many jokes in the pantheon of
Jewish humour. 'I Bernard Cohen', one of them goes, 'of 111 West
Street, Stamford Hill, garment manufacturer, desire to give £100
—anonymous.'

It is this weakness that is perhaps the most powerful of all the
J.P.A.'s secret weapons. And it is one that they use vigorously
and, some would say, ruthlessly. It is seen at its most effective at
their annual fund raising dinners, where everything is done to
foster a competitive spirit. Each year's campaign starts in January
and lasts until the Day of Atonement, which usually falls at the
end of the following September. The whole affair is carefully
stage managed throughout: it begins with a grand dinner, usually
at Claridge's or the Savoy, and is attended by the most prominent
and wealthiest members of the community. Further dinners for
each of the trade committees, descending somewhat in grandeur
but organized on similar lines, are held in the following months.
The J.P.A. pays a great deal of attention to the planning of these
dinners, for the amount raised at the first one sets the tone, so
Lavy Bakstansky, the J.P.A. director says, for the rest of the
dinners. The guests are carefully selected, and by the time the
dinner starts the J.P.A. organizers who have been discreetly
circulating during the pre-dinner cocktails have a pretty shrewd
idea of exactly who 'the big givers' will be and how much they
will donate. Some like Sir Isaac Wolfson, who has regularly given
£100,000 for the last seven years (this is a personal gift and does
not include the annual £50,000 set aside each year for Israel by the
Wolfson Foundation), can be relied upon; others have to be
persuaded; either directly by the canvassers or during the after-
dinner session when, along with the brandy and cigars, the names
of the donors and the amounts they have given are slowly read

out by the chairman in descending order, starting with the name of the largest donor in the hope that by the time he has finished at least some will have been persuaded to increase the number they were first thinking of. 'We believe in calling out names. You can't be a gentleman when raising money,' says Bakstansky. It is a pressure that is often increased by the knowledge that your fellow diners and donors are often your suppliers and customers as well. 'Yes, I suppose you could say I've been "invited",' said my neighbour at the textile trade dinner, which I attended shortly after the opening of the 1969 campaign.

It is an exercise not designed to spare anybody's feelings. At the dinner I went to not only were the amounts that each had given read out, but every time they exceeded (or fell short) of last year's donation that too was mentioned. And when the chairman came to one donation that was markedly smaller than the rest there was a distinct mutter of 'disgraceful'. By the time the evening's ceremonies had ended another £777,000 had been raised for Israel. It may be a tough way to raise money but it is undeniably effective.

P

Chapter Eleven

Conclusion

'Why pick on us?' a man who is now chairman of a large super-market chain asked me, echoing a centuries-old Jewish complaint. 'We are just businessmen like everybody else.'

That may be true today. The great Jewish businesses of the nineteenth and early twentieth centuries are, as the impact of their founding fathers fades, fast losing their distinguishing character-istic. The patriarch, immortalized in oils and surrounded in heavy gilt, may still preside over the board room table; there may still be, as there are at Rothschilds or Marks and Spencer, members of the family to keep his memory alive; but for the most part the classic figure of the Jewish entrepreneur is in retreat. The job has been accomplished; the empire built; the fortune made. The task now is altogether more humdrum. What is needed is modernization and rationalization—the constant process of adjustment that has to take place if the business is to prosper or even stay alive. But this is a managerial, not an entrepreneurial function and more often than not it is a task that is being done by non-Jewish outsiders, free from emotional and family ties with the business. At Mon-tague Burton a former management consultant is now in control; at Tesco where McKinseys, the ubiquitous American consultants have been called in, they are for the first time looking outside the family for a new managing director, and even at Marks and Spencer, the influence of Lord Marks and Lord Sieff is on the wane.

226

But this ineluctable transition is not the main theme of this book. It may not be legitimate now, as the supermarket chairman implied, to single out modern Jewish businessmen for special comment. But at the same time it is difficult to ignore the achievements of their fathers and grandfathers. They may not all have become Rothschilds and Wolfsons, but even so a surprisingly large number—more than their distribution in the population would warrant—have turned their hands to business—often with considerable success.

Throughout the nineteenth century it was, as we have seen, the ingenuity and initiative of the German-Jewish bankers and financiers that led them to play a large part in making London the financial capital of the world; in the early years of the twentieth century the energy and resourcefulness of the Russo-Jewish immigrants were directed towards the building of the massive retailing multiples and chains—the Marks and Spencers, the Montague Burtons and the Great Universal Stores—that now dominate Britain's high streets. One only has to take a walk down Oxford Street to perceive the results of this revolution. In the last fifty years the Jews have transformed the tailoring business, have given mass-market retailing a hefty push in the right direction and have had an invigorating effect on the radio business, the furniture trades and on entertainment. Two out of the three major cinema chains, Odeon and Granada, were built by Jewish entrepreneurs and today a sizeable chunk of the entertainment business, stretching from Associated Television to London's Palladium, is in the hands of the three Grade brothers—an ebullient trio who started life as tap-dancers in the music halls of the East End. In the mid-twentieth century the sons of the immigrants have made a similar impact on the property business. What is more, this impetus came from below. These developments were not the work of giant corporations seeking new outlets for expansion but the result of hundreds, if not thousands, of individual initiatives: the work of men struggling to better their lot, to drag themselves up out of the ranks of the *lumpenproletariat* and gain admission to middle-class society. They were in every sense exceptional men.

But they had to be, for, as Professor J. A. Schumpeter points out in his monumental *Capitalism, Socialism and Democracy*:

> To undertake new things is difficult and constitutes a distinct economic function, first because they lie outside of the routine tasks which everybody understands and, secondly, because the environment resists in many ways that vary, according to social conditions, from simple refusal either to finance or buy a new thing, to physical attack on the man who tries to produce it. To act with confidence beyond the range of familiar beacons and overcome that resistance requires aptitudes that are present in only a small fraction of the population and that define the entrepreneurial type as well as the entrepreneurial function. This function does not essentially consist in either inventing anything or otherwise creating the conditions which the enterprise exploits. It consists in getting things done.

But why was it the Jews who got things done? This is the fundamental question, and the first point to be made is that I do not subscribe to the idea that the Jews are *inherently* better businessmen; that inbuilt into the Jewish character is a flair for business that has somehow been denied to others. Other considerations apart, it seems to me that despite the work of Professor Jensen, who in the States has tried to show that racial background has a bearing on intelligence and aptitude, the available evidence is too slim and too inconclusive to support such a thesis. What I do believe is that the Jews, by reason of their history and their culture, have inherited a whole system of values which when combined with the environment in which they have found themselves has led them to behave in quite specific and identifiable ways. And the more hostile and unfriendly the environment, the more marked this characteristic behaviour becomes.

To take environment first. Though England of the 1880s was

an infinitely more tolerant country than the Russo–Polish empire from which the Jews had fled, the East End was not a particularly comfortable place. The overcrowding was so severe, the conditions were so squalid and the competition so intense that merely to survive, let alone to succeed, called for extraordinary individual effort and resourcefulness. To this must be added the widespread suspicion and hostility with which Jews were regarded. James Johnson and his friends of the British Brothers' League may not have achieved their objectives but they were sufficiently active and vociferous to make the Jews of the East End, in whose minds the memories of the indignities they had suffered were still very fresh, feel acutely uncomfortable. Nor did the Aliens' Act of 1905, which for the first time restricted immigrant rights to enter the country freely, do much to reassure them.

In this situation the Jews' natural instinct was to explore every avenue of escape, as other immigrants have done both before and after them. In the eighteenth century it was the Quakers and other nonconformists who, labouring under similar handicaps to the Jews, made the running in banking and brewing to such good effect that in 1939 Sir Montague Burton could justly apply the compliment that is usually paid to members of his own community and say: 'This comparative handful of people, whose number does not exceed twenty thousand in Great Britain, have made a contribution out of all proportion to their numbers.' In the late 1960s it has been the Pakistanis and the Cypriots who have taken up the Jews' traditional role in the lower reaches of the clothing trade, demonstrating in the process that they are just as opportunistic as any Jew.

But the Jews of late Victorian England, the fathers of the Clores and the Wolfsons, were in a special situation. Their handicaps may have been great but so were their opportunities: there was not one but many avenues of escape open to them. At the very moment of their arrival, England was standing at the threshold of a consumer boom that was nothing short of revolutionary. As we have seen in the space of little more than two generations the

whole machinery for feeding, clothing and entertaining the increasingly prosperous working class was erected. And as the Jews
had already been heavily involved in these areas in their native
Russia they were extraordinarily well placed to cater for similar
needs in their new home.

But important though it is, the nature of the environment and
the opportunities it presented is only part of the explanation. The
grinding poverty of the East End undoubtedly provided the
necessary stimulus, but what is remarkable is the vigour of the
Jews' reaction. Historical accident may explain why so many Jews
gravitated first towards finance and later towards shopkeeping,
property dealing and tailoring, but the basic question remains: if
the opportunities were there, why was it that the Jews were
among the first to spot and seize them?

The answer is necessarily complicated and made up of a number
of strands that have to be untangled. In the first place the immigrants of the 1880s were, unlike the present-day West Indian
immigrants, who have so far displayed none of their entrepreneurial flair, an urban people, accustomed to living in towns
and used to handling money. The emotional shock of being up-
rooted and forced to leave their homes was undoubtedly great,
but at the same time there was, in a very large number of cases,
surprisingly little economic dislocation or unemployment. When
the German doctors and dentists who fled from Hitler in the 1930s
arrived in Israel they found little demand for their services and so
they became taxi drivers and bricklayers. (One of the most popular
jokes in Israel concerns a group of German refugees on a building
site. As the bricks are passed from hand to hand, the men are
heard to say: '*Danke schön, Herr Doktor. Bitte schön, Herr Doktor.*')
The immigrants to Britain experienced no such painful break:
the East End community to which they were drawn was, so they
quickly found, economically and socially remarkably similar to
the ones they had so abruptly left. And thousands discovered it
was just as easy (or difficult) to be a tailor or a shopkeeper in
Whitechapel as it had been in Vilna or Lodtz.

To take up a business career, preferably on one's own account, was for the majority of the immigrants the obvious thing to do. Though the professional and social barriers which had forced the Huguenots, and later the Quakers, into trade had largely collapsed by 1880, few of those arriving from Russia, Poland and Lithuania had either the education or resources to become doctors, dentists or lawyers. Much as they might have wished, as Isaac Wolfson's father did, to pursue their Talmudic studies according to Jewish custom, their first responsibility was to look after themselves, their wives and their families. So it was only to be expected they should choose to practise the trades they already knew.

The conditions in which they carried on their trades were in themselves a spur to achievement.* In many ways the teeming ghettoes of the East End and the large provincial cities provided the best possible training ground for a successful business career: they were, in a sense, ideal business nurseries for the budding entrepreneur. To succeed in building up a business of any size in the East End, whether it be tailoring, shopkeeping or whatever, required quite unusual energy and stamina. And it is significant, I think, that the majority of those whose careers I have discussed are the sons and grandsons of the original immigrants. The handicaps were so great that few of the first generation managed to erect companies of any size but at least they provided the necessary platform from which the upward leap could be made.

* This is not an exclusively British or indeed a peculiarly Jewish phenomenon. In 1965 a group of American sociologists from Michigan State University conducted a series of depth interviews with a number of entrepreneurs in an attempt to discover what the motive forces were. What emerged was that a disproportionately large percentage were either first- or second-generation immigrants. By contrast, the sociologists found in the business community at large only 5 per cent of its leaders were foreign-born and only 20 per cent had immigrant fathers. After similar interviews with a cross-section of 'corporation men', the sociologists concluded: 'The entrepreneur ... needs the kind of education that prepared him for surviving in the "open". Very often this means that his first education comes from being shoved into the open at a very early stage and learning how to survive by his wits and his ability to deal with others. The kind of training he needs cannot be learned in the ordinary school with its neat, orderly educational process for socializing the child to take his place in established society. He has to learn how to build a structure of relationships outside the established organizations.'

Energy, stamina and above all self-reliance—these are some of the most notable characteristics of the men whose careers we have been discussing. Though it is by no means universally true (Alec Colman, the property developer, for example, continued to live with his parents until he was well into his mid-twenties) many of the tycoons made the break with their families when they were still very young. The reasons vary: Sir Isaac Wolfson may remain faithful to the memory of his father, but that did not stop him breaking away from the family furniture business and setting off for London when he was twenty-three; Sir John Cohen's departure from the family home in Hackney was prompted partly by his dislike of his father's tailoring business and partly by the uneasy family atmosphere which grew up after his mother's death; and Louis Mintz, the rag trade king, took his first independent steps on the commercial road while he was still at school, joining forces with a man who is now a well-known barrister, to sell sweets to his schoolmates in the playground during the lunch hour.

It may have been easier, for the reasons I have just explained, for the Jews to adapt themselves to the commercial cut and thrust of life in the East End. But this still does not wholly account for the Jews' astonishing success as businessmen. Clearly there are specific hereditary and environmental factors at work. The Jews are no longer as distinctive a community as they once were. Over the years the differences have become blurred and indistinct. But in the early twentieth century contemporary observers with no particular axe to grind were in no doubt at all that the immigrants were, when compared with their English neighbours, very unusual people indeed. It was in their attitude to work that the differences were most marked. Whereas the English workman was content for the most part to remain an employee, the overriding desire of the majority of the immigrants was to control their own destiny by becoming their own masters. In 1902 a poor Jewish immigrant of no particular consequence or importance called Angor Wilchenski was asked by Her Majesty's Royal

Commissioners inquiring into alien immigration to outline his philosophy. Wilchenski replied: 'I neither smoke nor drink and believe in everything that will make me better off.' It was this aspect that struck Beatrice Potter so forcibly. In 1889 she wrote:*

> As an industrial competitor the Polish Jew is fettered by no definite standard of life; it rises and falls with his opportunities; he is not depressed by penury, and he is not demoralized by gain. Thus the immigrant Jew, fresh from the sorrowful experiences of his race, seems to justify by his existence those strange assumptions which figured for man in the political economy of Ricardo—an Always Enlightened Selfishness, seeking employment or profit with an absolute mobility of body and mind, without pride, without preference, without interests outside the struggle for the existence and welfare of the individual and the family. We see these assumptions verified in the Jewish inhabitants of Whitechapel; and in the East End trades we may watch the prophetic deduction of the Hebrew economist actually fulfilled—in a perpetually recurring bare subsistence wage for a great majority of manual workers.

It is not difficult to see why the Jews were prepared to struggle so hard to become their own masters. Firstly it was no more than straightforward common sense. Even the dullest 'greener' in the humblest tailoring shop could see the attractions of owning the business rather than being at someone's beck and call. The prospects on the cutting-room floor were so limited and the pay so poor that the man who remained an employee had little or no chance of escape. Secondly the Jews were so low on the economic scale that they could afford to take risks. The history of the Jews has been so fraught with tragedies and disasters that they have learned to seize the main chance while the going remains good. Thirdly there is the Jewish optimism that Beatrice Potter spoke of. The out-worker with the tumbledown shed and a couple of

* Op. cit.

ancient Singer machines in some East End backstreet may know in his heart of hearts that he will never be Sir Montague Burton, but as long as he is his own boss there is always a chance; anyway he will keep on trying.

The fourth reason is more complex and is perhaps the most important of all. The Jews have been persecuted for so long, forced to move from one place to another, that they have in self-defence constructed their own survival kit. A consciousness of their own identity, to which I shall come later, is the basic ingredient of this package but I think a desire for independence is also part of it. This desire and the ambition that goes with it is a trait that has been etched deep into the Jewish character. Historically the Jews have always been attracted to those trades and professions which offer scope for individual enterprise: from property dealing at one end of the spectrum to taxi driving at the other. As late as 1955 the loan department of the Jewish Welfare Board could report: 'The committee continue to find that the high wages being offered do not seem to lessen the number of prospective borrowers who prefer to be their own masters, rather than take jobs which might make them more money.'

Again it is not difficult to see why. As we saw in the previous chapter, at the back (and sometimes at the forefront) of every Jew's mind lies the fear, no matter how secure or how well-regarded he and his fellow Jews might be, that anti-semitism might rear its head. After all the memory of Sir Oswald Mosley and his Blackshirts is still fresh. And if, as Sir John Cohen put it, 'we have to take up our bundle and run', the knowledge that one's bundle is of a useful size is infinitely comforting. The need to set out on one's own and acquire that bundle might not seem so pressing now, but to the immigrants of the 1880s the pressures were very strong.

The undoubted existence of an anti-semitic undercurrent in industry and elsewhere had a profound effect on the Jewish pattern of employment—and thus on the nature of Jewish achievement. In 1880 it was certainly true that to be a Jew was a distinct disability. Industry may not have been a closed shop, but the chances of a humble Jew climbing the managerial ladder of any large manufacturing firm and reaching the top in open competition with the Gentiles was, or perhaps more significantly, was seen to be extremely slim. Even today anti-semitism is still to be found both in industry and the City. In the early 1950s the officials of the Cambridge University Appointments' Board made the following, private comments about a couple of Jewish undergraduates they had interviewed. 'Not very appetizing looking—short and Jewy with wet palms but seems a versatile chap and quite a figure anyhow in the bridge and chess world ... ' 'I fear an unattractive chap—if only because one is instinctively drawn to feel this about the chosen race from which he must surely stem. Small, sallow, raven hair and fleshy nose. *I think more of the reaction of potential employers than my own, of course* [my italics].' When challenged about these remarks (which were, incidentally, never intended to be passed on to potential employers and were written solely for the officials' own guidance), the Appointments' Board defended itself by pointing out that they were reflecting industry's views, not their own. As they were men who were, by the nature of their job, in day-to-day contact with industry they were in a good position to know what the views were.

It is the fear of exposure to prejudice of this kind, coupled with an ambition to be one's own master, that has led so many Jews to seek self-employment. It is a feeling that even someone as well balanced and sophisticated as Arnold Weinstock, managing director of the biggest electrical combine in Britain, has experienced. Weinstock, the son of an immigrant North London tailor, started his career as a five-pound-a-week clerk in the Admiralty in Bath. After a short spell he left for a job in a Jewish property firm. And one of the reasons for his leaving, so he says, was the belief that it was impossible for a Jew to become Permanent Secretary of the Admiralty—'deputy secretary perhaps, but top man, no'. As it happens, Weinstock has been proved wrong. In the last twenty years a number of Jews have become extremely distinguished and powerful civil servants, among them, Sir Eric Roll, former chief economic adviser to the late lamented Department of Economic Affairs and now a banker with Warburgs. But the point is not what the Jews have achieved but what Arnold Weinstock *believed* they could achieve.*

It is not only Jewish businessmen who display this hunger for independence. It also partially explains why so many Jews become doctors, dentists and lawyers. 'I was not brought up as a Jew,' a solicitor who has built up a large and successful practice told me. 'But when I found I was going to be treated like one, I determined to act like one. I think I am an example of a chap who would never have built up his own practice and would have probably been content to have been a partner in a large firm. But when I realized I would never be president of the Law Society or a senior partner in one of the large firms, I said to myself: "I'll show them I am as good as the next man, if not better." I think that part of being a Jew means one is determined to do much better than the other chap.'

These then were the external pressures—the poverty of the ghetto, the existence, whether real or imaginary, of anti-semitism and the desire, prompted by this fear, for independence and the security it was seen to bring. But they were not the only forces which drove the Polish and Russian Jews onwards and upwards. Much of the pressure was, I think, internal; its source being the Jewish community itself—or more specifically that part of it whose attitudes and values had been fashioned in the ghettoes of Eastern Europe.

In the first place the very existence of such a self-conscious, tightly knit community, forced to struggle for existence in an alien environment, was in itself a source of comfort and support.

---

* Even in manufacturing industry the Jews are beginning to make their mark. Apart from Lord Melchett himself, two of the senior directors at the British Steel Corporation are Jewish. But it is worth noting that they have got where they are not by climbing the managerial ladder but have been brought in from outside for their special expertise as bankers, scientists or lawyers.

The owner-driver instinct was one of the factors which prompted many men to set out on the road to fame and fortune, but though the journey was often a hard and solitary one it was not entirely so. Once the community was established and had put down roots in alien soil there grew up a special kind of freemasonry that is characteristic of minority groups everywhere. Writing about the Quakers in the eighteenth century, Professor Peter Mathias has said:* 'Legal restraints, the sense of social separateness and a common faith made the Meeting House and the Chapel the focus of a communal life of great resilience and tenacity. Here is a body of mutual confidence and mutual trust.' Substitute synagogue for meeting house and the same is true of the Jews. If anything their sense of togetherness and common identity was even stronger than the Quakers. The Jews had only just emerged from the suffocating atmosphere of the Russian ghetto which, while offering them a measure of protection against persecution also, by virtue of its existence, kept the memories of their tragic history alive and ever-present.

This awareness of a shared fate and a common identity was undoubtedly helpful when it came to business. The atmosphere of the ghetto may have been charged with a spirit of cut-throat competition, with each man striving for himself and his family, but it was tempered by a certain charity; by the willingness of one Jew to help another, if only because he knew that circumstances might change and that one day he might himself need a helping hand. However predatory the careers of men like Sir Isaac Wolfson might seem in retrospect, in their early years at least the tycoons relied heavily on the support both of their families and on that wider community of their fellow Jews. Their style of business was so direct and personal they naturally found it easier to do deals with people who spoke the same language and shared the same attitudes and assumptions. On this confidence and understanding whole empires have been built, for when they came to look for lieutenants to staff their growing businesses the

* Op. cit.

same principles applied. The old boy network, for all its public-school overtones, is not an exclusively Gentile phenomenon: old Etonians have one system, the Jews have another. Just as middle-class, public-school-educated bankers are at their happiest doing business with other middle-class, public-school bankers, so the Jews preferred to do business with other Jews. One of the features of the rise of the commercial aristocracy was the extent to which bankers married bankers' daughters. Among the Jews in the early twentieth century the same phenomenon occurred. Furniture men married the daughters of other furniture men, thereby cementing the existing commercial links still further.

This aspect is characteristic of many minority groups. But in one sense the Jews were exceptional, just as the East European ghettoes were exceptional. Behind their walls there flourished a very special kind of society: hierarchical, status-conscious and with its own particular and long-cherished set of values. Set high among them was a respect for, and a love of, learning. 'Learning gives prestige, respect, authority and status,' say Zbrowski and Herzog in their study of ghetto society, *Life is with People*, a much better book than its *schmaltzy* title implies. 'In the synagogue, the men who sit along the Eastern Wall, the *mizrakh*, are pre-eminently the learned and the rabbi, as the most learned of all, has the most honoured seat of all—next to the Ark where the Torah is kept.' In traditional Jewish society a parent's very first obligation was to instil in his children a knowledge of Jewish law. 'Thou shalt', he was told in the first of the Jewish Scriptures' 613 Commandments, 'teach them [God's commandments] diligently unto thy children and thou shall talk of them when thou sittest down, and when thou walkest by the way, when thou liest down and when thou risest up.'

Even after the immigrants had left their native Russia they continued to observe these precepts. Louis Mintz, for example, was brought up in just such a tradition. After he finished school at four o'clock he did not return home as other children did but went on to spend four or five hours each evening at the local *heder*—the Hebrew name for a theological school for young children—being instructed by the rabbi in the intricacies of the Talmud. This in itself was, with its emphasis on logical analysis, a formidable intellectual discipline—and one which even those Jews like Arnold Weinstock who did not pass through the Talmudic mill seem to have inherited as part of their intellectual equipment. Unlike most of the property developers and super-marketeers, Weinstock does not openly identify with the Jewish community—the only sign of his allegiance is a cigarette box on the board room table embossed with a seven-branched cande-labra—and plays next to no part in its communal affairs. Even so Weinstock, as he himself admits, owes a good deal to his back-ground and cultural inheritance. 'I am conscious of having in-herited something of the Talmudic tradition without, curiously enough, ever having learnt a word of Hebrew. I was out of the Jewish community for years, but as I get older I get just that bit more aware of Jewish values, though it is an intellectual aware-ness, not a religious one.' Weinstock has not built a business but has made an existing one more profitable and efficient by a programme of ruthless rationalization and simplification. 'Man-agement', he says, 'is the arrangement of the most economical use of resources.' Such a definition might seem obvious to the point of banality, but few managers have the intellectual equip-ment or the necessary courage of their own convictions to carry this maxim through to its logical conclusion. This Weinstock has done. And in the process he has displayed a mental toughness and a capacity for analytical thought which is all too rare in British industry.

When combined with an inherited love of the things of the mind this analytical power does much to explain the massive intellectual achievements of the Jews. As Nathan Glazer, the American sociologist, has pointed out in a perceptive essay:* 'With fields of action now available wider than simply the end-less exploration of the Talmud, young Jews poured into the

* *The Jewish Role in Student Activism.*

universities, wherever they could, exploring every new intellectual realm, and helping to create quite a few of them.' Much of this intellectual vigour found expression in the universities and the professions but it is also, as we have seen with Weinstock and Marks and Spencer, noticeable among Jewish businessmen. They may not have been more intelligent than their business rivals but the habit of asking the question 'why?'—one of the basic tools of Talmudic inquiry—has undoubtedly proved helpful in solving the day-to-day problems of business.

A love of learning was one feature of immigrant society; a desire for wealth was another. 'Historically, traditionally, ideally,' say Zbrowski and Herzog,* 'learning has been and is regarded as the primary value and wealth as subsidiary or com- plementary. But economic pressures and outside influences have made of wealth a constant contender for first place in the value hierarchy. Both the force of outside pressures and the force of tradition are demonstrated by the extent to which wealth as a status criterion is translatable into a substitute for, or an equi- valent of, learning.'

Wealth was valued and sought after not so much for the material comforts it brought but for the respect and prestige that is attached to it—particularly if it is used in the service of the community.† As Howard Brotz, a young Jewish sociologist, has observed:‡ 'Wealth in the ghetto was the basis of high social status in so far as it typically made possible the conference of indulgences and, obversely, independence of charity of other Jews.' That so many rich Jews should place such emphasis on charity is, I think, an indication of the extent to which this tradition still survives. Few of the millionaires I talked to would

* Op. cit.

† If there is any validity in the thesis first advanced by Max Weber in his *Protest- antism and the Spirit of Capitalism* that there is a link between the value system of a society and the economic behaviour of its members, then it is here, it can be argued, that the Jewish religious ethic has played a part. Like Puritanism it plays down the importance of the afterlife and stresses that it is what a man does in his lifetime that determines his future happiness.

‡ 'An analysis of social stratification within Jewish Society in London.'

admit that a desire for money in itself was the main motive force. 'Money has never been my God,' Sir John Cohen said to me. 'I've never bothered about it.' However sceptical one may be about the disclaimers of the very rich, Sir John is not an unduly ostentatious man and that may well be true. But even so, in one sense money must have been important for, without the commercial success and the money that goes with it, Sir John would not have achieved the respect which he himself admits he craved for. 'I had to do something for myself,' he said. 'I felt that if I wasn't to get on people would not respect me. I would just be one of the masses.'

This attitude to wealth as status symbol is not confined to a handful of millionaires but is widely held throughout the Jewish community, whose lay leaders are, after all, almost without exception businessmen. Even in the synagogue it is possible to tell a man's financial status at a glance. Unlike the Anglican Church the United Synagogue charges its members for their seats: at Edgware the annual rental ranges from thirty-five to fifteen pounds and, naturally, the richer people choose the most expensive seats ... It was in Edgware in 1965 that Dr Ernest Krausz asked a cross-section of the Jewish community there what forces *should* determine an individual's social standing. Over 24 per cent said education; 37 per cent listed character and behaviour and only 5½ per cent mentioned money. But when Dr Krausz asked them what they thought actually *did* affect status a very different finding emerged. 'Most respondents', Dr Krausz reported, 'said that in practice money plays the most important part in social position.'

Whether it will continue to do so is a very open question. The people that Dr Krausz was talking to in Edgware were for the most part the sons and daughters of immigrants and as such only a step away from the ghetto, its culture and its memories. 'This area', Howard Brotz, a sociologist who visited neighbouring Hendon in 1955, wrote,* 'is the East End of twenty-five years

* Op. cit.

Q

ago, but an East End whose members have become more prosperous and assimilated to the culture of their host society.' But society, and especially Jewish society, is never static. The ambitions of the immigrants and their children have largely been fulfilled. The majority of the Jews in England now enjoy middle-class incomes and display middle-class attitudes. There are still, of course, poor Jews. But the existence of the Welfare State ensures that their children will not have to struggle as they did. Harry Alexander, an East End tailor whom I visited in the winter of 1968–9, working in a backyard shed that Beatrice Potter would instantly have recognized, would, if he had had his wish, have become a violinist. As it was, he remained a tailor—more prosperous than his father perhaps but still a tailor. He is proud of his work, but he takes even greater pleasure in the fact that his son is training to be an accountant and his daughter is a student at the London School of Economics. The Jews will probably always produce more than their quota of businessmen, but let the melting pot boil for another twenty-five years or so and it may no longer be possible or indeed meaningful to talk of the Jewish business.

Bibliography

GENERAL

Aris, S., 'The Jewish Entrepreneur', *New Society*, January 30th, 1964.

Bagehot, W., *Lombard Street* (Smith Elder, London, 1873).

Barou, Dr N., *The Jews in Work and Trade* (The Trades Advisory Council, 3rd edition, London, 1948).

Beddington Behrens, Sir E., *Look Back, Look Forward* (Macmillan, London, 1963).

Bermant, C., *Troubled Eden, an Anatomy of British Jewry* (Valentine Mitchell, London, 1969).

Birmingham, S., *Our Crowd, the Great Jewish Families of New York* (Longmans, London, 1968).

Blake, R., *Disraeli* (Eyre and Spottiswoode, London, 1966).

Booth, C., *Life and Labour of the People of London*, 9 vols (Macmillan, London, 1902).

Brotz, H., 'An analysis of social stratification within Jewish Society in London', Ph.D. thesis, 1951.

Bull, G. and A. Vice, *Bid for Power* (Elek, London, 1958).

Clapham, Sir J., *An Economic History of Modern Britain 1850–1886* (Cambridge University Press, Cambridge, 1950–52).

Clarke, W. M., *The City in the World Economy* (The Institute of Economic Affairs, London, 1965).

Collins, O. and others, *The Enterprising Man* (Bureau of Business and Economic Research, Michigan State University, 1965).

Corti, Count E., *The Rise of the House of Rothschild*, translated from the German by Brian and Beatrice Lunn, 2 vols (Gollancz, London, 1928).

D'Arcy Hart, R., *The Samuel Family of Liverpool and London* (Routledge and Kegan Paul, London, 1958).

243

Deutscher, I., *The Non-Jewish Jew and Other Essays* (Oxford University Press, Oxford, 1968).

Dickson, P. G. M., *The Financial Revolution in England, 1688–1756* (Macmillan, London, 1967).

Dubnow, S. M., *History of the Jews in Russia and Poland*, 3 vols (The Jewish Publication Society of America, Philadelphia, 1918).

Emden, P., *Jews of Britain* (Sampson Low Marston, London, 1943).

Emden, P., *Quakers in Commerce, a Record of Business Achievement* (Sampson Low Marston, London, 1940).

Evans–Gordon, W., *The Alien Immigrant* (Heinemann, London, 1903).

Ferris, P., *The City* (Gollancz, London, 1960).

Foot, P., *Immigration and Race in British Politics* (Penguin, London, 1965).

Freedman, M., *A Minority in Britain* (Valentine Mitchell, London, 1955).

Gartner, L. P., *The Jewish Immigrant in England, 1870–1914* (Allen and Unwin, London, 1948).

Glazer, N., 'The Jewish Role in Student Activism' (*Fortune*, January 1969).

Henriques, R., *Marcus Samuel, First Viscount Bearsted and Founder of Shell* (Barrie and Rockliff, London, 1960).

Henriques, R., *Sir Robert Waley-Cohen* (Secker and Warburg, London, 1966).

Herberg, W., *Protestant, Catholic, Jew, an Essay in American Religious Sociology* (Doubleday Anchor, New York, 1960).

Jackson, S., *The Sassoons* (Heinemann, London, 1968).

Krausz, E., 'Jews in Britain: Integrated or Apart?' paper given to the Institute of Race Relations' 4th annual conference, September 1969.

Krausz, E., *Leeds Jewry* (Heffer, Cambridge, 1963).

Krausz, E., 'Occupation and Social Advancement in Anglo-Jewry', *The Jewish Journal of Sociology*, vol. IV, no. 1, June 1962.

Landa, M. J., *The Alien Problem and Its Remedy* (P. S. King, London, 1911).

Lipman, V. D., *A Century of Social Service. The History of the Jewish Board of Guardians* (Routledge and Kegan Paul, London, 1959).

Lipman, V. D., *Social History of the Jews in England 1850–1950* (Watts, London, 1954).

Litvinoff, B., *A Peculiar People, Inside the Jewish World Today* (Weidenfeld and Nicholson, London, 1969).

Macaulay, Lord, 'Civil Disabilities of the Jews' in *Collected Essays*, edited by Hugh Trevor-Roper (Fontana, London, 1965).

Marriott, O., *The Property Boom* (Hamish Hamilton, London, 1967).

Mathias, P., *The First Industrial Nation. An Economic History of Britain, 1700–1914* (Methuen, London, 1969).

Meyer, C. and C. Black, *The Makers of our Clothes* (Duckworth, London, 1909).

Mitchell, Y., *The Family* (Heinemann, London, 1967).

Montagu, L. H., *Samuel Montagu, a Character Sketch* (Truslove and Hanson, privately printed, 1913).

Morton, F., *The Rothschilds* (Secker and Warburg, London, 1962).

Plumb, J. H., *Sir Robert Walpole*, 2 vols (Cresset Press, London, 1956).

Rees, G., *St. Michael, a History of Marks and Spencer* (Weidenfeld and Nicholson, London, 1969).

Roth, C., *History of the Jews in England* (Oxford University Press, Oxford, 1941).

Roth, C., *The Magnificent Rothschilds* (Robert Hale, London, 1939).

Rumyaneck, J., 'The social and economic development of Jews in England, 1730–1860', Ph.D. thesis, 1933.

Russell, C. and H. S. Lewis, *The Jew in London, a Study of Racial Character and Present-Day Conditions* (Unwin, London, 1900).

Schumpeter, J., *Capitalism, Socialism and Democracy* (Unwin University Books, London, 1930).

Sombart, W., *The Jews and Modern Capitalism*, translated from the German by M. Epstein (Collier Books, New York, 1962).

Stewart, M. and L. Hunter, *The Needle is Threaded* (Heinemann and Newman Neame, London, 1964).

Sutherland, L., *The Brothers Goldsmid and the Financing of the Napoleonic Wars* (Transactions of the Jewish Historical Society, vol. 14).

Sutherland, L., *Samson Gideon, an Eighteenth Century Jewish Financier* (Transactions of the Jewish Historical Society, vol. 17).

Thomas, J., *History of the Leeds Clothing Industry*, Occasional Papers no. 1 (Yorkshire Bulletin of Economic and Social Research, 1955).

Truptil, R. J., *British Banks and the Money Market* (Jonathan Cape, London, 1936).

Weber, M., *The Protestant Ethic and the Spirit of Capitalism* (Unwin University Books, London, 1930).

Wechsberg, J., *The Merchant Bankers* (Weidenfeld and Nicholson, London, 1966).

Weisgal, M. W. and J. Carmichael (eds), *Chaim Weizmann, a Biography by Several Hands* (Weidenfeld and Nicholson, London, 1962).

Yaffe, J., *The American Jews, Portrait of a Split Personality* (Random House, New York, 1968).

Young, G. K., *Merchant Banking, Practice and Prospects* (Weidenfeld and Nicholson, London, 1966).

Zborowski, M. and E. Herzog, *Life is with People, The Culture of the Shtetl* (Schocken, New York, 1962).

OFFICIAL SOURCES

House of Commons Select Committee on Emigration and Immigration (Foreigners), S.P. 1888, XI and S.P. 1889, X.

Report to the Board of Trade on the Sweating System in the East End of London by the Labour Correspondent of the Board, S.P. 1887, LXXXIX.

Report to the Board of Trade on the Sweating System in Leeds by the Labour Correspondent of the Board, S.P. 1887, LXXXVI.

Royal Commission on Alien Immigration: Report and Minutes of Evidence, 2 vols, Cmd. 1742 (H.M.S.O., 1903).

Index

Roth, Professor C., 53
Rothschild, Amschel, 66
Rothschild, Baron Edmond de, 72
Rothschild, Edmund, 77
Rothschild, Evelyn, 77
Rothschild, Hon. Jacob, 73, 76–9
Rothschild, James (Jacob), 65, 66
Rothschild, Karl, 66
Rothschild, Lady Charlotte, and erection
    of tenements, 37, 46, 209
Rothschild, Leo, 77
Rothschild, Lionel, 48, 64: elected to
    House of Commons, 50
Rothschild, Mayer Amschel, 62, 66
Rothschild, Nathaniel, Third Lord,
    77 n, 213
Rothschild, Nathan Mayer, founder of
    British house of Rothschild, 48, 50,
    64–8: and Elector of Hesse, 62, 65; in
    Manchester, 62, 65; death, 64; and
    Napoleonic Wars, 65; and Waterloo,
    65 n; bullion broker to Government,
    65; dominant figure on Stock
    Exchange, 65
Rothschild, Nathan Mayer, first Lord:
    and improvement of conditions in
    East End, 46; obtains peerage, 50
Rothschild, Solomon, 66
Rothschild family and banking business,
    42, 43, 46, 47, 50, 62, 64–9, 75, 118,
    121, 164, 226, 227: acquisition of
    country estates, 48; and purchase of
    Suez Canal, 61; financial assistance to
    Disraeli, 61; international scope of
    business, 66–8; family unity, 67–8;
    observance of Jewish practices, 71;
    and Israel, 72–3; involvement with
    Jewish business, 73; increase in
    number of partners, 76; at present
    day, 76–80; introduction of outside
    talent, 77
Royal Commission on Alien Immigra-
    tion (1902–3), 27–9, 33, 38–40, 86, 89,
    93, 97, 101, 232–3
Rubin, Sol, 209
Russia, 24–9: assassination of Alexander
    II, 24; anti-semitic riots, 25;
    Elizabethgrad pogroms, 25–6; May
    Laws, 26–7, 29; restrictions on Jews,
    27; emigration of Jews, 29

Russian Jewish immigrants in England,
    29–41, 86–9, 229–31, 236: accusations
    against them, 33; concentration in
    East End of London, 34–40, 86–9;
    powers of assimilation, 39–41

SACHER FAMILY, 161
Sainsbury, John, and Sainsbury's Stores,
    22, 95, 148
Sainsbury, Lord, 156 and n
St Helens, and Pilkington family, 160
St Michael (Rees), 170 n
Saipe, Louis, 120
Salmon, Barnett, 177, 181, 182
Salmon, Geoffrey, 177–9, 184–5
Salmon, Ivor, 179
Salmon, Sir Julian, 179
Salmon and Gluckstein, 181–4: tobacco
    business in East End, 181–2; venture
    into catering, 182–3; chain of teashops,
    183; sale of tobacco business, 183–4;
    and J. Lyons, 184
Salmon family, 176–9, 185
Salomons, Sir David, first Jewish Lord
    Mayor of London, 17 n, 50
Sampson, Jack, 110
Samson Gideon (Sutherland), 57 n, 58 n
Samuel, H., jewellers, 131–2
Samuel, M. (firm), 62, 69, 80, 81, 84;
    see also Hill, Philip
Samuel, Sir Harold, 22, 74, 190, 193,
    204, 205: acquires City of London
    Real Property Company, 187, 198–
    200; and Regent Street Arcade, 197
Samuel, Sir Herbert (Visc Samuel),
    44
Samuel, Sir Marcus (First Visc.), 18, 62,
    69, 80
Samuel, Sir Stuart Montagu, 51
Samuel Montagu and Co., 62, 70–71,
    75, 84
Samuel family, 42, 43, 47, 50, 51
Sassoon, David, 49, 67
Sassoon, E. D., banking business, 67
Sassoon, Elias, 67
Sassoon, S. D., 49
Sassoon, Sir Edward, 49
Sassoon family, 43, 49, 67: divisions, 67
Sassoons, The (Jackson), 67
Schroeder, Henry J., 62